Classic Writings in Anarchist Criminology

A Historical Dismantling of Punishment and Domination

EDITED BY

Anthony J. Nocella II,
Mark Seis,
and Jeff Shantz

Foreword by Ruth Kinna
Afterword by Luis A. Fernandez

What People are Saying About this Book:

"This book is an outstanding collection of classic writings on anarchism ... a great scholarly resource on the history of alternatives to punishment, prisons, and punitive justice."—Dr. Erik Juergensmeyer, Editor, *Green Theory and Praxis Journal*

"*Classic Writings in Anarchist Criminology* is must-read book for those who know the criminal justice system is broken, and wants effective solutions. This collection lays out the theoretical foundation for scholars, politicians, practices, and activists to create sound solutions, sure to challenge the failing criminal justice system."—Dr. Amber E. George, Editor, *Journal for Critical Animal Studies*

"*Classic Writings in Anarchist Criminology* is a book that every person that is interested in criminology must read."—Madelynne Kinoshita, Save the Kids

"This book shows that there is a long brilliant history of people working to dismantle domination, control, and punishment."—Poetry Behind the Walls

"A rich and provocative collection of writings that contribute to current abolitionist movements—examining past thinkers enables us to better examine our current problems and imagine alternative solutions!"—Dr. Jason Del Gandio, co-editor of *Spontaneous Combustion: The Eros Effect and Global Revolution*

"*Classic Writings in Anarchist Criminology* brings together an outstanding collection of essays written by some of the most intelligent and influential anarchists that have ever walked the earth. Importantly, their arguments continue to burn with a ferocious intensity, bringing new understanding and insight as to why social justice alternatives to crime and punishment are needed. My hope is that this powerful book will spark—or reignite—a beautiful spirit of revolt, resistance, and commitment to freedom for all, within those fortunate enough to read it."—Dr. Richard J. White, Sheffield Hallam University

Classic Writings in Anarchist Criminology
© 2020 Anthony J. Nocella II, Mark Seis, and Jeff Shantz
Foreword © 2020 Ruth Kinna
Afterword © 2020 Luis A. Fernandez

This edition © 2020 AK Press (Chico, Edinburgh)

ISBN: 978-1-84935-379-3
E-ISBN: 978-1-84935-380-9
Library of Congress Control Number: 2019911062

AK Press   AK Press
370 Ryan Ave. #100   33 Tower St.
Chico, CA 95973   Edinburgh EH6 7BN
USA   Scotland
www.akpress.org   www.akuk.com
akpress@akpress.org   ak@akedin.demon.co.uk

The above addresses would be delighted to provide you with the latest AK Press
distribution catalog, which features books, pamphlets, zines, and stylish apparel
published and/or distributed by AK Press. Alternatively, visit our websites for
the complete catalog, latest news, and secure ordering.

Cover design by Josh MacPhee | Antumbra Design
Printed in the USA on acid-free, recycled paper

This book is dedicated to everyone, human and nonhuman, that is locked up, tortured, and confined in every jail, detention, prison, cage, tank, handcuff, cell, padded room, unit, and chain.

CONTENTS

ACKNOWLEDGEMENTS   We, the editors, would like to thank everyone at AK Press for believing in and supporting this book. We could not think of a better press to publish this book with than AK Press. We would also like to thank our academic departments for their support and friendship. Thank you to our human and nonhuman family and friends. Nothing is possible without others. We are all dependent on others; no one is an island. Thank you also to those today and through history who identified as anarchists and fought for the liberation and freedom for all. Finally, we would like to thank Richard J. White, Jason Del Gandio, Luis A. Fernandez, Madelynne Kinoshita, Amber E. George, and Erik Juergensmeyer who wrote reviews of the book prior to publication.

FOREWORD

Ruth Kinna

One of the exhibits in the Kropotkin House Museum in Dmitrov, near Moscow, is a pencil or charcoal sketch by Kropotkin depicting him in his prison cell. The space is small, dark, and frightening and it perfectly captures the isolation and bleakness of incarceration.

Kropotkin was hardly the only anarchist to gain personal experience of the prison system or to use his reflections on his imprisonment to think more broadly about the operation of the bourgeois justice system and the punishment regimes that are integral to it. As the editors of this pioneering collection argue, anarchist critique draws anarchists magnetically toward its analysis. That is not to say that anarchism is defined by criminology (understood in a narrow sense) but that the anarchist refusal to recognize the justice of our current political arrangements effectively criminalizes the doctrines anarchists espouse and encourages anarchists to place questions of order at the heart of their social theory. Anarchists often wrote about prison because, like Alexander Berkman, they were deeply affected by their experiences. Anarchists analyzed crime, punishment, discipline, and social compliance because of the critiques of power, domination, and authority they advanced.

Looking again at the substantial body of work that anarchists produced on crime and criminology reminds us of the practical force of anarchist critique. The eloquent arguments that anarchists put to their accusers were intended to highlight the translation of legal norms into policy. When the Chicago anarchists explained the tyrannical nature of the property laws enshrined in the constitution and protected by the state, they were not simply making a technical point about justice and injustice. They were explaining the consequences of the power asymmetries that the justice system upheld for millions of dispossessed and exploited peoples. It did not follow, Albert Parsons argued, "that because a man is a judge he is also just." Leaving questions of individual virtue aside, the American courts were packed:

"candidates for judgeships, throughout the United States" were "named by corporation and monopoly influences." More than one Chief Justice had been appointed to the bench of the US Supreme Court at the behest of "leading railway magnates." No wonder, then, that justice was systematically denied to the poor and unemployed. Parsons described the streets of Chicago filled with "30,000 men in compulsory idleness; destitution, misery and want upon every hand" facing "the First Regiment out in a street-riot drill ... practicing a street-riot drill for the purpose of mowing down these wretches ... the working people are to be slaughtered in cold blood, and ... men are drilling upon the streets of the cities of America to butcher their fellow men when they demand the right to work and partake of the fruits of their labor." How far things have changed since 1887 is a moot point. Of course, situations vary across the globe and unemployment is only one of the issues that attracts aggressive policing. But the thrust of Parsons's analysis is about the institutionalization of injustice, the legality of violent repression and the unreasonable measures deployed to regulate disadvantage.

Revisiting anarchist criminology also draws attention to the alternatives that anarchists propose when they attack the prevailing order. The anarchist critique of bourgeois justice was targeted, not generalized. Indeed, it was predicated on an alternative conception of justness. Those who followed Proudhon described justice as immanent, and understood it as a contingent idea, simultaneously a condition and a practice that emerged from individual reflection or reason and social engagement. Like Nietzsche, anarchists denied the possibility of making absolute, universal moral judgments and the possibility that justice could be externally imposed. Justice emerged as part of a social process. Thus in attacking the unfairness and corruption of bourgeois justice systems, anarchists did not dismiss the possibility that rules could be broken, that norms could be transgressed or that harms could be inflicted. The point that Kropotkin made in "Law and Authority" was that military, clerical, and political elites adopted community rules and customs and gave them a new spin. Law corrupted established social practices and fixed them authoritatively so that they could always be enforced coercively and changed only when it suited the ruling elites.

Two of the pressing questions that this important and unique collection raises, then, are about the persistence of the social relations that historical anarchists decried as partial, tyrannous, and deadening and the conditions of justice that anarchists preferred in order to root alternative just practices.

Introduction

THE ORIGINS AND IMPORTANCE OF CLASSIC ANARCHIST CRIMINOLOGY

Mark Seis, Anthony J. Nocella II, and Jeff Shantz

Why Criminology and Criminal Justice Studies Need an Anarchist Perspective

Criminology and criminal justice are inherently biased disciplines of study. Both criminology and criminal justice presuppose that capitalism and the state are natural representations of human nature and therefore serve as a baseline for civilized society. Furthermore, criminology and criminal justice presume that the legal apparatuses that buttress state capitalism are, as Jeffery Reiman argues, the "minimum neutral ground rules" for a civilized society.[1] These unquestioned assumptions underlie the curriculums of the overwhelming majority of criminology and criminal justice programs taught in the United States and abroad.

This book examines these unquestioned assumptions by referencing the works of classic anarchist thinkers who have methodically and painstakingly deconstructed these unquestioned assumptions by drawing attention to the inevitable fact that state capitalism is the source of crime and criminal behavior and immense human suffering. Capitalism is legalized inequality and theft. Laws, police, courts, and prisons exist to enforce the rights of the owners of capital to steal the wealth produced by workers, making them desperate, poor, and dependent on low wages, which do not allow the majority of working people to acquire the necessities of life. Further, the criminal justice system criminalizes and normalizes the extremely stratified inequality endemic to state capitalism based on race, ethnicity, gender, and physical and mental ability. People of color and people with disabilities are disproportionately marginalized and imprisoned, and women

1   Jeffery Reiman, *The Rich Get Richer and the Poor Get Prison: Ideology, Class, and Criminal Justice* (New York: Allyn & Bacon, 2010).

disproportionately end up the poorest of all, suffering the indignities of poverty and patriarchy. In short, state capitalism criminalizes the impoverished conditions created by capitalism. This makes the state capitalist criminal justice system the most racist, classist, and sexist institution in the United States.

This is why the fields of criminology and criminal justice need to entertain the anarchist critique if they are to call themselves academic disciplines. Criminology and criminal justice have been persistent in their misguided critiques of anarchists and anarchism without rigorously addressing the issues raised by anarchist theory and praxis.

Anarchism is a living idea based on free association and mutual aid. Anarchism emphasizes maximum human liberty while acknowledging the natural social inclination for humans to work for the mutual benefit of each other. Anarchists reject government, hierarchy, domination, private property, and coercive authority. Anarchists hold the position that freedom is contingent upon equality and that equality is the product of freely associating individuals working collectively to assure that all have equal access to collectively produced wealth. As such, anarchism rejects the privatization of wealth by state capitalism and the authoritarian distribution of collective wealth by state socialism. Anarchists believe that states are unnecessary and that social organization is best left to free associating individuals to decide their fate through direct forms of democratic organizations. There may be many manifestations of anarchist types of organization but the one similarity they share is the idea that people should be completely free to associate in the creation of social organizations designed to structure social life.[2]

One of the most fundamental, unquestioned premises of criminology and criminal justice is the notion that states are the consequence of human nature. Based on social contract theorists like Thomas Hobbes, John Locke, and Jean-Jacques Rousseau, criminology and criminal justice assume that society would be impossible without states, even though human society has existed without states for the majority of human history.[3] Hobbes's notion that life is "short,

2   The above descriptions are taken from numerous definitions of anarchism outlined in Iain McKay, *An Anarchist FAQ: Volume One* (Oakland: AK Press, 2008).
3   Earnest Barker, ed., *Social Contract: Essays by Locke, Hume, and Rousseau* (London: Oxford University Press, 1960).

brutish and nasty" without some form of sovereign power to bring order to our lives is probably one of the most damaging unquestioned assumptions underlying state power.[4] How often do we hear it touted by agents of the state that police power represents the "thin blue line," which separates us from the evils of "anarchy" and an orderly, civilized life? According to Locke and Hobbes, and to some degree Rousseau, humans are simply incapable of organizing themselves in orderly ways without the threat of state violence to serve as both a deterrent and, if need be, an executioner of aberrant behavior. In short, the state prevents what criminology and criminal justice cannons presuppose is a Hobbesian "war of all against all."[5] Criminology and criminal justice rarely ask whether state capitalism is, by its nature, violent and its behavior aberrant, and thus a legitimate form of social organization. Several anarchists included in this edition deconstruct the primary unquestioned assumption of criminology and criminal justice: that states are necessary products of human nature rather than organized forms of human subjugation and oppression.[6]

Another major unquestioned assumption examined in this collection of articles is the social construction and protection of private property and capital accumulation as one of the major purposes legitimizing state power. It is presupposed by mainstream criminology and criminal justice that private ownership of the means of production is a human right that should be protected by the legal apparatus of the state. In fact, the overwhelming majority of crimes committed under state capitalism are property-related crimes committed by those who are marginalized from the means of production, not to mention the colossal crimes committed by those who own the means of production. Both street crime and white collar/corporate crime are the direct products of capitalist economics. Street crimes are committed precisely because people are marginalized and lack access and opportunity. Those who work and produce are excluded from claiming the wealth they create because of the unquestioned assumption of private property. White collar and corporate crime are the products

4   Ibid.
5   Ibid.
6   See for example, the articles included in this text on Alexander Berkman, Peter Kropotkin, Emma Goldman, and Mikhail Bakunin. See also: Peter Kropotkin, *Anarchism: A Collection of Revolutionary Writings* (Mineola, NY: Dover Publications, 2002).

of greed created by the prioritization of the pursuit of wealth over moral and social issues pertaining to collective responsibility and justice. In short, those who take food because they are hungry are thieves. Those who work hard but have little are unfortunate. Those who find non-state-sanctioned ways to acquire the necessities of life are criminals. Owners of production who exploit and poison workers and contaminate our environment are heroes of industry. Rarely are their behaviors criminalized, and if they are, the punishment is lenient. The majority of criminological theory and criminal justice policy is constructed to legitimize, validate, and perpetuate the injustices of private property and ownership.

Anarchists reject the concept of private property because the Earth and its accompanying resources and wealth are the collective inheritance of all human and nonhuman life. The idea that the Earth's wealth and resources can be monopolized and owned by a few is patently absurd. In addition, anarchists reject the notion that those who think they own property have the right to exploit and deny others access to these collectively owned or built resources, whether land, machinery, or buildings. The fact that the criminal justice system protects the right of the few to steal the collective inheritance of the earth and to deny access to the collective needs of fellow humans is nothing other than theft, making the owners of so-called capital the real criminals of the Earth and humanity.

Another major unquestioned assumption of criminology and criminal justice is that punishment through the deprivation of liberty equals justice. The notion that we have implicitly given our consent to state power inherent in the concept of a social contract assumes that individuals have given up some of their liberty to seek sanctuary in state-mandated legal codes assumed to be in the best interest of the individual. Despite this *prima facie* fallacy, criminology and criminal justice treat prisons as legitimate and even humane ways to deal with marginalized populations. Incarceration is the mechanism used to legitimize structural racism, classism, sexism, and every other form of injustice endemic to state capitalist systems. It is no surprise that people of color in the US and throughout the colonized world are disproportionately represented in the prison industrial complex. Who consents to live a life of inequality and exploitation? Who knowingly and willingly gives up their liberty to arbitrary and capricious authorities masquerading as arbiters of moral virtue and civic order?

If the criminal justice system is not, as anarchists contend, the defender of a democratically decided civic order, then its main purpose must be to bully and coerce people into conforming to a system of systemic violence. Police, courts, and prisons are the institutions used to enforce a particular ideology that rationalizes inequality and social injustices. The criminal justice system has enforced genocide and ethnocide against Indigenous peoples, supported slavery, outlawed women's suffrage and made legal other crimes of patriarchy, prohibited LGBTQ people's right to exist, and enabled ecocide. In addition, the criminal justice system has defended the capitalist's right to exploit workers by depriving them of unions, equitable pay, and safe workplaces. Given the criminal justice system's track record of enforcing injustice, it seems only logical that anarchism, with its emphasis on theoretical deconstruction of state capitalism and actions directed against the state and its institutions of exploitation, is, as Jeff Ferrell argues, inherently criminological.[7]

How Anarchism Contributes to Criminology and Criminal Justice

Anarchism provides a key understanding to the roots of crime and conflict in society. By problematizing the nature of the state and capitalism, alternatives to the existing forms of domination become possible realities rather than just abstract ideas. Anarchism provides the critical understanding that makes social change urgent, especially with respect to institutionalized forms of classism, racism, and sexism protected by police, courts, and prisons.

Anarchism examines and works to end domination and oppressions such as racism, classism, sexism, ableism, ageism, statism, elitism, homophobia, transphobia, colonialism, and fascism.[8] Literacy with anarchism means one can no longer be ignorant of injustices

7   Jeff Ferrell, "Against the law: Anarchist criminology" in D. MacLean and D. Milovanovic, eds., *Thinking Critically about Crime* (Vancouver: Collective Press, 1997).
8   Randall Amster, A. P. DeLeon, Luis A. Fernandez, Anthony J. Nocella II, and Deric Shannon, eds., *Contemporary Anarchist Studies: An Introductory Anthology of Anarchy in the Academy* (New York: Routledge, 2009).

committed by states and their laws, police, courts, prisons, and armies.[9] Addressing injustice means being truly criminological; it means being informed of root causes of conflict, which are not thoroughly entertained within conventional criminological programs.[10] Ending domination in all of its manifestations makes the conditions of human life more free with respect to human expression, initiative, creativity, and social organization. Anarchist criminology is based on root causes of conflict and advocates for the abolition of police, prisons, punishment, and punitive justice.[11]

While mainstream criminology and criminal justice are not without their own definitions of fairness and equality, they fail to consider the fundamental structural inequality inherent in capitalism. As noted above, the laws created in the capitalist system are not neutral; they favor the interests of the owners of capital. Equality before the law is a fallacy. If equality before the law were true, then how would it be possible for a homeless person to be in violation of the law if s/he is squatting in a vacant privately-owned building? Private property makes people homeless. Juries determining the fate of the accused do so based on whether a law was violated, not on the social context of whether society and the law are just. Anarchists understand the capitalist system is rigged in favor of those who own private capital, and challenge the system of capitalism accordingly.

Anarchist criminology, theories, perspectives, and practices that address social harms and the unjust social relations that cause and maintain harm, have been present from the inception of criminology as a field of research, scholarship, and practice. Yet, formally trained criminologists and concerned members of society alike probably have little familiarity with the vibrant and vital histories of anarchist contributions to criminological understandings and analyses, specifically anarchist ideas, proposals, practices, and critiques. Illiteracy of anarchism has stunted criminology and criminal justice studies by perpetuating ineffectual policy solutions to problems only solvable by imagining a world without states and private ownership of capital.

9   Luis A. Fernandez, *Policing Dissent: Social Control and the Anti-Globalization Movement* (New Brunswick, NJ: Rutgers University Press, 2008).
10   H. E. Pepinsky, *Peacemaking: Reflections of a Radical Criminologist* (Ottawa: University of Ottawa Press, 2006).
11   Angela Y. Davis, *Are Prisons Obsolete?* (New York: Seven Stories Press, 2003).

The ever-present examples of direct democracy, communalism, and mutual aid that are present daily in contemporary society are most often ignored by conventional criminology and criminal justice studies.[12] These alternative voices need to be heard and heeded by conventional criminology and criminal justice if we are to reduce and remove sources of social injustice.[13]

Writers including Pierre-Joseph Proudhon and Peter Kropotkin wrote on issues of crime, deviance, and punishment in the 1800s. Kropotkin and others, like Emma Goldman and Voltairine de Cleyre, explicitly critiqued and challenged formal criminology and criminologists in various writings. Kropotkin and de Cleyre offered incisive criticisms of Cesare Lombroso's attempts at a scientific criminology that lacked science. These and other anarchists also contested criminal justice system practices—from laws that reflect nothing more than economic, political, and moral preferences of elites to the brutality of prisons, and to the impacts of what today are called labeling and stigma.[14]

Anarchist criminology has supported and reinforced the voices and perspectives of community-based movements and the views, ideas, and practices of resistance movements in rethinking issues of crime and justice. Anarchist criminology has been part of movements for social transformation, rebellion, insurrection, and revolution—for a new world in which social harms are mitigated as much as possible and no groups wield coercive authority against the others.

Anarchism emerges and develops within and in response and opposition to state managed industrial capitalism's associated harms ranging from enclosures, to dispossessions, to displacements, to mass murder and genocide, to slavery and exploitation.[15] Anarchist movements pose challenges to liberal democratic states that have legalized and institutionalized the social harms of industrial capitalism. Likewise, anarchists oppose and challenge the state's

12   Jeff Shantz, *Commonist Tendencies: Mutual Aid Beyond Communism* (Brooklyn: Punctum Books, 2013).

13   Mumia Abu-Jamal, *All Things Censored* (New York: Seven Stories Press, 2000).

14   Anthony J. Nocella II, "The Rise of the Terrorization of Dissent," in Mechthild E. Nagel and Anthony J. Nocella II, eds., *The End of Prisons: Reflections from the Decarceration Movement* (New York: Rodopi, 2013), 13–30.

15   Jeff Shantz and José Brendan Macdonald, *Beyond Capitalism: Building Democratic Alternatives for Today and the Future* (New York: Bloomsbury Publishing, 2013).

legalization and institutionalization of the prison industrial complex and the state's criminalizing of dissent, resistance, and individual social reformers.

Notably, anarchists are among the first, in that context of emerging criminology to go to the roots of issues like crime, conflict, and violence, and to locate such social problems in structures and systems of inequality, competition, and private property. Take, for example, Alexander Berkman, included in this collection of essays, who writes:

> Don't you see that the conditions of his whole life have made him what he is? And don't you see that the system which keeps up such conditions is a greater criminal than the petty thief? The law will step in and punish him, but is it not the same law that permits those bad conditions to exist and upholds the system that makes criminals? ... Think it over and see if it is not the law itself, the government, which really creates crime by compelling people to live in conditions that make them bad. See how law and government uphold and protect the biggest crime of all, the mother of all crimes, the capitalistic wage system, and then proceeds to punish the poor criminal.[16]

While early mainstream or hegemonic criminology was focusing on individual choices (classical theory) or individual pathologies (positivism), anarchists were situating crime within economic, political, and social relations.

Anarchists were among the first to question the power relations involved in definitions of crime and in the morality of the elite imposing their will on society. Take, for example, this classic critique of state power by Proudhon:

> To be governed is to be, at every wheel and turn and every movement, noted, registered, inventoried, priced, stamped, rated, appraised, levied, patented, licensed, authorized, annotated, admonished, thwarted, reformed, overhauled and corrected. It is to be, on the pretext of public usefulness and in the name of the general interest, taxed, exercised, ransomed, exploited,

16   Alexander Berkman, *What is Anarchism?* (Oakland: AK Press, 2003), 22–23.

monopolized, brow-beaten, pressured, bamboozled and robbed:
then at the slightest sign of resistance, at the first murmur of com-
plaint, repressed, fined, vilified, irritated, hounded, reprimanded,
knocked senseless, disarmed ... imprisoned, shot, mown down,
tried, convicted, deported ... and, to cap it all, toyed with, gulled,
offended and dishonored. So much for government, so much for
justice, so much for its morality.[17]

Anarchists were critiquing state power while the emerging discipline of criminology was legitimating state power by defending
the inequality of capitalism as constituted in the criminal justice system. One can clearly see these critiques in the works included in this
collection, especially those by Berkman, Goldman, Kropotkin, and
Proudhon.

Why Have Mainstream Criminology and Criminal Justice Ignored Anarchism?

As discussed above, criminology and criminal justice are biased disciplines founded on unquestioned assumptions and blind inquiry,
obviating the need to contextualize the historical foundations of the
study of criminology and criminal justice. Introductory criminology and criminal justice textbooks do not ask how social systems and
structures create crime. Instead, they ask why people commit crimes
in existing social systems and structures and how we can control and
reduce crime within existing social systems and structures. Questions
about how the social order is constructed to create crime are sorely
lacking with respect to the epistemological focus of the discipline.

In some cases, even critical criminological theories like neo-Marx-
ism have been notably dismissive of anarchist critiques, ignoring
counter-hegemonic anarchist histories and theories contributing to
criminology. This dismissiveness distorts the nature of critical perspectives in criminology and their development. This dismissiveness
also ignores the historically relevant fact that the earliest critical writings on criminology are anarchist in origin and influence.

17   Pierre-Joseph Proudhon, in Daniel Guérin, ed., *No Gods No Masters: An Anthology of Anarchism, Book One* (Oakland: AK Press, 1998), 80.

Criminology textbooks, those books that serve as gatekeeping and discipline-framing functions, make no mention of anarchism and anarchist theory. The exclusion or marginalization of anarchism within criminology has implications and impacts in the non-academic world as well. It is not merely an academic issue by any means. The exclusion of anarchism reinforces normative statist notions of law and order and tells the public that states and their police forces and criminal justice systems are the neutral baseline for "civilized" people, rather than historically situated, central institutions of social injustice, class violence, inequality, and societal harm.

Anarchist criminology threatens the status quo because it promotes alternatives to state capitalism, private property, police, courts, and prisons, and promotes instead social organization based on mutual aid, free association, and transformative practices of justice.[18] The neglect of anarchism in criminology denies people key insights into transformative justice practices. Transformative justice starts with the cause of crime rather than the crime itself, and it seeks to deal with an offense as a transformative opportunity to mitigate wrongs, especially among offender, victim, and community. Transformative justice is focused on the abolition of prison, police, and punishment, and recognizes issues of oppression and identity, which restorative justice does not recognize during the accountability, forgiveness, and healing process. Indigenous people, many who operated without states, practiced a transformative type of justice, making this practice comparable to many of the ideas embedded in anarchism, especially those ideas seeking to eliminate coercive authority, hierarchy, and domination. In an anarchist society, state definitions of crime would disappear, but conflict between humans would remain. The nonhierarchical and non-coercive strategies defining transformative justice will, to some degree, always be necessary. The silencing of anarchist criminology renders real-world, social-justice alternatives unfathomable, suggesting that state-centric scholarly perspectives on crime, punishment and research are the norm with respect to criminological research and analysis. This means that even critical approaches to crime and punishment have state-oriented solutions, despite the inevitable fact that the state is the antecedent cause of crime and social injustice.

18   Anthony J. Nocella II, "An overview of the history and theory of transformative justice," *Peace & Conflict Review* 6, Issue 1 (2012): 1–10.

Anarchist criminology has supported and reinforced the voices and perspectives of community-based movements and the views, ideas, and practices of resistance movements in rethinking issues of crime and justice. Anarchist criminology has been part of movements for social transformation, rebellion, insurrection, and revolution—for a new world in which social harms are mitigated as much as possible and no groups wield coercive authority against others. Simply put, anarchist movements pose challenges to liberal democratic states, which have legalized and institutionalized the social harms of capital. Likewise, anarchists oppose and challenge the state's legalization and institutionalization of the prison industrial complex and the state's criminalizing of dissent, resistance, and individual social reformers.

Given the counter-hegemonic perspective of anarchism, it becomes imperative to criminology and criminal justice to employ anarchist principles if the discipline is ever going to be a force for the application of justice in society. What is at stake for mainstream criminology and criminal justice is to be relevant by truly understanding the critiques levied by anarchism. Entrenched, unquestioned assumptions about the nature of social reality are not easily surrendered. Business as usual is the way of power and its accompanying entrenched bureaucratic structures. This text challenges the heart and soul of mainstream criminology and criminal justice to defend its preference for a political and economic system that perpetuates social injustice and inequality. If criminology and criminal justice want to be taken seriously as academic disciplines, then they need to defend themselves from the critiques raised by this volume of articles.

An Urgent Resource for Today

This is a groundbreaking volume, unique in criminology. It is the first collection to bring together in one place significant documents in anarchist criminology—writings on crime, punishment, repression, authoritarianism, and moral and social regulation. These are works that lay the foundations of anarchist criminology. This collection shows the diversity of anarchist perspectives, the richness of anarchist analysis, and the potency of anarchist challenges to statist perspectives on crime, deviance, and punishment. The writings collected here show that anarchists were among the earliest to offer critiques of state practice and among the first to directly criticize academic or formal perspectives in criminology.

The works here show the readiness of anarchists to offer alternatives to address social harms and their capacity to locate solutions to social problems in real world practices of social justice, including revolutionary movements. The writings in this collection show that anarchists effectively identified the sources of social problems in social structures and relations of inequality, and recognized that the institutions preferred by mainstream criminologists as would-be solutions to social problems were actually the causes or enablers of those harms in the first place. Police, courts, prisons, and the law can never be solutions when capitalism and the state are inherently biased systems predicated on perpetuating and normalizing inequality and violence. The dismantling of capitalism and the state obviates the need for the institutions comprising the criminal justice system. This collection will help readers to rethink the nature of criminological theories and histories of criminology as social scientific practice. It is indispensable in helping the reader to rethink the notion of justice and systems of justice as well. It shows that the history of criminology is not what hegemonic criminology and the dominant criminology textbooks have told us it is.

The writers collected here reveal a vital, alternative criminology that has run alongside, intersected with, and challenged mainstream criminology throughout its history—from the very beginning. Some of these works, such as Michael Schwab's response to Cesare Lombroso, will be new for both anarchists and criminologists. Articles by Berkman, Goldman, Kropotkin, and to some degree all the articles included in this collection will shed a spotlight on neglected areas in criminological analysis dealing with the unquestioned assumptions of state power, capitalism, and the legitimacy of criminal justice institutions. This is the foundation and framework for a re-envisioning of criminology and a re-orienting of the discipline as a field of analysis, research, and scholarship. At the same time, it provides essential literacy for criminology and criminal justice teachers and students, activists, organizers, and all those working to change the world positively and end the state and capitalist systems of exploitation, oppression, and repression.

This volume can provide a starting point for uncovering or recovering a criminology that has perhaps been forced underground but has been historically present since the inception of the study of crime and criminal justice. This is a work that will be eye-opening both for criminologists who have been denied a crucial part of their own history and for anarchists who have keen concerns about issues of state violence, repression, and criminalization and who will now have some important resources to draw on in one text.

This collection arrives at a crucial moment in social struggles, as serious and vibrant movements openly call into question the existing institutions, agencies, practices, and perspectives of justice in state capitalist liberal democracies like Canada and the United States. These social movements, bristling with revolutionary potential, call into question the continued operation of systems of criminal in/justice and seriously raise the prospect of abolition and radical alternatives. From Idle No More to Black Lives Matter, to the movements for missing and murdered Indigenous women, these movements provide an insurgent criminology of communities directly impacted by statist criminal in/justice. Anarchism has influenced many movements over the years, such as environmentalism, animal liberation, feminism, disability justice, prison abolition, political prisoner support, and labor unions.[19]

As much as ever, anarchist criminology provides important insights into the character of criminal justice systems as forces of domination and brutality and offers crucial ideas for positive alternatives based in the needs of communities of the dominated and oppressed.[20] It is hoped that the writings presented here will contribute to those community movements of transformation and offer useful resources, ideas, and examples of positive change and assertive opposition to statist power.[21]

19   See for example the following: Paul Avrich, *Anarchist Voices* (Oakland: AK Press, 2005); Steven Best and Anthony J. Nocella II, eds., *Igniting a Revolution: Voices in Defense of the Earth* (Oakland: AK Press, 2006); Anthony J. Nocella II, R. White, and E. Cudworth, eds., *Anarchism and Animal Liberation: Essays on Complementary Elements of Total Liberation* (Jefferson, NC: McFarland, 2015); Ashanti Alston, "One journey into and out of the anarchist .... BLACK!," http://www.anarchistpanther.net.
20   Daniel Guérin, *Anarchism: From Theory to Practice* (New York: Monthly Review Press, 1970).
21   Jeff Shantz, *Against All Authority: Anarchism and the Literary Imagination* (Upton Pyne, UK: Imprint Academic, 2011).

PART ONE

WILLIAM GODWIN
(1756–1836)

William Godwin's work predates the naming of anarchism as a formal political project but is considered to be its most important precursor or progenitor in Western Enlightenment thought, and an alternative to classical criminological perspectives, such as those of Cesare Beccaria and Jeremy Bentham.

Godwin situates the issues of criminology on their proper ground. Criminal justice and law rest on nothing other than coercion. This is their basis, form, and means; despite whatever more palatable dressing they might be given. Social coercion of one class over another is inherently unjust and unstable. Coercion cannot secure anything resembling social peace; rather it only ensures that injustice, inequality, and conflict persist throughout society. For Godwin, laws and criminal justice are not expressions of a social contract or individual rationality, as Bentham or Beccaria might have it, but coercion—they are force by other means.

Chapter 1 is taken from *An Enquiry Concerning Political Justice, Book VII: Of Crimes And Punishments* (London: G.G and J. Robinson, 1793).

An Enquiry Concerning Political Justice
Book VII: Of Crimes And Punishments
William Godwin

**CHAPTER I: LIMITATIONS OF THE DOCTRINE OF
PUNISHMENT WHICH RESULT FROM THE PRINCIPLES OF
MORALITY**
**Definition of punishment.—Nature of crime.—Retributive justice not
independent and absolute.—Not to be vindicated from the system of
nature.—Desert a chimerical property.—Conclusion.**

The subject of punishment is perhaps the most fundamental in the science of politics. Men associated for the sake of mutual protection and benefit. It has already appeared, that the internal affairs of such associations are of infinitely greater importance than their external.[1] It has appeared that the action of society in conferring rewards and superintending opinion is of pernicious effect.[2] Hence it follows that government, or the action of the society in its corporate capacity, can scarcely be of any utility, except so far as it is requisite for the suppression of force by force; for the prevention of the hostile attack of one member of the society upon the person or property of another, which prevention is usually called by the name of criminal justice, or punishment.

Before we can properly judge of the necessity or urgency of this action of government, it will be of some importance to consider the precise import of the word punishment. I may employ force to counteract the hostility that is actually committing on me. I may employ force to compel any member of the society to occupy the post that I conceive most conducive to the general advantage, either in the mode of impressing soldiers and sailors, or by obliging a military officer

1   Book V, Chap. XX. [Ed. Note: The Book references are to other sections of *An Enquiry Concerning Political Justice*.]
2   Book V, Chap. XII, passim.

or a minister of state to accept or retain his appointment. I may put an innocent man to death for the common good, either because he is infected with a pestilential disease, or because some oracle has declared it essential to the public safety. None of these, though they consist in the exertion of force for some moral purpose, comes within the import of the word punishment. Punishment is generally used to signify the voluntary infliction of evil upon a vicious being, not merely because the public advantage demands it, but because there is apprehended to be a certain fitness and propriety in the nature of things, that render suffering, abstractedly from the benefit to result, the suitable concomitant of vice.

The justice of punishment therefore, in the strict import of the word, can only be a deduction from the hypothesis of free-will, and must be false, if human actions be necessary. Mind, as was sufficiently apparent when we treated of that subject,[3] is an agent, in no other sense than matter is an agent. It operates and is operated upon, and the nature, the force and line of direction of the first, is exactly in proportion to the nature, force and line of direction of the second. Morality in a rational and designing mind is not essentially different from morality in an inanimate substance. A man of certain intellectual habits is fitted to be an assassin, a dagger of a certain form is fitted to be his instrument. The one or the other excites a greater degree of disapprobation, in proportion as its fitness for mischievous purposes appears to be more inherent and direct. I view a dagger on this account with more disapprobation than a knife, which is perhaps equally adapted for the purposes of the assassin; because the dagger has few or no beneficial uses to weigh against those that are hurtful, and because it has a tendency by means of association to the exiting of evil thoughts. I view the assassin with more disapprobation than the dagger, because he is more to be feared, and it is more difficult to change his vicious structure or take from him his capacity to injure. The man is propelled to act by necessary causes and irresistible motives, which, having once occurred, are likely to occur again. The dagger has no quality adapted to the contraction of habits, and, though it have committed a thousand murders, is not at all more likely (unless so far as those murders, being known, may operate as a slight associated motive with the

3   Book IV, Chap. VI.

possessor) to commit murder again. Except in the articles here spec-
ified, the two cases are exactly parallel. The assassin cannot help the
murder he commits any more than the dagger.

These arguments are merely calculated to set in a more perspic-
uous light a principle, which is admitted by many by whom the doctrine of necessity has never been examined; that the only measure
of equity is utility, and whatever is not attended with any beneficial
purpose, is not just. This is so evident a proposition that few reasonable and reflecting minds will be found inclined to reject it. Why
do I inflict suffering on another? If neither for his own benefit nor
the benefit of others, can that be right? Will resentment, the mere
indignation and horror I have conceived against vice, justify me in
putting a being to useless torture? "But suppose I only put an end to
his existence." What, with no prospect of benefit either to himself
or others? The reason the mind easily reconciles itself to this supposition is that we conceive existence to be less a blessing than a curse
to a being incorrigibly vicious. But in that case the supposition does
not fall within the terms of the question: I am in reality conferring a
benefit. It has been asked, "If we conceive ourselves two beings, each
of them solitary, but the first virtuous and the second vicious, the
first inclined to the highest acts of benevolence, if his situation were
changed for the social, the second to malignity, tyranny and injustice,
do we not feel that the first is entitled to felicity in preference to the
second?" If there be any difficulty in the question, it is wholly caused
by the extravagance of the supposition. No being can be either virtuous or vicious who has no opportunity of influencing the happiness
of others. He may indeed, though now solitary, recollect or imagine
a social state; but this sentiment and the propensities it generates can
scarcely be vigorous, unless he have hopes of being at some future
time restored to that state. The true solitaire cannot be considered as
a moral being, unless the morality we contemplate be that which has
relation to his own permanent advantage. But, if that be our meaning, punishment, unless for reform, is peculiarly absurd. His conduct
is vicious because it has a tendency to render him miserable: shall we
inflict calamity upon him, for this reason only because he has already
inflicted calamity upon himself? It is difficult for us to imagine to
ourselves a solitary intellectual being, whom no future accident shall
ever render social. It is difficult for us to separate even in idea virtue

and vice from happiness and misery; and of consequence not to imagine that, when we bestow a benefit upon virtue, we bestow it where it will turn to account; and, when we bestow a benefit upon vice, we bestow it where it will be unproductive. For these reasons the question of a solitary being will always be extravagant and unintelligible, but will never convince.

It has sometimes been alledged that the very course of nature has annexed suffering to vice, and has thus led us to the idea of punishment. Arguments of this sort must be listened to with great caution. It was by reasonings of a similar nature that our ancestors justified the practice of religious persecution: "Heretics and unbelievers are the objects of God's indignation; it must therefore be meritorious in us to mal-treat those whom God has cursed." We know too little of the system of the universe, are too liable to error respecting it, and see too small a portion of the whole, to entitle us to form our formal principles upon an imitation of what we conceive to be the course of nature.

It is an extreme error to suppose that the course of nature is something arbitrarily adjusted by a designing mind. Let us once conceive a system of percipient beings to exist, and all that we know of the history of man follows from that conception as so many inevitable consequences. Mind, beginning to exist, must have begun from ignorance, must have received idea after idea, must have been liable to erroneous conclusions from imperfect conceptions. We say that the system of the universe has annexed happiness to virtue and pain to vice. We should speak more accurately if we said, that virtue would not be virtue nor vice be vice, if this connection could cease. The office of the principle, whether mind or whatever else, to which the universe owes its existence, is less that of fabricating than conducting; is not the creation of truth, and the connecting ideas and propositions which had no original relation to each other, but the rendering truth, the nature of which is unalterable, an active and vivifying principle. It cannot therefore be good reasoning to say, the system of nature annexes unhappiness to vice, or in other words vice brings its own punishment along with it, therefore it would be unjust in us not by a positive interference to render that punishment double.

Thus it appears, whether we enter philosophically into the principle of human actions, or merely analyse the ideas of rectitude and justice which have the universal consent of mankind, that, accurately speaking, there is no such thing as desert. It cannot be just that we should inflict suffering on any man, except so far as it tends to good. Hence it follows that the strict acceptation of the word punishment by no means accords with any sound principles of reasoning. It is right that I should inflict suffering, in every case where it can be clearly shown that such infliction will produce an overbalance of good. But this infliction bears no reference to the mere innocence or guilt of the person upon whom it is made. An innocent man is the proper subject of it, if it tend to good. A guilty man is the proper subject of it under no other point of view. To punish him upon any hypothesis for what is past and irrecoverable and for the consideration of that only, must be ranked among the wildest conceptions of untutored barbarism. Every man upon whom discipline is administered, is to be considered as to the rationale of this discipline as innocent. Xerxes was not more unreasonable when he lashed the waves of the sea, than that man would be who inflicted suffering on his fellow, from a view to the past, and not from a view to the future.

It is of the utmost importance that we should bear these ideas constantly it mind during our whole examination of the theory of punishment. This theory would in the past transactions of man-kind have been totally different, if the had divested themselves of all emotions of anger and resentment, if they had considered the man who torments another for what he has done, as upon par with the child who beats the table; if they had figured to their imagination, and then properly estimated, the man, who should shut up in prison some atrocious criminal, and afterwards torture him at stated periods, merely in consideration of the abstract congruity of crime and pun-ishment, without any possible benefit to others or to himself; if they had regarded infliction as that which was to be regulated solely by the dispassionate calculation of the future, without suffering the past, in itself considered, for a moment to enter into the account.

CHAPTER II: GENERAL DISADVANTAGES OF COERCION
Conscience in matters of religion considered—In the conduct of life.— Best practicable criterion of duty—Not the decision of other men—But of our own understanding.—Tendency of coercion.—Its various classes considered.

Having thus precluded all ideas of punishment or retribution strictly so called, it belongs to us in the farther discussion of this interesting subject, to think merely of that coercion, which has usually been employed against persons convicted of past injurious action, for the purpose of preventing further mischief. And here we will first consider what is the quantity of evil which accrues from all such coercion, and secondly examine the cogency of the various reasons by which this coercion is recommended. It will not be possible wholly to avoid repetition of some of the reasons which occurred in the preliminary discussion of the exercise of private judgment.[4] But those reasonings will now be extended, and derive additional advantage from a fuller arrangement.

It is commonly said that no man ought to be compelled in matters of religion to act contrary to the dictates of his conscience. Religion is a principle which the practice of all ages has deeply impressed upon the mind. He that discharges what his own apprehensions prescribe to him on the subject, stands approved to the tribunal of his own mind, and, conscious of rectitude in his intercourse with the author of nature, cannot fail to obtain the greatest of those advantages, whatever may be their amount, which religion has to bestow. It is in vain that I endeavour by persecuting statutes to compel him to resign a false religion for a true. Arguments may convince, but persecution cannot. The new religion, which I oblige him to profess contrary to his conviction, however pure and holy it may be in its own nature, has no benefits in store for him. The sublimest worship becomes transformed into a source of corruption, when it is not consecrated by the testimony of a pure conscience. Truth is the second object in this respect, integrity of heart is the first: or rather a proposition, that in its abstract nature is truth itself, converts into rank falsehood and mortal poison, if it be professed with the lips only, and abjured by the understanding. It is then the foul garb of hypocrisy. Instead of elevating the mind above sordid temptations, it perpetually reminds the worshipper of the abject pusillanimity to which he has yielded. Instead of filling him with sacred confidence, it overwhelms with confusion and remorse.

The inference that has been made from these reasonings is, that

4   Book II, Chap. VI

criminal law is eminently misapplied in affairs of religion, and that its true province is civil misdemeanours. But this inference is false. It is only by an unaccountable perversion of reason, that men have been induced to affirm that religion is the sacred province of conscience, and that the moral duty may be left undefined to the decision of the magistrate. What, is it of no consequence whether I be the benefactor of my species, or their bitterest enemy? whether I be an informer, or a robber, or a murderer? whether I be employed as a soldier to extirpate my fellow beings, or be called upon as a citizen to contribute my property to their extirpation? whether I tell the truth with that firmness and unreserve which ardent philanthropy will not fail to inspire, or suppress science lest I be convicted of blasphemy, and fact lest I be convicted of a libel? whether I contribute my efforts for the furtherance of political justice, or quietly submit to the exile of a family of whose claims I am an advocate, or to the subversion of liberty for which every man should be ready to die? Nothing can be more clear, than that the value of religion, or of any other species of abstract opinion, lies in its moral tendency. If I should be ready to set at nought the civil power for the sake of that which is the means, how much more when it rises in contradiction to the end?

Of all human concerns morality is the most interesting. It is the perpetual associate of our transactions: there is no situation in which we can be placed no alternative that can be presented to our choice, respecting which duty is silent. "What is the standard of morality and duty?" Justice. Not the arbitrary decrees that are in force in a particular climate; but those laws of eternal reason that are equally obligatory wherever man is to be found. "But the rules of justice often appear to us obscure, doubtful and contradictory; what criterion shall be applied to deliver us from uncertainty?" There are but two criterions possible the decisions of other men's wisdom, and the decisions of our own understanding. Which of these is conformable to the nature of man? Can we surrender our own understandings? However we may strain after implicit faith, will not conscience in spite of ourselves whisper us, "This decree is equitable, and this decree is founded in mistake?" Will there not be in the minds of the votaries of superstition, a perpetual dissatisfaction, a desire to believe what is dictated to them, accompanied with a want of that in which belief consists, evidence and conviction? If we could surrender our understandings, what sort of beings should we become? By the terms of the proposition we should not be rational: the nature of things would prevent us from being moral, for morality is the judgment of reason, employed in determining on the effects to result from the different kinds of conduct we may observe.

Hence it follows that there is no criterion of duty to any man but in the exercise of his private judgment. Whatever attempts to prescribe to his conduct, and to deter him from any course of action by penalties and threats, is an execrable tyranny. There may be some men of such inflexible virtue as to set human ordinances at defiance. It is generally believed that there are others so depraved, that, were it not for penalties and threats, the whole order of society would be subverted by their excesses. But what will become of the great mass of mankind, who are neither so virtuous as the first, nor so degenerate as the second? They are successfully converted by positive laws into latitudinarians and cowards. They yield like wax to the impression that is made upon them. Directed to infer the precepts of duty from the *dicta* of the magistrate, they are too timid to resist, and too short sighted to detect the imposition. It is thus that the mass of mankind have been condemned to a tedious imbecility.

There is no criterion of duty to any man but in the exercise of his private judgment. Has coercion any tendency to enlighten the judgment? Certainly not. Judgment is the perceived agreement or disagreement of two ideas, the perceived truth or falsehood of any proposition. Nothing can aid this perception, that does not set the ideas in a clearer light, that does not afford new evidence of the substantialness or unsubstantialness of the proposition. The direct tendency of coercion is to set our understanding and our fears, our duty and our weakness at variance with each other. And how poor spirited a refuge does coercion afford? If what you require of me is duty, are there no reasons that will prove it to be such? If you understand more of eternal justice than I, and are thereby fitted to instruct me, cannot you convey the superior knowledge you possess from your understanding into mine? Will you set your wit against one who is intellectually a child, and because you are better informed than I, assume, not to be my preceptor, but my tyrant? Am I not a rational being? Could I resist your arguments, if they were demonstrative? The odious system of coercion, first annihilates the understanding of the subject, and then of him that adopts it. Dressed in the supine prerogatives of a master, he is excused from cultivating the faculties of a man. What would not man have been, long before this, if the proudest of us had no hopes but in argument, if he knew of no resort beyond, and if he were obliged to sharpen his faculties, and collect his powers, as the only means of effecting his purposes?

Let us reflect for a moment upon the species of argument, if argument it is to be called, that coercion employs. It avers to its victim that he must necessarily be in the wrong, because I am more vigorous and more cunning than he. Will vigour and cunning be always on the side of truth? Every such exertion implies in its nature a species of contest. This contest may be decided before it is brought to open trial by the despair of one of the parties. But it is not always so. The thief that by main force surmounts the strength of his pursuers, or by stratagem and ingenuity escapes from their toils, so far as this argument is valid proves the justice of his cause. Who can refrain from indignation when he sees justice thus miserably prostituted? Who does not feel, the moment the contest begins, the full extent of the absurdity that this appeal includes? It is not easy to decide which of the two is most deeply to be deplored, the magistracy, the representative of the social system, that declares war against one of its members, in the behalf of justice, or in the behalf of oppression. In the first we see truth throwing aside her native arms and her intrinsic advantage, and putting herself upon a level with falsehood. In the second we see falsehood confident in the casual advantage she possesses, artfully extinguishing the new born light that would shame her in the midst of her usurped authority. The exhibition in both is that of an infant crushed in the merciless grasp of a giant. No sophistry can be more palpable than that which pretends to bring the two parties to an impartial hearing. Observe the consistency of this reasoning. We first vindicate political coercion, because the criminal has committed an offence against the community at large, and then pretend, while we bring him to the bar of the community, the offended party, that we bring him before an impartial umpire. Thus in England, the king by his attorney is the prosecutor, and the king by his representative is the judge. How long shall such odious inconsistencies impose on mankind? The pursuit commenced against the supposed offender is the *posse comitatus*, the armed force of the whole, drawn out in such portions as may be judged necessary; and when seven millions of men have got one poor, unassisted individual in their power, they are then at leisure to torture or to kill him, and to make his agonies a spectacle to glut their ferocity.

The argument against political coercion is equally good against the infliction of private penalties between master and slave, and between parent and child. There was in reality, not only more of gallantry, but more of reason in the Gothic system of trial by duel, than in these. The trial of force is over in these as we have already said, before the exertion of force is begun. All that remains is the leisurely infliction of torture, my power to inflict it being placed in my joints and my sinews. This whole argument may be subjected to an irresistible dilemma. The right of the parent over his child lies either in his superior strength or his superior reason. If in his strength, we have only to apply this right universally, in order to drive all morality out of the world. If in his reason, in that reason let him confide. It is a poor argument of my superior reason, that I am unable to make justice be apprehended and felt in the most necessary cases, without the intervention of blows.

Let us consider the effect that coercion produces upon the mind of him against whom it is employed. It cannot begin with convincing; it is no argument. It begins with producing the sensation of pain, and the sentiment of distaste. It begins with violently alienating the mind from the truth with which we wish it to be impressed. It includes in it a tacit confession of imbecility. If he who employs coercion against me could mould me to his purposes by argument, no doubt he would. He pretends to punish me because his argument is important, but he really punishes me because his argument is weak.

CHAPTER III: OF THE PURPOSES OF COERCION
Nature of defence considered. — Coercion for restraint — For
reformation. — Supposed uses of adversity — Defective — Unnecessary. —
Coercion for example — 1. Nugatory. — The necessity of political coercion
arises from the defects of political institution. — 2. Unjust. — Unfeeling
character of this species of coercion.

Proceed we to consider three principal ends that coercion proposes to itself restraint, reformation and example. Under each of these heads the arguments on the affirmative side must be allowed to be cogent, not irresistible. Under each of them considerations will occur, that will oblige us to doubt universally of the propriety of coercion. In this examination I shall take it for granted that the persons with whom I am reasoning allow, that the ends of restraint and example may be sufficiently answered in consistency with the end of reformation, that is, without the punishment of death. To those by whom this is not allowed in the first instance, the subsequent reasonings will only apply with additional force.

The first and most innocent of all the classes of coercion is that which is employed in repelling actual force. This has but little to do with any species of political institution, but may nevertheless deserve to be first considered. In this case I am employed (suppose, for example, a drawn sword is pointed at my own breast or that of another, with threats of instant destruction) in preventing a mischief that seems about inevitably to ensue. In this case there appears to be no time for experiments. And yet even here meditation will not leave us without our difficulties. The powers of reason and truth are yet unfathomed. That truth which one man cannot communicate is less than a year, another can communicate in a fortnight. The shortest term may have an understanding commensurate to it. When Marius said with a stern look and a commanding countenance to the soldier that was sent down into his dungeon to assassinate him, "Wretch, have you the temerity to kill Marius!" and with these few words drove him to flight; it was, that he had so energetic an idea compressed in his mind, as to make its way with irresistible force to the mind of his executioner. If there were falsehood and prejudice mixed with this idea, can we believe that truth is not more powerful than they? It would be well for the human species, if they were all in this respect like Marius, all accustomed to place an intrepid confidence in the single energy of intellect. Who shall say what there is that would be impossible to men with these habits? Who shall say how far the whole species might be improved, were they accustomed to despise force in others, and did they refuse to employ it for themselves?

But the coercion we are here considering is exceedingly different. It is employed against an individual whose violence is over. He is at present engaged in no hostility against the community or any of its members. He is quietly pursuing those occupations which are beneficial to himself, and injurious to none. Upon what pretence is this man to be the subject of violence? For restraint? Restraint from what? "From some future injury which it is to be feared he will commit." This is the very argument which has been employed to justify the most execrable of all tyrannies. By what reasonings have the inquisition, the employment of spies and the various kinds of public censure directed against opinion been vindicated? Because there is an intimate connection between men's opinions and their conduct: because immoral sentiments lead by a very probable consequence to immoral actions. There is not more reason, in many cases at least, to apprehend that the man who has once committed robbery will commit it again, than the man who dissipates his property at the gaming-table, or who is accustomed to profess that upon any emergency he will not scruple to have recourse to this expedient. Nothing can be more obvious than that, whatever precautions may be allowable with respect to the future, justice will reluctantly class among these precautions any violence to be committed on my neighbour. Nor are they oftener unjust than they are superfluous. Why not arm myself with vigilance and energy, instead of locking up every man whom my imagination may bid me fear, that I may spend my days in undisturbed inactivity? If communities, instead of aspiring, as they have hitherto done, to embrace a vast territory, and to glut their vanity with ideas of empire, were contented with a small district with a proviso of confederation in cases of necessity, every individual would then live under the public eye, and the disapprobation of his neighbours, a species of coercion, not derived from the caprice of men, but from the system of the universe, would inevitably oblige him either to reform or to emigrate.—The sum of the argument under this head is, that all coercion for the sake of restraint is punishment upon suspicion, a species of punishment, the most abhorrent to reason, and arbitrary in its application, that can be devised.

The second object which coercion may be imagined to propose to itself is reformation. We have already seen various objections that may be offered to it in this point of view. Coercion cannot convince, cannot conciliate, but on the contrary alienates the mind of him against whom it is employed. Coercion has nothing in common with reason, and therefore can have no proper tendency to the generation of virtue. Reason is omnipotent: if my conduct be wrong, a very simple statement, flowing from a clear and comprehensive view, will make it appear to be such; nor is there any perverseness that can resist the evidence of which truth is capable.

But to this it may be answered, "that this view of the subject may indeed be abstractedly true, but that it is not true relative to the present imperfection of human faculties. The grand requisite for the reformation and improvement of the human species, seems to consist in the rousing of the mind. It is for this reason that the school of adversity has so often been considered as the school of virtue. In an even course of easy and prosperous circumstances the faculties sleep. But, when great and urgent occasion is presented, it should seem that the mind rises to the level of the occasion. Difficulties awaken vigour and engender strength; and it will frequently happen that the more you check and oppress me, the more will my faculties swell, till they burst all the obstacles of oppression."

The opinion of the excellence of adversity is built upon a very obvious mistake. If we will divest ourselves of paradox and singularity, we shall perceive that adversity is a bad thing, but that there is something else that is worse. Mind can neither exist nor be improved without the reception of ideas. It will improve more in a calamitous, than a torpid state. A man will sometimes be found wiser at the end of his career, who has been treated with severity, than with neglect. But because severity is one way of generating thought, it does not follow that it is the best.

It has already been shown that coercion absolutely considered is injustice. Can injustice be the best mode of disseminating principles of equity and reason? Oppression exercised to a certain extent is the most ruinous of all things. What is but this, that has habituated mankind to so much ignorance and vice for so many thousand years? Can that which in its genuine and unlimited state is the worst, become by a certain modification and diluting the best of all things? All coercion sours the mind. He that suffers it, is practically persuaded of the want of a philanthropy sufficiently enlarged in those with whom he is most intimately connected. He feels that justice prevails only with great limitations, and that he cannot depend upon being treated with justice. The lesson which coercion reads to him is, "Submit to force, and abjure reason. Be not directed by the convictions of your understanding, but by the basest part of your nature, the dread of present pain, and the pusillanimous terror of the injustice of others." It was thus Elizabeth of England and Frederic of Prussia were educated in the school of adversity. The way in which they profited by this discipline was by finding resources in their own minds, enabling them to regard unmoved the violence that was employed against them. Can this be the best possible mode of forming men to virtue? If it be, perhaps it is farther requisite that the coercion we use should be flagrantly unjust, since the improvement seems to lie not in submission, but resistance.

But it is certain that truth is adequate to awaken the mind without the aid of adversity. Truth does not consist in a certain number of unconnected propositions, but in evidence that shows them reality and their value. If I apprehend the value of any pursuit, shall I not engage in it? If I apprehend it clearly, shall I not engage in it zealously? If you would awaken my mind in the most effectual manner, tell me the truth with energy. For that purpose, thoroughly understand it yourself, impregnate your mind with its evidence, and speak from the clearness of your view, and the fullness of conviction. Were we accustomed to an education, in which truth was never neglected from indolence, or told in a way treacherous to its excellence, in which the preceptor subjected himself to the perpetual discipline of finding the way to communicate it with brevity and force, but without prejudice and acrimony, it cannot be doubted, but such an education would be much more effectual for the improvement of the mind, than all the modes of angry or benevolent coercion that can be devised.

The last object which coercion proposes is example. Glad legislators confined their views to reformation and restraint, their exertions of power, though mistaken, would still have borne the stamp of humanity. But, at the moment vengeance presented itself as a stimulus on the one side, or the exhibition of a terrible example on the other, no barbarity was then thought too great. Ingenious cruelty was busied to find new means of torturing the victim, or of rendering the spectacle impressive and horrible.

It has long since been observed that this system of policy constantly fails of its purpose. Farther refinements in barbarity produce a certain impression so long as they are new, but this impression soon vanishes, and the whole scope of a gloomy invention is exhausted in vain.[5] The

5   Beccaria, *Dei Delitti e delle Pene.*

reason of this phenomenon is that, whatever may be the force with which novelty strikes the imagination, the unchangeable principles of reason speedily recur, and assert their indestructible empire. We feel the emergencies to which we are exposed, and we feel, or we think we feel, the dictates of truth directing to their relief. Whatever ideas we form in opposition to the mandates of law, we draw, with sincerity, though it may be with some mixture of mistake, from the unalterable conditions of our existence. We compare them with the despotism which society exercises in its corporate capacity, and the more frequent is our comparison, the greater are our murmurs and indignation against the injustice to which we are exposed. But indignation is not a sentiment that conciliates; barbarity possesses none of the attributes of persuasion. It may terrify; but it cannot produce in us candour and docility. Thus ulcerated with injustice, our distresses, our temptations, and all the eloquence of feeling present themselves again and again. Is it any wonder they should prove victorious?

With what repugnance shall we contemplate the present forms of human society, If we recollect that the evils which they thus mercilessly avenge, owe their existence to the vices of those very forms? It is a well known principle of speculative truth, that true self love and social prescribe to us exactly the same species of conduct.[6] Why is this acknowledged in speculation and perpetually contradicted in practice? Is there any innate perverseness in man that continually hurries him to his own destruction? This is impossible, for man is thought, and, till thought began, he had no propensities either to good or evil. My propensities are the fruit of the impressions that have been made upon me the good always preponderating because the inherent nature of things is more powerful than any human institutions. The original sin of the worst men, is in the perverseness of these institutions, the opposition they produce between public and private good, the monopoly they create of advantages which reason directs to be left in common. What then can be more shameless than for society to make an example of those whom she has goaded to the breach of order instead of amending her own institutions, which, by straining order into tyranny, produced the mischief? Who can tell how rapid would be our progress towards the total annihilation of

6   Book IV, Chap. IX.

civil delinquency, if we did but enter upon the business of reform in the right manner?

Coercion for example, is liable to all the same objections as coercion for restraint or reformation, and to certain other objections peculiar to itself. It is employed against a person now not in the commission of offence, and of whom we can only suspect that he ever will offend. It supersedes argument reason and conviction, and requires us to think such a species of conduct our duty, because such is the good pleasure of our superiors, and because, as we are taught by the example in question, they will make us rue our stubbornness if we think otherwise. In addition to this it is to be remembered that, when I am made to suffer as an example to others, I am treated myself with supercilious neglect, as if I were totally incapable of feeling and morality. If you inflict pain upon me, you are either just or unjust. If you be just, it should seem necessary that there should be something in me that makes me the fit subject of pain either desert, which is absurd, or mischief I may be expected to perpetrate, or lastly a tendency to reformation. If any of these be the reason why the suffering I undergo is just, then example is out of the question: it may be an incidental consequence of the procedure, but it can form no part of its principle. It must surely be a very inartificial and injudicious scheme for guiding the sentiments of mankind; to fix upon an individual as a subject of torture or death, respecting whom this treatment has no direct fitness, merely that we may bid others look on, and derive instruction from his misery. This argument will derive additional force from the reasonings of the following chapter.

CHAPTER IV: OF THE APPLICATION OF COERCION

Delinquency and coercion incommensurable—External action no proper subject of criminal animadversion—How far capable of proof.—Iniquity of this standard in a moral—And in a political view.—Propriety of a retribution to be measured by the intention of the offender considered.—Such a project would overturn criminal law—Would abolish coercion.—Inscrutability, 1. Of motives—Doubtfulness of history—Declarations of sufferers.—2. Of the future conduct of the offender—Uncertainty of evidence—Either of the facts—Or the intention.—Disadvantages of the defendant in a criminal suit.

A farther consideration, calculated to show, not only the absurdity of coercion for example, but the iniquity of coercion in general, is, that delinquency and coercion are in all cases incommensurable. No standard of delinquency ever has been or ever can be discovered. No two crimes were ever alike, and therefore the reducing them explicitly or implicitly to general classes, which the very idea of example implies, is absurd. Nor is it less absurd to attempt to proportion the degree of suffering to the degree of delinquency, when the latter can never be discovered. Let us endeavour to clear in the most satisfactory manner the truth of these propositions.

Man, like every other machine the operations of which can be made the object of our senses, may he said, relatively, not absolutely speaking, to consist of two parts, the external and the internal. The form which his actions assume is one thing; the principle from which they flow is another. With the former it is possible we should be acquainted; respecting the latter there is no species of evidence that can adequately inform us. Shall we proportion the degree of suffering to the former or the latter, to the injury sustained by the community, or to the quantity of ill intention conceived by the offender? Some philosophers, sensible of the inscrutability of intention, have declared in favour of our attending to nothing but the injury sustained. The humane and benevolent Beccaria has treated this as a truth of the utmost importance, "unfortunately neglected by the majority of political institutors, and preserved only in the dispassionate speculation of philosophers."[7]

It is true that we may in many instances be tolerably informed respecting external actions, and that there will at first sight appear to be no great difficulty in reducing them to general rules. Murder, according to this system, will be the exertion of any species of action affecting my neighbour, so as that the consequences terminate in death. The difficulties of the magistrate are much abridged upon this principle, though they are by no means annihilated. It is well known how many subtle disquisitions, ludicrous or tragical according to the temper with which we view them, have been introduced to determine in each particular instance, whether the action were or were not the real occasion of the death. It never can be demonstratively ascertained.

---

7   "Questa è una di quelle palpabili verità, che per una maravigliosa combinazione di circostanze non fono con decifa sicurezza conosciute, che da alcuni pochi penfatori uomini d' ogni nazione, e d' ogni secolo." *Dei Delitti d delle Pene.*

But, dismissing this difficulty, how complicated is the iniquity of treating all instances alike, in which one man has occasioned the death of another? Shall we abolish the imperfect distinctions, which the most odious tyrannies have hitherto thought themselves compelled to admit, between chance medley, manslaughter and malice prepense? Shall we inflict on the man who, in endeavouring to save the life of a drowning fellow creature, oversets a boat and occasions the death of a second, the same suffering, as on him who from gloomy and vicious habits is incited to the murder of his benefactor? In reality the injury sustained by the community is by no means the same in these two cases, the injury sustained by the community is to be measured by the antisocial dispositions of the offender, and, if that were the right view of the subject, by the encouragement afforded to similar dispositions from his impunity. But this leads us at once from the external action to the unlimited consideration of the intention of the actor. The iniquity of the written laws of society is of precisely the same nature, though not of so atrocious a degree, in the confusion they actually introduce between varied intentions, as if this confusion were unlimited. The delinquencies recited upon a former occasion, of "one man that commits murder, to remove a troublesome observer of his depraved dispositions, who will otherwise counteract and expose him to the world; a second, because he cannot bear the ingenuous sincerity with which he is told of his vices; a third, from his intolerable envy of superior merit; a fourth, because he knows that his adversary mediates an act pregnant with extensive mischief, and perceives no other mode by which its perpetration can be prevented; a fifth, in defence of his father's life or his daughter's chastity; and any of these, either from momentary impulse, or any of the infinite shades of deliberation"[8];—are delinquencies all of them unequal, and entitled to a very different censure in the court of reason. Can a system that levels these inequalities, and confounds these differences, be productive of good? That we may render men beneficent towards each other, shall we subvert the very nature of right and wrong? Or is not this system, from whatever pretenses introduced, calculated in the most powerful manner to produce general injury? Can there be a more flagrant injury than to inscribe as we do in effect upon our

8   Book II, Chap. VI, p. 131.

courts of judgment "This is the Hall of Justice, in which the principles of right and wrong are daily and systematically slighted, and offenses of a thousand different magnitudes are confounded together, by the insolent supineness of the legislator, and the unfeeling selfishness of those who have engrossed the produce of the general labour to their sole emolument!"

But suppose, secondly, that we were to take the intention of the offender and the future injury to be apprehended, as the standard of inflictions. This would no doubt be a considerable improvement. This would be the true mode of reconciling coercion and justice, if for reasons already assigned they were neat in their own nature incompatible. It is earnestly to be desired that this mode of administering retribution should be seriously attempted. It is to be hoped that men will one day attempt to establish an accurate criterion, and not go on for ever, as they have hitherto done, with a sovereign contempt of equity and reason. This attempt would lead by a very obvious process to the abolition of all coercion.

It would immediately lead to the abolition of all criminal law. An enlightened and reasonable judicature would have recourse, in order to decide upon the cause before them, to no code but the code of reason. They would feel the absurdity of other men's teaching them what they should think, and pretending to understand the case before it happened, better than they who had all the circumstances of the case under their inspection. They would feel the absurdity of bringing every error to be compared with a certain number of measures previously invented, and compelling it to agree with one of them. But we shall shortly have occasion to return to this topic.[9]

The greatest advantage that would result from men's determining to govern themselves in the suffering to be inflicted by the motives of the offender and the future injury to be apprehended, would consist in their being taught how vain and iniquitous it is in them to attempt to wield the rod of retribution. Who is it that in his sober reason will pretend to assign the motives that influenced me in any article of my conduct, and upon them to found a grave, perhaps a capital, penalty against me? The attempt would be presumptuous and absurd, even though the individual who was to judge me, had made the longest

9   Chap. VIII.

observation of my character, and been most intimately acquainted with the series of my actions. How often does a man deceive himself in the motives of his conduct, and assign it to one principle when it in reality proceeds from another? Can we expect that a mere spectator should form a judgment sufficiently correct, when he who has all the sources of information in his hands, is nevertheless mistaken? Is it not to this hour a dispute among philosophers whether I be capable of doing good to my neighbour for his own sake? "To ascertain the intention of a man it is necessary to be precisely informed of the actual impression of the objects upon his senses, and of the previous disposition of his mind, both of which vary in different persons, and even in the same person at different times, with a rapidity commensurate to the succession of ideas, passions and circumstances."[10] Meanwhile the individuals, whose office it is to judge of this inscrutable mystery, are possessed of no previous knowledge, utter strangers to the person accused, and collecting their own lights from the information of two or three ignorant and prejudiced witnesses.

What a vast train of actual and possible motives enter into the history of a man, who has been incited to destroy the life of another? Can you tell how much in these there was of apprehended justice and how much of inordinate selfishness? how much of sudden passion, and how much of rooted depravity? how much of intolerable provocation, and how much of spontaneous wrong? how much of that sudden insanity which hurries the mind into a certain action by a sort of incontinence of nature almost without any assignable motive, and how much of incurable habit? Consider the uncertainty of history. Do we not still dispute whether Cicero were more a vain or a virtuous man, whether the heroes of ancient Rome were impelled by vain glory or disinterested benevolence, whether Voltaire were the stain of his species, or their most generous and intrepid benefactor? Upon these subjects moderate men perpetually quote upon us the impenetrableness of the human heart. Will moderate men pretend that we have not a hundred times more evidence upon which to found

10 "Questa [l'intenzione] dipende dalla impressione attuale degli oggetti, et dalla precedente disposizione della mente: esse variano in tutti gli nomini e in ciascun nomo calla velocissina successione delle idee, delle passion, e delle circoflanze." He adds, "Sarebbe dunque necessario formare non folo un codice particolare per ciascun cittadino, ma una nuova legge ad ogni delitto."

our judgment in these cases, than in that of the man who was tried last week at the Old Bailey? This part of the subject will be put in a striking light, if we recollect the narratives that have been written by condemned criminals. In how different a light do they place the transactions that proved fatal to them, from the construction that was put upon them by their judges? And yet these narratives were written under the most awful circumstances, and many of them without the least hope of mitigating their fate, and with marks of the deepest sincerity. Who will say that the judge with his slender pittance of information was more competent to decide upon the motives, than the prisoner after the severest scrutiny of his own mind? How few are the trials which an humane and a just man can read, terminating in a verdict of guilty, without feeling an uncontrolable repugnance against the verdict? If there be any sight more humiliating than all others, it is that of a miserable victim acknowledging the justice of a sentence, against which every enlightened reasoner exclaims with horror.

But this is not all. The motive, when ascertained, is only a subordinate part of the question. The point upon which only society can equitably animadvert, if it had any jurisdiction in the case, is a point, if possible, still more inscrutable than that of which we have been treating. A legal inquisition into the minds of men, considered by itself, all rational enquirers have agreed to condemn. What we want to ascertain is, not the intention of the offender, but the chance of his offending again. For this purpose we reasonably enquire first into his intention. But, when we have found this, our task is but begun. This is one of our materials, to enable us to calculate the probability of his repeating his offense or being imitated by others. Was this an habitual state of his mind, or was it a crisis in his history likely to remain an unique? What effect has experience produced on him, or what likelihood is there that the uneasiness and suffering that attend the perpetration of eminent wrong may have worked a salutary change in his mind? Will he hereafter be placed in circumstances that shall propel him to the same enormity? Precaution is in the nature of things a step in the highest degree precarious. Precaution that consists in inflicting injury on another, will at all times be odious to an equitable mind. Meanwhile be it observed, that all which has been said upon the uncertainty of crime, tends to aggravate the injustice of coercion for the sake of example. Since the crime upon which I animadvert in one man can never be the same as the crime of another, it is as if I should award a grievous penalty against persons with one eye, to prevent any man in future from putting out his eyes by design.

One more argument calculated to prove the absurdity of the attempt to proportion delinquency and suffering to each other may be derived from the imperfection of evidence. The veracity of witnesses will be to an impartial spectator a subject of continual doubt. Their competence, so far as relates to just observation and accuracy of understanding, will be still more doubtful. Absolute impartiality it would be absurd to expect from them. How much will every word and every action come distorted by the medium through which it is transmitted? The guilt of a man, to speak in the phraseology of law, may be proved either by direct or circumstantial evidence. I am found near to the body of a man newly murdered. I come out of his apartment with a bloody knife in my hand or with blood upon my clothes. If, under these circumstances and unexpectedly charged with murder, I falter in my speech or betray perturbation in my countenance, this is an additional proof. Who does not know that there is not a man in England, however blameless a life he may lead, who is secure that he shall not end it at the gallows? This is one of the most obvious and universal blessings that civil government has to bestow. In what is called direct evidence, it is necessary to identify the person of the offender. How many instances are there upon record of persons condemned upon this evidence, who after their death have been proved entirely innocent? Sir Walter Raleigh, when a prisoner in the Tower, heard some high words accompanied with blows under his window. He enquired of several eye witnesses who entered his apartment in succession, into the nature of the transaction. But the story they told varied in such material circumstances, that he could form no just idea of what had been done. He applied this to prove the vanity of history. The parallel would have been more striking if he had applied it to criminal suits.

But supposing the external action, the first part of the question to be ascertained, we have next to discover through the same garbled and confused medium the intention. How few men should I choose to entrust with the drawing up a narrative of some delicate and interesting transaction of my life? How few, though, corporally speaking, they were witnesses of what was done, would justly describe my motives, and properly report and interpret my words? And yet in an affair, that involves my life, my fame and my future usefulness, I am obliged to trust to any vulgar and casual observer.

A man properly confident in the force of truth, would consider a public libel upon his character as a trivial misfortune. But a criminal trial in a court of justice is inexpressibly different. Few men, thus circumstanced, can retain the necessary presence of mind and freedom from embarrassment. But, if they do, it is with a cold and unwilling ear that their tale is heard. If the crime charged against them be atrocious, they are half condemned in the passions of mankind, before their cause is brought to a trial. All that is interesting to them is decided amidst the first burst of indignation; and it is well if their story be impartially estimated, ten years after their body has mouldered in the grave. Why, if a considerable time elapse between the trial and the execution, do we find the severity of the public changed to compassion? For the same reason that a master, if he do not beat his slave in the moment of resentment, often feels a repugnance to the beating him at all. Not so much, as is commonly supposed, from forgetfulness of the offence, as that the sentiments of reason have time to recur, and he feels in a confused and indefinite manner the injustice of coercion. Thus every consideration tends to show, that a man tried for a crime is a poor deserted individual with the whole force of the community conspiring his ruin. The culprit that escapes, however conscious of innocence, lifts up his hands with astonishment, and can scarcely believe his senses, having such mighty odds against him. It is easy for a man who desires to shake off an imputation under which he labours, to talk of being put on his trial, but no man ever seriously wished for this ordeal, who knew what a trial was.

PART TWO

PIERRE-JOSEPH PROUDHON
(1809–1865)

Pierre-Joseph Proudhon is famously the first public figure to describe their political orientation as anarchist—and to declare "anarchist" as a positive assertion in opposition to archist tyranny. Proudhon argued that anarchy, as self-organization, rather than being a condition of chaos and disorder, is the true form of order in conditions of freedom. The Circle-A symbol, ubiquitous in urban centers as a graffiti tag of resistance, is believed to be taken from Proudhon's proposition that anarchy is order (the A in the O).

Proudhon provides criminological perspectives that predate the emergence of the formal academic criminology of Lombroso. His work is unique in analyzing private property, social violence broadly, and in contributing an analysis of war as an ongoing everyday condition of life in statist societies of economic injustice.

Chapter 2 taken from The Works of P. J. Proudhon, Volume I, translated from French by Benjamin R. Tucker (Princeton, MA, Benj. R. Tucker, 1876).

CHAPTER 2

What is Property? An Inquiry into the
Principle of Rights and of Government
Pierre-Joseph Proudhon

Chapter II: Property considered as a Natural Right.—Occupation and
Civil Law as Efficient Bases of Property.

DEFINITIONS.

The Roman law defined property as the right to use and abuse one's
own within the limits of the law—*jus utendi et abutendi re suâ, quatenus
juris ratio patitur*. A justification of the word *abuse* has been attempted, on the ground that it signifies, not senseless and immoral abuse,
but only absolute domain. Vain distinction! invented as an excuse for
property, and powerless against the frenzy of possession, which it neither prevents nor represses. The proprietor may, if he chooses, allow
his crops to rot under foot; sow his field with salt; milk his cows on
the sand; change his vineyard into a desert, and use his vegetable-
garden as a park: do these things constitute abuse, or not? In the matter of property, use and abuse are necessarily indistinguishable.

According to the Declaration of Rights, published as a preface to
the Constitution of '93, property is "the right to enjoy and dispose
at will of one's goods, one's income, and the fruit of one's labor and
industry."

Code Napoléon, article 544: "Property is the right to enjoy and
dispose of things in the most absolute manner, provided we do not
overstep the limits prescribed by the laws and regulations."

These two definitions do not differ from that of the Roman law:
all give the proprietor an absolute right over a thing; and as for the
restriction imposed by the code,—*provided we do not overstep the limits
prescribed by the laws and regulations,*—its object is not to limit property, but to prevent the domain of one proprietor from interfering

with that of another. That is a confirmation of the principle, not a limitation of it.

There are different kinds of property: 1. Property pure and simple, the dominant and seigniorial power over a thing; or, as they term it, *naked property*. 2. *Possession*. "Possession," says Duranton, "is a matter of fact, not of right." Toullier: "Property is a right, a legal power; possession is a fact." The tenant, the farmer, the *commandité*, the usufructuary, are possessors; the owner who lets and lends for use, the heir who is to come into possession on the death of a usufructuary, are proprietors. If I may venture the comparison: a lover is a possessor, a husband is a proprietor.

This double definition of property—domain and possession—is of the highest importance; and it must be clearly understood, in order to comprehend what is to follow.

From the distinction between possession and property arise two sorts of rights: the *jus in re*, the right *in* a thing, the right by which I may reclaim the property which I have acquired, in whatever hands I find it; and the *jus ad rem*, the right *to* a thing, which gives me a claim to become a proprietor. Thus the right of the partners to a marriage over each other's person is the *jus in re*; that of two who are betrothed is only the *jus ad rem*. In the first, possession and property are united; the second includes only naked property. With me who, as a laborer, have a right to the possession of the products of Nature and my own industry,—and who, as a proletaire, enjoy none of them,—it is by virtue of the *jus ad rem* that I demand admittance to the *jus in re*.

This distinction between the *jus in re* and the *jus ad rem* is the basis of the famous distinction between *possessoire* and *pétitoire*,—actual categories of jurisprudence, the whole of which is included within their vast boundaries. *Pétitoire* refers to every thing relating to property; *possessoire* to that relating to possession. In writing this memoir against property, I bring against universal society an *action pétitoire*: I prove that those who do not possess to-day are proprietors by the same title as those who do possess; but, instead of inferring therefrom that property should be shared by all, I demand, in the name of general security, its entire abolition. If I fail to win my case, there is nothing left for us (the proletarian class and myself) but to cut our throats: we can ask nothing more from the justice of nations; for, as the code of procedure (art. 26) tells us in its energetic style, *the plaintiff who has been non-suited in an action pétitoire, is debarred thereby from bringing an action possessoire.* If, on the contrary, I gain the case, we must then commence an *action possessoire*, that we may be reinstated in the enjoyment of the wealth of which we are deprived by property. I hope that we shall not be forced to that extremity; but these two actions cannot be prosecuted at once, such a course being prohibited by the same code of procedure.

Before going to the heart of the question, it will not be useless to offer a few preliminary remarks.

§ 1.—PROPERTY AS A NATURAL RIGHT.

The Declaration of Rights has placed property in its list of the natural and inalienable rights of man, four in all: *liberty, equality, property, security*. What rule did the legislators of '93 follow in compiling this list? None. They laid down principles, just as they discussed sovereignty and the laws; from a general point of view, and according to their own opinion. They did every thing in their own blind way.

If we can believe Toullier: "The absolute rights can be reduced to three: *security, liberty, property*." Equality is eliminated by the Rennes professor; why? Is it because *liberty* implies it, or because property prohibits it? On this point the author of "Droit Civil Expliqué" is silent: it has not even occurred to him that the matter is under discussion.

Nevertheless, if we compare these three or four rights with each other, we find that property bears no resemblance whatever to the others; that for the majority of citizens it exists only potentially, and as a dormant faculty without exercise; that for the others, who do enjoy it, it is susceptible of certain transactions and modifications which do not harmonize with the idea of a natural right; that, in practice, governments, tribunals, and laws do not respect it; and finally that everybody, spontaneously and with one voice, regards it as chimerical.

Liberty is inviolable. I can neither sell nor alienate my liberty; every contract, every condition of a contract, which has in view the alienation or suspension of liberty, is null: the slave, when he plants his foot upon the soil of liberty, at that moment becomes a free man. When society seizes a malefactor and deprives him of his liberty, it is a case of legitimate defence: whoever violates the social compact by the commission of a crime declares himself a public enemy; in attacking the liberty of others, he compels them to take away his own. Liberty is the original condition of man; to renounce liberty is to renounce the nature of man: after that, how could we perform the acts of man?

Likewise, equality before the law suffers neither restriction nor exception. All Frenchmen are equally eligible to office: consequently, in the presence of this equality, condition and family have, in many cases, no influence upon choice. The poorest citizen can obtain judgment in the courts against one occupying the most exalted station. Let the millionaire, Ahab, build a château upon the vineyard of Naboth: the court will have the power, according to the circumstances, to order the destruction of the château, though it has cost millions; and to force the trespasser to restore the vineyard to its original state, and pay the damages. The law wishes all property, that has been legitimately acquired, to be kept inviolate without regard to value, and without respect for persons.

The charter demands, it is true, for the exercise of certain political rights, certain conditions of fortune and capacity; but all publicists know that the legislator's intention was not to establish a privilege, but to take security. Provided the conditions fixed by law are complied with, every citizen may be an elector, and every elector eligible. The right, once acquired, is the same for all; the law compares neither persons nor votes. I do not ask now whether this system is the best; it is enough that, in the opinion of the charter and in the eyes of every one, equality before the law is absolute, and, like liberty, admits of no compromise.

It is the same with the right of security. Society promises its members no half-way protection, no sham defence; it binds itself to them as they bind themselves to it. It does not say to them, "I will shield you, provided it costs me nothing; I will protect you, if I run no risks thereby." It says, "I will defend you against everybody; I will save and avenge you, or perish myself." The whole strength of the State is at the service of each citizen; the obligation which binds them together is absolute.

How different with property! Worshipped by all, it is acknowledged by none: laws, morals, customs, public and private conscience, all plot its death and ruin.

To meet the expenses of government, which has armies to

support, tasks to perform, and officers to pay, taxes are needed. Let all contribute to these expenses: nothing more just. But why should the rich pay more than the poor? That is just, they say, because they possess more. I confess that such justice is beyond my comprehension.

Why are taxes paid? To protect all in the exercise of their natural rights—liberty, equality, security, and property; to maintain order in the State; to furnish the public with useful and pleasant conveniences.

Now, does it cost more to defend the rich man's life and liberty than the poor man's? Who, in time of invasion, famine, or plague, causes more trouble,—the large proprietor who escapes the evil without the assistance of the State, or the laborer who sits in his cottage unprotected from danger?

Is public order endangered more by the worthy citizen, or by the artisan and journeyman? Why, the police have more to fear from a few hundred laborers, out of work, than from two hundred thousand electors!

Does the man of large income appreciate more keenly than the poor man national festivities, clean streets, and beautiful monuments? Why, he prefers his country-seat to all the popular pleasures; and when he wants to enjoy himself, he does not wait for the greased pole!

One of two things is true: either the proportional tax affords greater security to the larger tax-payers, or else it is a wrong. Because, if property is a natural right, as the Declaration of '93 declares, all that belongs to me by virtue of this right is as sacred as my person; it is my blood, my life, myself: whoever touches it offends the apple of my eye. My income of one hundred thousand francs is as inviolable as the grisette's daily wage of seventy-five centimes; her attic is no more sacred than my suite of apartments. The tax is not levied in proportion to strength, size, or skill: no more should it be levied in proportion to property.

If, then, the State takes more from me, let it give me more in return, or cease to talk of equality of rights; for otherwise, society is established, not to defend property, but to destroy it. The State, through the proportional tax, becomes the chief of robbers; the State sets the example of systematic pillage: the State should be brought to the bar of justice at the head of those hideous brigands, that execrable mob which it now kills from motives of professional jealousy.

But, they say, the courts and the police force are established to restrain this mob; government is a company, not exactly for insurance, for it does not insure, but for vengeance and repression. The premium which this company exacts, the tax, is divided in proportion to property; that is, in proportion to the trouble which each piece of property occasions the avengers and repressers paid by the government.

This is any thing but the absolute and inalienable right of property. Under this system the poor and the rich distrust, and make war upon, each other. But what is the object of the war? Property. So that property is necessarily accompanied by war upon property. The liberty and security of the rich do not suffer from the liberty and security of the poor; far from that, they mutually strengthen and sustain each other. The rich man's right of property, on the contrary, has to be continually defended against the poor man's desire for property. What a contradiction!

In England they have a poor-rate: they wish me to pay this tax. But what relation exists between my natural and inalienable right of property and the hunger from which ten million wretched people are suffering? When religion commands us to assist our fellows, it speaks in the name of charity, not in the name of law. The obligation of benevolence, imposed upon me by Christian morality, cannot be imposed upon me as a political tax for the benefit of any person or poor-house. I will give alms when I see fit to do so, when the sufferings of others excite in me that sympathy of which philosophers talk, and in which I do not believe: I will not be forced to bestow them. No one is obliged to do more than comply with this injunction: *In the exercise of your own rights do not encroach upon the rights of another*; an injunction which is the exact definition of liberty. Now, my possessions are my own; no one has a claim upon them: I object to the placing of the third theological virtue in the order of the day.

Everybody, in France, demands the conversion of the five per cent bonds; they demand thereby the complete sacrifice of one species of property. They have the right to do it, if public necessity requires it; but where is the just indemnity promised by the charter? Not only does none exist, but this indemnity is not even possible; for, if the indemnity were equal to the property sacrificed, the conversion would be useless.

The State occupies the same position to-day toward the bond-holders that the city of Calais did, when besieged by Edward III, toward its notables. The English conqueror consented to spare its inhabitants, provided it would surrender to him its most distinguished citizens to do with as he pleased. Eustache and several others offered themselves; it was noble in them, and our ministers should recommend their example to the bondholders. But had the city the right to surrender them? Assuredly not. The right to security is absolute; the country can require no one to sacrifice himself. The soldier standing guard within the enemy's range is no exception to this rule. Wherever a citizen stands guard, the country stands guard with him: to-day it is the turn of the one, to-morrow of the other. When danger and devotion are common, flight is parricide. No one has the right to flee from danger; no one can serve as a scapegoat. The maxim of Caiaphas—*it is right that a man should die for his nation*—is that of the populace and of tyrants; the two extremes of social degradation.

It is said that all perpetual annuities are essentially redeemable. This maxim of civil law, applied to the State, is good for those who wish to return to the natural equality of labor and wealth; but, from the point of view of the proprietor, and in the mouth of conversionists, it is the language of bankrupts. The State is not only a borrower, it is an insurer and guardian of property; granting the best of security, it assures the most inviolable possession. How, then, can it force open the hands of its creditors, who have confidence in it, and then talk to them of public order and security of property? The State, in such an operation, is not a debtor who discharges his debt; it is a stock-company which allures its stockholders into a trap, and there, contrary to its authentic promise, exacts from them twenty, thirty, or forty per cent. of the interest on their capital.

That is not all. The State is a university of citizens joined together under a common law by an act of society. This act secures all in the possession of their property; guarantees to one his field, to another his vineyard, to a third his rents, and to the bondholder, who might have bought real estate but who preferred to come to the assistance of the treasury, his bonds. The State cannot demand, without offering an equivalent, the sacrifice of an acre of the field or a corner of the vineyard; still less can it lower rents: why should it have the right to diminish the interest on bonds? This right could not justly exist, unless the bondholder could invest his funds elsewhere to equal advantage; but being confined to the State, where can he find a place to invest them, since the cause of conversion, that is, the power to borrow to better advantage, lies in the State? That is why a government, based on the principle of property, cannot redeem its annuities without the consent of their holders. The money deposited with the republic is property which it has no right to touch while other kinds of property are respected; to force their redemption is to violate the social contract, and outlaw the bondholders.

The whole controversy as to the conversion of bonds finally reduces itself to this: —

Question. Is it just to reduce to misery forty-five thousand families who derive an income from their bonds of one hundred francs or less?

Answer. Is it just to compel seven or eight millions of tax-payers to pay a tax of five francs, when they should pay only three?

It is clear, in the first place, that the reply is in reality no reply; but, to make the wrong more apparent, let us change it thus: Is it just to endanger the lives of one hundred thousand men, when we can save them by surrendering one hundred heads to the enemy? Reader, decide!

All this is clearly understood by the defenders of the present system. Yet, nevertheless, sooner or later, the conversion will be effected and property be violated, because no other course is possible; because property, regarded as a right, and not being a right, must of right perish; because the force of events, the laws of conscience, and physical and mathematical necessity must, in the end, destroy this illusion of our minds.

To sum up: liberty is an absolute right, because it is to man what impenetrability is to matter,—a *sine qua non* of existence; equality is an absolute right, because without equality there is no society; security is an absolute right, because in the eyes of every man his own liberty and life are as precious as another's. These three rights are absolute; that is, susceptible of neither increase nor diminution; because in society each associate receives as much as he gives,—liberty for liberty, equality for equality, security for security, body for body, soul for soul, in life and in death.

But property, in its derivative sense, and by the definitions of law, is a right outside of society; for it is clear that, if the wealth of each was social wealth, the conditions would be equal for all, and it would be a contradiction to say: *Property is a man's right to dispose at will of social property*. Then if we are associated for the sake of liberty, equality, and security, we are not associated for the sake of property; then if property is a *natural* right, this natural right is not *social*, but *anti-social*. Property and society are utterly irreconcilable institutions. It is as impossible to associate two proprietors as to join two magnets by their opposite poles. Either society must perish, or it must destroy property.

If property is a natural, absolute, imprescriptible, and inalienable right, why, in all ages, has there been so much speculation as to its origin?—for this is one of its distinguishing characteristics. The origin of a natural right! Good God! who ever inquired into the origin of the rights of liberty, security, or equality? They exist by the same right that we exist; they are born with us, they live and die with us. With property it is very different, indeed. By law, property can exist without a proprietor, like a quality without a subject. It exists for the human being who as yet is not, and for the octogenarian who is no more. And yet, in spite of these wonderful prerogatives which savor of the eternal and the infinite, they have never found the origin of property; the doctors still disagree. On one point only are they in harmony: namely, that the validity of the right of property depends upon the authenticity of its origin. But this harmony is their condemnation. Why have they acknowledged the right before settling the question of origin?

Certain classes do not relish investigation into the pretended titles to property, and its fabulous and perhaps scandalous history. They wish to hold to this proposition: that property is a fact; that it always has been, and always will be. With that proposition the *savant* Proudhon[1] commenced his "Treatise on the Right of Usufruct," regarding the origin of property as a useless question. Perhaps I would subscribe to this doctrine, believing it inspired by a commendable love of peace, were all my fellow-citizens in comfortable circumstances; but, no! I will not subscribe to it.

The titles on which they pretend to base the right of property are two in number: *occupation* and *labor*. I shall examine them successively,

---

1   The Proudhon here referred to is J. B. V. Proudhon; a distinguished French jurist, and distant relative of the author—*Translator* [Benjamin Tucker].

under all their aspects and in detail; and I remind the reader that, to whatever authority we appeal, I shall prove beyond a doubt that property, to be just and possible, must necessarily have equality for its condition.

§ 2.—Occupation, as the Title to Property.

It is remarkable that, at those meetings of the State Council at which the Code was discussed, no controversy arose as to the origin and principle of property. All the articles of Vol. II, Book 2, concerning property and the right of accession, were passed without opposition or amendment. Bonaparte, who on other questions had given his legists so much trouble, had nothing to say about property. Be not surprised at it: in the eyes of that man, the most selfish and wilful person that ever lived, property was the first of rights, just as submission to authority was the most holy of duties.

The right of *occupation*, or of the *first occupant*, is that which results from the actual, physical, real possession of a thing. I occupy a piece of land; the presumption is, that I am the proprietor, until the contrary is proved. We know that originally such a right cannot be legitimate unless it is reciprocal; the jurists say as much.

Cicero compares the earth to a vast theatre: *Quemadmodum theatrum cum commune sit, recte tamen dici potest ejus esse eum locum quem quisque occuparit.*

This passage is all that ancient philosophy has to say about the origin of property.

The theatre, says Cicero, is common to all; nevertheless, the place that each one occupies is called *his own*; that is, it is a place *possessed*, not a place *appropriated*. This comparison annihilates property; moreover, it implies equality. Can I, in a theatre, occupy at the same time one place in the pit, another in the boxes, and a third in the gallery? Not unless I have three bodies, like Geryon, or can exist in different places at the same time, as is related of the magician Apollonius.

According to Cicero, no one has a right to more than he needs: such is the true interpretation of his famous axiom—*suum quidque cujusque sit,* to each one that which belongs to him—an axiom that has been strangely applied. That which belongs to each is not that which each *may* possess, but that which each *has a right* to possess.

Now, what have we a right to possess? That which is required for our labor and consumption; Cicero's comparison of the earth to a theatre proves it. According to that, each one may take what place he will, may beautify and adorn it, if he can; it is allowable: but he must never allow himself to overstep the limit which separates him from another. The doctrine of Cicero leads directly to equality; for, occupation being pure toleration, if the toleration is mutual (and it cannot be otherwise) the possessions are equal.

Grotius rushes into history; but what kind of reasoning is that which seeks the origin of a right, said to be natural, elsewhere than in Nature? This is the method of the ancients: the fact exists, then it is necessary, then it is just, then its antecedents are just also. Nevertheless, let us look into it.

"Originally, all things were common and undivided; they were the property of all." Let us go no farther. Grotius tells us how this original communism came to an end through ambition and cupidity; how the age of gold was followed by the age of iron, &c. So that property rested first on war and conquest, then on treaties and agreements. But either these treaties and agreements distributed wealth equally, as did the original communism (the only method of distribution with which the barbarians were acquainted, and the only form of justice of which they could conceive; and then the question of origin assumes this form: how did equality afterwards disappear?)—or else these treaties and agreements were forced by the strong upon the weak, and in that case they are null; the tacit consent of posterity does not make them valid, and we live in a permanent condition of iniquity and fraud.

We never can conceive how the equality of conditions, having once existed, could afterwards have passed away. What was the cause of such degeneration? The instincts of the animals are unchangeable, as well as the differences of species; to suppose original equality in human society is to admit by implication that the present inequality is a degeneration from the nature of this society,—a thing which the defenders of property cannot explain. But I infer therefrom that, if Providence placed the first human beings in a condition of equality, it was an indication of its desires, a model that it wished them to realize in other forms; just as the religious sentiment, which it planted in their hearts, has developed and manifested itself in various ways. Man has but one nature, constant and unalterable: he pursues it through instinct, he wanders from it through reflection, he returns to it through judgment; who shall say that we are not returning now? According to Grotius, man has abandoned equality; according to me, he will yet return to it. How came he to abandon it? Why will he return to it? These are questions for future consideration.

Reid writes as follows: —

"The right of property is not innate, but acquired. It is not grounded upon the constitution of man, but upon his actions. Writers on jurisprudence have explained its origin in a manner that may satisfy every man of common understanding.

"The earth is given to men in common for the purposes of life, by the bounty of Heaven. But to divide it, and appropriate one part of its produce to one, another part to another, must be the work of men who have power and understanding given them, by which every man may accommodate himself, *without hurt to any other*.

"This common right of every man to what the earth produces, before it be occupied and appropriated by others, was, by ancient moralists, very properly compared to the right which every citizen had to the public theatre, where every man that came might occupy an empty seat, and thereby acquire a right to it while the entertainment lasted; but no man had a right to dispossess another.

"The earth is a great theatre, furnished by the Almighty, with perfect wisdom and goodness, for the entertainment and employment of all mankind. Here every man has a right to accommodate himself as a spectator, and to perform his part as an actor; but without hurt to others."

Consequences of Reid's doctrine.

1. That the portion which each one appropriates may wrong no one, it must be equal to the quotient of the total amount of property to be shared, divided by the number of those who are to share it;

2. The number of places being of necessity equal at all times to that of the spectators, no spectator can occupy two places, nor can any actor play several parts;

3. Whenever a spectator comes in or goes out, the places of all contract or enlarge correspondingly: for, says Reid, "*the right of property is not innate, but acquired;*" consequently, it is not absolute; consequently, the occupancy on which it is based, being a conditional fact, cannot endow this right with a stability which it does not possess

itself. This seems to have been the thought of the Edinburgh professor when he added: —

"A right to life implies a right to the necessary means of life; and that justice, which forbids the taking away the life of an innocent man, forbids no less the taking from him the necessary means of life. He has the same right to defend the one as the other. To hinder another man's innocent labor, or to deprive him of the fruit of it, is an injustice of the same kind, and has the same effect as to put him in fetters or in prison, and is equally a just object of resentment."

Thus the chief of the Scotch school, without considering at all the inequality of skill or labor, posits *a priori* the equality of the means of labor, abandoning thereafter to each laborer the care of his own person, after the eternal axiom: *Whoso does well, shall fare well.*

The philosopher Reid is lacking, not in knowledge of the principle, but in courage to pursue it to its ultimate. If the right of life is equal, the right of labor is equal, and so is the right of occupancy. Would it not be criminal, were some islanders to repulse, in the name of property, the unfortunate victims of a shipwreck struggling to reach the shore? The very idea of such cruelty sickens the imagination. The proprietor, like Robinson Crusoe on his island, wards off with pike and musket the proletaire washed overboard by the wave of civilization, and seeking to gain a foothold upon the rocks of property. "Give me work!" cries he with all his might to the proprietor: "don't drive me away, I will work for you at any price." "I do not need your services," replies the proprietor, showing the end of his pike or the barrel of his gun. "Lower my rent at least." "I need my income to live upon." "How can I pay you, when I can get no work?" "That is your business." Then the unfortunate proletaire abandons himself to the waves; or, if he attempts to land upon the shore of property, the proprietor takes aim, and kills him.

We have just listened to a spiritualist; we will now question a materialist, then an eclectic: and having completed the circle of philosophy, we will turn next to law.

According to Destutt de Tracy, property is a necessity of our nature. That this necessity involves unpleasant consequences, it would be folly to deny. But these consequences are necessary evils which do not invalidate the principle; so that it as unreasonable to rebel against property on account of the abuses which it generates, as to complain of life because it is sure to end in death. This brutal and pitiless philosophy promises at least frank and close reasoning. Let us see if it keeps its promise.

"We talk very gravely about the conditions of property, ... as if it was our province to decide what constitutes property.... It would seem, to hear certain philosophers and legislators, that at a certain moment, spontaneously and without cause, people began to use the words *thine* and *mine;* and that they might have, or ought to have, dispensed with them. But *thine* and *mine* were never invented."

A philosopher yourself, you are too realistic. *Thine* and *mine* do not necessarily refer to self, as they do when I say *your* philosophy, and *my* equality; for *your* philosophy is you philosophizing, and *my* equality is I professing equality. *Thine* and *mine* oftener indicate a relation,—*your* country, *your* parish, *your* tailor, *your* milkmaid; *my* chamber, *my* seat at the theatre, *my* company and *my* battalion in the National Guard. In the former sense, we may sometimes say *my* labor, *my* skill, *my* virtue; never *my* grandeur nor *my* majesty: in the latter sense only, *my* field, *my* house, *my* vineyard, *my* capital,—precisely as the banker's clerk says *my* cash-box. In short, *thine* and *mine* are signs and expressions of personal, but equal, rights; applied to things outside of us, they indicate possession, function, use, not property.

It does not seem possible, but, nevertheless, I shall prove, by quotations, that the whole theory of our author is based upon this paltry equivocation.

"Prior to all covenants, men are, not exactly, as Hobbes says, in a state of *hostility,* but of *estrangement.* In this state, justice and injustice are unknown; the rights of one bear no relation to the rights of another. All have as many rights as needs, and all feel it their duty to satisfy those needs by any means at their command."

Grant it; whether true or false, it matters not. Destutt de Tracy cannot escape equality. On this theory, men, while in a state of *estrangement,* are under no obligations to each other; they all have the right to satisfy their needs without regard to the needs of others, and consequently the right to exercise their power over Nature, each according to his strength and ability. That involves the greatest inequality of wealth. Inequality of conditions, then, is the characteristic feature of estrangement or barbarism: the exact opposite of Rousseau's idea. But let us look farther: —

"Restrictions of these rights and this duty commence at the time when covenants, either implied or expressed, are agreed upon. Then appears for the first time justice and injustice; that is, the balance between the rights of one and the rights of another, which up to that time were necessarily equal."

Listen: *rights were equal*; that means that each individual had the right to *satisfy his needs without reference to the needs of others*. In other words, that all had the right to injure each other; that there was no right save force and cunning. They injured each other, not only by war and pillage, but also by usurpation and appropriation. Now, in order to abolish this equal right to use force and stratagem,—this equal right to do evil, the sole source of the inequality of benefits and injuries,—they commenced to make *covenants either implied or expressed*, and established a balance. Then these agreements and this balance were intended to secure to all equal comfort; then, by the law of contradictions, if isolation is the principle of inequality, society must produce equality. The social balance is the equalization of the strong and the weak; for, while they are not equals, they are strangers; they can form no associations,—they live as enemies. Then, if inequality of conditions is a necessary evil, so is isolation, for society and inequality are incompatible with each other. Then, if society is the true condition of man's existence, so is equality also. This conclusion cannot be avoided.

This being so, how is it that, ever since the establishment of this balance, inequality has been on the increase? How is it that justice and isolation always accompany each other? Destutt de Tracy shall reply: —

"*Needs* and *means*, *rights* and *duties*, are products of the will. If man willed nothing, these would not exist. But to have needs and means, rights and duties, is to *have*, to *possess*, something. They are so many kinds of property, using the word in its most general sense: they are things which belong to us."

Shameful equivocation, not justified by the necessity for generalization! The word *property* has two meanings: 1. It designates the quality which makes a thing what it is; the attribute which is peculiar to it, and especially distinguishes it. We use it in this sense when we say *the properties of the triangle* or of *numbers; the property of the magnet*, &c. 2. It expresses the right of absolute control over a thing by a free and intelligent being. It is used in this sense by writers on jurisprudence. Thus, in the phrase, *iron acquires the property of a magnet*, the word *property* does not convey the same idea that it does in this one: *I have acquired this magnet as my property*. To tell a poor man that he HAS property because he HAS arms and legs,—that the hunger from which he suffers, and his power to sleep in the open air are his property,—is to play upon words, and to add insult to injury.

"The sole basis of the idea of property is the idea of personality. As soon as property is born at all, it is born, of necessity, in all its fulness. As soon as an individual knows *himself*,—his moral personality, his capacities of enjoyment, suffering, and action,—he necessarily sees also that this *self* is exclusive proprietor of the body in which it dwells, its organs, their powers, faculties, &c. ... Inasmuch as artificial and conventional property exists, there must be natural property also; for nothing can exist in art without its counterpart in Nature."

We ought to admire the honesty and judgment of philosophers! Man has properties; that is, in the first acceptation of the term, faculties. He has property; that is, in its second acceptation, the right of domain. He has, then, the property of the property of being proprietor. How ashamed I should be to notice such foolishness, were I here considering only the authority of Destutt de Tracy! But the entire human race, since the origination of society and language, when metaphysics and dialectics were first born, has been guilty of this puerile confusion of thought. All which man could call *his own* was identified in his mind with his person. He considered it as his property, his wealth; a part of himself, a member of his body, a faculty of his mind. The possession of things was likened to property in the powers of the body and mind; and on this false analogy was based the right of property,—*the imitation of Nature by art*, as Destutt de Tracy so elegantly puts it.

But why did not this ideologist perceive that man is not proprietor even of his own faculties? Man has powers, attributes, capacities; they are given him by Nature that he may live, learn, and love: he does not own them, but has only the use of them; and he can make no use of them that does not harmonize with Nature's laws. If he had absolute mastery over his faculties, he could avoid hunger and cold; he could eat unstintedly, and walk through fire; he could move mountains, walk a hundred leagues in a minute, cure without medicines and by the sole force of his will, and could make himself immortal. He could say, "I wish to produce," and his tasks would be finished with the words; he could say. "I wish to know," and he would know; "I love," and he would enjoy. What then? Man is not master of himself, but may be of his surroundings. Let him use the wealth of Nature, since he can live only by its use; but let him abandon his pretensions to the title of proprietor, and remember that he is called so only metaphorically.

To sum up: Destutt de Tracy classes together the external *productions* of Nature and art, and the *powers* or *faculties* of man, making both of them species of property; and upon this equivocation he hopes to establish, so firmly that it can never be disturbed, the right of property. But of these different kinds of property some are *innate*, as memory, imagination, strength, and beauty; while others are *acquired*, as land, water, and forests. In the state of Nature or isolation, the strongest and most skilful (that is, those best provided with innate property) stand the best chance of obtaining acquired property. Now, it is to prevent this encroachment and the war which results therefrom, that a balance (justice) has been employed, and covenants (implied or expressed) agreed upon: it is to correct, as far as possible, inequality of innate property by equality of acquired property. As long as the division remains unequal, so long the partners remain enemies; and it is the purpose of the covenants to reform this state of things. Thus we have, on the one hand, isolation, inequality, enmity, war, robbery, murder; on the other, society, equality, fraternity, peace, and love. Choose between them!

M. Joseph Dutens—a physician, engineer, and geometrician, but a very poor legist, and no philosopher at all—is the author of a "Philosophy of Political Economy," in which he felt it his duty to break lances in behalf of property. His reasoning seems to be borrowed from Destutt de Tracy. He commences with this definition of property, worthy of Sganarelle: "Property is the right by which a thing is one's own." Literally translated: Property is the right of property.

After getting entangled a few times on the subjects of will, liberty, and personality; after having distinguished between *immaterial-natural* property, and *material-natural* property, a distinction similar to Destutt de Tracy's of innate and acquired property,—M. Joseph Dutens concludes with these two general propositions: 1. Property is a natural and inalienable right of every man; 2. Inequality of property is a necessary result of Nature,—which propositions are convertible into a simpler one: All men have an equal right of unequal property.

He rebukes M. de Sismondi for having taught that landed property has no other basis than law and conventionality; and he says himself, speaking of the respect which people feel for property, that "their good sense reveals to them the nature of the *original contract* made between society and proprietors."

He confounds property with possession, communism with equality, the just with the natural, and the natural with the possible. Now he takes these different ideas to be equivalents; now he seems to distinguish between them, so much so that it would be infinitely easier to refute him than to understand him. Attracted first by the title of the work, "Philosophy of Political Economy," I have found, among the author's obscurities, only the most ordinary ideas. For that reason I will not speak of him.

M. Cousin, in his "Moral Philosophy," page 15, teaches that all morality, all laws, all rights are given to man with this injunction: "*Free being, remain free.*" Bravo! master; I wish to remain free if I can. He continues: —

"Our principle is true; it is good, it is social. Do not fear to push it to its ultimate.

"1. If the human person is sacred, its whole nature is sacred; and particularly its interior actions, its feelings, its thoughts, its voluntary decisions. This accounts for the respect due to philosophy, religion, the arts industry, commerce, and to all the results of liberty. I say respect, not simply toleration; for we do not tolerate a right, we respect it."

I bow my head before this philosophy.

"2. My liberty, which is sacred, needs for its objective action an instrument which we call the body: the body participates then in the sacredness of liberty; it is then inviolable. This is the basis of the principle of individual liberty.

"3. My liberty needs, for its objective action, material to work upon; in other words, property or a thing. This thing or property naturally participates then in the inviolability of my person. For instance, I take possession of an object which has become necessary and useful in the outward manifestation of my liberty. I say, 'This object is mine since it belongs to no one else; consequently, I possess it legitimately.' So the legitimacy of possession rests on two conditions. First, I possess only as a free being. Suppress free activity, you destroy my power to labor. Now it is only by labor that I can use this property or thing, and it is only by using it that I possess it. Free activity is then the principle of the right of property. But that alone does not legitimate possession. All men are free; all can use property by labor. Does that mean that all men have a right to all property? Not at all. To possess legitimately, I must not only labor and produce in my capacity of a free being, but I must also be the first to occupy the property. In short, if labor and production are the principle of the right of property, the fact of first occupancy is its indispensable condition.

"4. I possess legitimately: then I have the right to use my property as I see fit. I have also the right to give it away. I have also the right to bequeath it; for if I decide to make a donation, my decision is as valid after my death as during my life."

In fact, to become a proprietor, in M. Cousin's opinion, one must take possession by occupation and labor. I maintain that the element of time must be considered also; for if the first occupants have occupied every thing, what are the new comers to do? What will become of them, having an instrument with which to work, but no material to work upon? Must they devour each other? A terrible extremity, unforeseen by philosophical prudence; for the reason that great geniuses neglect little things.

Notice also that M. Cousin says that neither occupation nor labor, taken separately, can legitimate the right of property; and that it is born only from the union of the two. This is one of M. Cousin's eclectic turns, which he, more than any one else, should take pains to avoid. Instead of proceeding by the method of analysis, comparison, elimination, and reduction (the only means of discovering the truth amid the various forms of thought and whimsical opinions), he jumbles all systems together, and then, declaring each both right and wrong, exclaims: "There you have the truth."

But, adhering to my promise, I will not refute him. I will only prove, by all the arguments with which he justifies the right of property, the principle of equality which kills it. As I have already said, my sole intent is this: to show at the bottom of all these positions that inevitable major, *equality*; hoping hereafter to show that the principle of property vitiates the very elements of economical, moral, and governmental science, thus leading it in the wrong direction.

Well, is it not true, from M. Cousin's point of view, that, if the liberty of man is sacred, it is equally sacred in all individuals; that, if it needs property for its objective action, that is, for its life, the appropriation of material is equally necessary for all; that, if I wish to be respected in my right of appropriation, I must respect others in theirs; and, consequently, that though, in the sphere of the infinite, a person's power of appropriation is limited only by himself, in the sphere of the finite this same power is limited by the mathematical relation between the number of persons and the space which they occupy? Does it not follow that if one individual cannot prevent another—his fellow-man—from appropriating an amount of material equal to his own, no more can he prevent individuals yet to come; because, while individuality passes away, universality persists, and eternal laws cannot be determined by a partial view of their manifestations? Must we not conclude, therefore, that whenever a person is born, the others must crowd closer together; and, by reciprocity of obligation, that if the new comer is afterwards to become an heir, the right of succession does not give him the right of accumulation, but only the right of choice?

I have followed M. Cousin so far as to imitate his style, and I am ashamed of it. Do we need such high-sounding terms, such sonorous phrases, to say such simple things? Man needs to labor in order to live; consequently, he needs tools to work with and materials to work upon. His need to produce constitutes his right to produce. Now, this right is guaranteed him by his fellows, with whom he makes an agreement to that effect. One hundred thousand men settle in a large country like France with no inhabitants: each man has a right to 1/100,000 of the land. If the number of possessors increases, each one's portion diminishes in consequence; so that, if the number of inhabitants rises to thirty-four millions, each one will have a right only to 1/34,000,000. Now, so regulate the police system and the government, labor, exchange, inheritance, &c., that the means of labor shall be shared by all equally, and that each individual shall be free; and then society will be perfect.

Of all the defenders of property, M. Cousin has gone the farthest. He has maintained against the economists that labor does not establish the right of property unless preceded by occupation, and against the jurists that the civil law can determine and apply a natural right, but cannot create it. In fact, it is not sufficient to say, "The right of property is demonstrated by the existence of property; the function of the civil law is purely declaratory." To say that, is to confess that there is no reply to those who question the legitimacy of the fact itself. Every right must be justifiable in itself, or by some antecedent right; property is no exception. For this reason, M. Cousin has sought to base it upon the *sanctity* of the human personality, and the act by which the will assimilates a thing. "Once touched by man," says one of M. Cousin's disciples, "things receive from him a character which transforms and humanizes them." I confess, for my part, that I have no faith in this magic, and that I know of nothing less holy than the will of man. But this theory, fragile as it seems to psychology as well as jurisprudence, is nevertheless more philosophical and profound than those theories which are based upon labor or the authority of the law. Now, we have just seen to what this theory of which we are speaking leads,—to the equality implied in the terms of its statement.

But perhaps philosophy views things from too lofty a standpoint, and is not sufficiently practical; perhaps from the exalted summit of speculation men seem so small to the metaphysician that he cannot distinguish between them; perhaps, indeed, the equality of conditions is one of those principles which are very true and sublime as generalities, but which it would be ridiculous and even dangerous to attempt to rigorously apply to the customs of life and to social transactions. Undoubtedly, this is a case which calls for imitation of the wise reserve of moralists and jurists, who warn us against carrying things to extremes, and who advise us to suspect every definition; because there is not one, they say, which cannot be utterly destroyed by developing its disastrous results—*Omnis definitio in jure civili periculosa est: parum est enim ut non subverti possit.* Equality of conditions,—a terrible dogma in the ears of the proprietor, a consoling truth at the poor-man's sick-bed, a frightful reality under the knife of the anatomist,—equality of conditions, established in the political, civil, and industrial spheres, is only an alluring impossibility, an inviting bait, a satanic delusion.

It is never my intention to surprise my reader. I detest, as I do death, the man who employs subterfuge in his words and conduct.

From the first page of this book, I have expressed myself so plainly and decidedly that all can see the tendency of my thought and hopes; and they will do me the justice to say, that it would be difficult to exhibit more frankness and more boldness at the same time. I do not hesitate to declare that the time is not far distant when this reserve, now so much admired in philosophers—this happy medium so strongly recommended by professors of moral and political science—will be regarded as the disgraceful feature of a science without principle, and as the seal of its reprobation. In legislation and morals, as well as in geometry, axioms are absolute, definitions are certain; and all the results of a principle are to be accepted, provided they are logically deduced. Deplorable pride! We know nothing of our nature, and we charge our blunders to it; and, in a fit of unaffected ignorance, cry out, "The truth is in doubt, the best definition defines nothing!" We shall know some time whether this distressing uncertainty of jurisprudence arises from the nature of its investigations, or from our prejudices; whether, to explain social phenomena, it is not enough to change our hypothesis, as did Copernicus when he reversed the system of Ptolemy.

But what will be said when I show, as I soon shall, that this same jurisprudence continually tries to base property upon equality? What reply can be made?

§ 3.—CIVIL LAW AS THE FOUNDATION AND SANCTION OF PROPERTY.
Pothier seems to think that property, like royalty, exists by divine right. He traces back its origin to God himself—*ab Jove principium.* He begins in this way:—

"God is the absolute ruler of the universe and all that it contains: *Domini est terra et plenitudo ejus, orbis et universi qui habitant in eo.* For the human race he has created the earth and all its creatures, and has given it a control over them subordinate only to his own. 'Thou madest him to have dominion over the works of thy hands; thou hast put all things under his feet,' says the Psalmist. God accompanied this gift with these words, addressed to our first parents after the creation: 'Be fruitful, and multiply and replenish the earth,'" &c.

After this magnificent introduction, who would refuse to believe the human race to be an immense family living in brotherly union, and under the protection of a venerable father? But, heavens! are brothers enemies? Are fathers unnatural, and children prodigal?

God gave the earth to the human race: why then have I received none? *He has put all things under my feet,*—and I have not where to lay my head! *Multiply,* he tells us through his interpreter, Pothier. Ah, learned Pothier! that is as easy to do as to say; but you must give moss to the bird for its nest.

"The human race having multiplied, men divided among themselves the earth and most of the things upon it; that which fell to each, from that time exclusively belonged to him. That was the origin of the right of property."

Say, rather, the right of possession. Men lived in a state of communism; whether positive or negative it matters little. Then there was no property, not even private possession. The genesis and growth of possession gradually forcing people to labor for their support, they agreed either formally or tacitly,—it makes no difference which,— that the laborer should be sole proprietor of the fruit of his labor; that is, they simply declared the fact that thereafter none could live without working. It necessarily followed that, to obtain equality of products, there must be equality of labor; and that, to obtain equality of labor, there must be equality of facilities for labor. Whoever without labor got possession, by force or by strategy, of another's means of subsistence, destroyed equality, and placed himself above or outside of the law. Whoever monopolized the means of production on the ground of greater industry, also destroyed equality. Equality being then the expression of right, whoever violated it was *unjust.*

Thus, labor gives birth to private possession; the right in a thing—*jus in re.* But in what thing? Evidently *in the product,* not *in the soil.* So the Arabs have always understood it; and so, according to Cæsar and Tacitus, the Germans formerly held. "The Arabs," says M. de Sismondi, "who admit a man's property in the flocks which he has raised, do not refuse the crop to him who planted the seed; but they do not see why another, his equal, should not have a right to plant in his turn. The inequality which results from the pretended right of the first occupant seems to them to be based on no principle of justice; and when all the land falls into the hands of a certain number of inhabitants, there results a monopoly in their favor against the rest of the nation, to which they do not wish to submit."

Well, they have shared the land. I admit that therefrom results a more powerful organization of labor; and that this method of distribution, fixed and durable, is advantageous to production: but how could this division give to each a transferable right of property in a thing to which all had an inalienable right of possession? In the terms of jurisprudence, this metamorphosis from possessor to proprietor is legally impossible; it implies in the jurisdiction of the courts the union of *possessoire* and *pétitoire*; and the mutual concessions of those who share the land are nothing less than traffic in natural rights. The original cultivators of the land, who were also the original makers of the law, were not as learned as our legislators, I admit; and had they been, they could not have done worse: they did not foresee the consequences of the transformation of the right of private possession into the right of absolute property. But why have not those, who in later times have established the distinction between *jus in re* and *jus ad rem*, applied it to the principle of property itself?

Let me call the attention of the writers on jurisprudence to their own maxims.

The right of property, provided it can have a cause, can have but one—*Dominium non potest nisi ex una causa contingere.* I can possess by several titles; I can become proprietor by only one—*Non ut ex pluribus causis idem nobis deberi potest, ita ex pluribus causis idem potest nostrum esse.* The field which I have cleared, which I cultivate, on which I have built my house, which supports myself, my family, and my livestock, I can possess: 1st. As the original occupant; 2d. As a laborer; 3d. By virtue of the social contract which assigns it to me as my share. But none of these titles confer upon me the right of property. For, if I attempt to base it upon occupancy, society can reply, "I am the original occupant." If I appeal to my labor, it will say, "It is only on that condition that you possess." If I speak of agreements, it will respond, "These agreements establish only your right of use." Such, however, are the only titles which proprietors advance. They never have been able to discover any others. Indeed, every right—it is Pothier who says it—supposes a producing cause in the person who enjoys it; but in man who lives and dies, in this son of earth who passes away like a shadow, there exists, with respect to external things, only titles of possession, not one title of property. Why, then, has society recognized a right injurious to itself, where there is no producing cause?

Why, in according possession, has it also conceded property? Why has the law sanctioned this abuse of power?

The German Ancillon replies thus: —

"Some philosophers pretend that man, in employing his forces upon a natural object,—say a field or a tree,—acquires a right only to the improvements which he makes, to the form which he gives to the object, not to the object itself. Useless distinction! If the form could be separated from the object, perhaps there would be room for question; but as this is almost always impossible, the application of man's strength to the different parts of the visible world is the foundation of the right of property, the primary origin of riches."

Vain pretext! If the form cannot be separated from the object, nor property from possession, possession must be shared; in any case, society reserves the right to fix the conditions of property. Let us suppose that an appropriated farm yields a gross income of ten thousand francs; and, as very seldom happens, that this farm cannot be divided. Let us suppose farther that, by economical calculation, the annual expenses of a family are three thousand francs: the possessor of this farm should be obliged to guard his reputation as a good father of a family, by paying to society ten thousand francs,—less the total costs of cultivation, and the three thousand francs required for the maintenance of his family. This payment is not rent, it is an indemnity.

What sort of justice is it, then, which makes such laws as this: —

"Whereas, since labor so changes the form of a thing that the form and substance cannot be separated without destroying the thing itself, either society must be disinherited, or the laborer must lose the fruit of his labor; and

"Whereas, in every other case, property in raw material would give a title to added improvements, minus their cost; and whereas, in this instance, property in improvements ought to give a title to the principal;

"Therefore, the right of appropriation by labor shall never be admitted against individuals, but only against society."

In such a way do legislators always reason in regard to property. The law is intended to protect men's mutual rights,—that is, the rights of each against each, and each against all; and, as if a proportion could exist with less than four terms, the law-makers always disregard the latter. As long as man is opposed to man, property offsets property, and the two forces balance each other; as soon as man is isolated, that is, opposed to the society which he himself represents, jurisprudence is at fault: Themis has lost one scale of her balance.

Listen to the professor of Rennes, the learned Toullier: —

"How could this claim, made valid by occupation, become stable and permanent property, which might continue to stand, and which might be reclaimed after the first occupant had relinquished possession?

"Agriculture was a natural consequence of the multiplication of the human race, and agriculture, in its turn, favors population, and necessitates the establishment of permanent property; for who would take the trouble to plough and sow, if he were not certain that he would reap?"

To satisfy the husbandman, it was sufficient to guarantee him possession of his crop; admit even that he should have been protected in his right of occupation of land, as long as he remained its cultivator. That was all that he had a right to expect; that was all that the advance of civilization demanded. But property, property! the right of escheat over lands which one neither occupies nor cultivates,— who had authority to grant it? who pretended to have it?

"Agriculture alone was not sufficient to establish permanent property; positive laws were needed, and magistrates to execute them; in a word, the civil State was needed.

"The multiplication of the human race had rendered agriculture necessary; the need of securing to the cultivator the fruit of his labor made permanent property necessary, and also laws for its protection. So we are indebted to property for the creation of the civil State."

Yes, of our civil State, as you have made it; a State which, at first, was despotism, then monarchy, then aristocracy, today democracy, and always tyranny.

"Without the ties of property it never would have been possible to subordinate men to the wholesome yoke of the law; and without permanent property the earth would have remained a vast forest. Let us admit, then, with the most careful writers, that if transient property, or the right of preference resulting from occupation, existed prior to the establishment of civil society, permanent property, as we know it to-day, is the work of civil law. It is the civil law which holds that, when once acquired, property can be lost only by the action of the proprietor, and that it exists even after the proprietor has relinquished possession of the thing, and it has fallen into the hands of a third party.

"Thus property and possession, which originally were confounded, became through the civil law two distinct and independent things; two things which, in the language of the law, have nothing whatever in common. In this we see what a wonderful change has been effected in property, and to what an extent Nature has been altered by the civil laws."

Thus the law, in establishing property, has not been the expression of a psychological fact, the development of a natural law, the application of a moral principle. It has literally *created* a right outside of its own province. It has realized an abstraction, a metaphor, a fiction; and that without deigning to look at the consequences, without considering the disadvantages, without inquiring whether it was right or wrong.

It has sanctioned selfishness; it has indorsed monstrous pretensions; it has received with favor impious vows, as if it were able to fill up a bottomless pit, and to satiate hell! Blind law; the law of the ignorant man; a law which is not a law; the voice of discord, deceit, and blood! This it is which, continually revived, reinstated, rejuvenated, restored, re-enforced—as the palladium of society—has troubled the consciences of the people, has obscured the minds of the masters, and has induced all the catastrophes which have befallen nations. This it is which Christianity has condemned, but which its ignorant ministers deify; who have as little desire to study Nature and man, as ability to read their Scriptures.

But, indeed, what guide did the law follow in creating the domain of property? What principle directed it? What was its standard?

Would you believe it? It was equality.

Agriculture was the foundation of territorial possession, and the original cause of property. It was of no use to secure to the farmer the fruit of his labor, unless the means of production were at the same time secured to him. To fortify the weak against the invasion of the strong, to suppress spoliation and fraud, the necessity was felt of establishing between possessors permanent lines of division, insuperable obstacles. Every year saw the people multiply, and the cupidity of the husbandman increase: it was thought best to put a bridle on ambition by setting boundaries which ambition would in vain attempt to overstep. Thus the soil came to be appropriated through need of the equality which is essential to public security and peaceable possession. Undoubtedly the division was never geographically equal; a multitude of rights, some founded in Nature, but wrongly interpreted and still more wrongly applied, inheritance, gift, and exchange; others, like the privileges of birth and position, the illegitimate creations of ignorance and brute force,—all operated to prevent absolute equality. But, nevertheless, the principle remained the same: equality had sanctioned possession; equality sanctioned property.

The husbandman needed each year a field to sow; what more convenient and simple arrangement for the barbarians,—instead of indulging in annual quarrels and fights, instead of continually moving their houses, furniture, and families from spot to spot,—than to assign to each individual a fixed and inalienable estate?

It was not right that the soldier, on returning from an expedition, should find himself dispossessed on account of the services which he had just rendered to his country; his estate ought to be restored to him. It became, therefore, customary to retain property by intent alone—*nudo animo;* it could be sacrificed only with the consent and by the action of the proprietor.

It was necessary that the equality in the division should be kept up from one generation to another, without a new distribution of the land upon the death of each family; it appeared therefore natural and just that children and parents, according to the degree of relationship which they bore to the deceased, should be the heirs of their ancestors. Thence came, in the first place, the feudal and patriarchal custom of recognizing only one heir; then, by a quite contrary application of the principle of equality, the admission of all the children to a share in their father's estate, and, very recently also among us, the definitive abolition of the right of primogeniture.

But what is there in common between these rude outlines of instinctive organization and the true social science? How could these men, who never had the faintest idea of statistics, valuation, or political economy, furnish us with principles of legislation?

"The law," says a modern writer on jurisprudence, "is the expression of a social want, the declaration of a fact: the legislator does not make it, he declares it." This definition is not exact. The law is a method by which social wants must be satisfied; the people do not vote it, the legislator does not express it: the *savant* discovers and formulates it. But in fact, the law, according to M. Ch. Comte, who has devoted half a volume to its definition, was in the beginning only the *expression of a want*, and the indication of the means of supplying it; and up to this time it has been nothing else. The legists—with mechanical fidelity, full of obstinacy, enemies of philosophy, buried in literalities—have always mistaken for the last word of science that which was only the inconsiderate aspiration of men who, to be sure, were well-meaning, but wanting in foresight.

They did not foresee, these old founders of the domain of property, that the perpetual and absolute right to retain one's estate,—a right which seemed to them equitable, because it was common,—involves the right to transfer, sell, give, gain, and lose it; that it tends, consequently, to nothing less than the destruction of that equality which they established it to maintain. And though they should have foreseen it, they disregarded it; the present want occupied their whole attention, and, as ordinarily happens in such cases, the disadvantages were at first scarcely perceptible, and they passed unnoticed.

They did not foresee, these ingenuous legislators, that if property is retainable by intent alone—*nudo animo*—it carries with it the right to let, to lease, to loan at interest, to profit by exchange, to settle annuities, and to levy a tax on a field which intent reserves, while the body is busy elsewhere.

They did not foresee, these fathers of our jurisprudence, that, if the right of inheritance is any thing other than Nature's method of preserving equality of wealth, families will soon become victims of the most disastrous exclusions; and society, pierced to the heart by one of its most sacred principles, will come to its death through opulence and misery.[2]

2   Here, especially, the simplicity of our ancestors appears in all its rudeness. After having made first cousins heirs, where there were no legitimate children, they could not so divide the property between two different branches as to prevent the simultaneous existence of extreme wealth and extreme poverty in the same family. For example: — James, dying, leaves two sons, Peter and John, heirs of his fortune: James's property is divided equally between them. But Peter has only one daughter, while John, his brother, leaves six sons. It is clear that, to be true to the principle of equality, and at the same time to that of heredity, the two estates must be divided in seven equal portions

They did not foresee. ... But why need I go farther?

The consequences are plain enough, and this is not the time to criticise the whole Code.

The history of property among the ancient nations is, then, simply a matter of research and curiosity. It is a rule of jurisprudence that the fact does not substantiate the right. Now, property is no exception to this rule: then the universal recognition of the right of property does not legitimate the right of property. Man is mistaken as to the constitution of society, the nature of right, and the application of justice; just as he was mistaken regarding the cause of meteors and the movement of the heavenly bodies. His old opinions cannot be taken for articles of faith. Of what consequence is it to us that the Indian race was divided into four classes; that, on the banks of the Nile and the Ganges, blood and position formerly determined the distribution of the land; that the Greeks and Romans placed property under the protection of the gods; that they accompanied with religious ceremonies the work of partitioning the land and appraising their goods? The variety of the forms of privilege does not sanction injustice. The faith of Jupiter, the proprietor,[3] proves no more against the equality of citizens, than do the mysteries of Venus, the wanton, against conjugal chastity.

among the children of Peter and John; for otherwise a stranger might marry Peter's daughter, and by this alliance half of the property of James, the grandfather, would be transferred to another family, which is contrary to the principle of heredity. Furthermore, John's children would be poor on account of their number, while their cousin, being an only child, would be rich, which is contrary to the principle of equality. If we extend this combined application of two principles apparently opposed to each other, we shall become convinced that the right of succession, which is assailed with so little wisdom in our day, is no obstacle to the maintenance of equality.

Under whatever form of government we live, it can always be said that *le mort saisit le vif*; that is, that inheritance and succession will last for ever, whoever may be the recognized heir. But the St. Simonians wish the heir to be designated by the magistrate; others wish him to be chosen by the deceased, or assumed by the law to be so chosen: the essential point is that Nature's wish be satisfied, so far as the law of equality allows. To-day the real controller of inheritance is chance or caprice; now, in matters of legislation, chance and caprice cannot be accepted as guides. It is for the purpose of avoiding the manifold disturbances which follow in the wake of chance that Nature, after having created us equal, suggests to us the principle of heredity; which serves as a voice by which society asks us to choose, from among all our brothers, him whom we judge best fitted to complete our unfinished work.

3   *Zeus klésios.*

The authority of the human race is of no effect as evidence in favor of the right of property, because this right, resting of necessity upon equality, contradicts its principle; the decision of the religions which have sanctioned it is of no effect, because in all ages the priest has submitted to the prince, and the gods have always spoken as the politicians desired; the social advantages, attributed to property, cannot be cited in its behalf, because they all spring from the principle of equality of possession.

What means, then, this dithyramb upon property?

"The right of property is the most important of human institutions."
...

Yes; as monarchy is the most glorious.

"The original cause of man's prosperity upon earth."

Because justice was supposed to be its principle.

"Property became the legitimate end of his ambition, the hope of his existence, the shelter of his family; in a word, the corner-stone of the domestic dwelling, of communities, and of the political State."

Possession alone produced all that.

"Eternal principle,— "

Property is eternal, like every negation, —

"Of all social and civil institutions."

For that reason, every institution and every law based on property will perish.

"It is a boon as precious as liberty."

For the rich proprietor.

"In fact, the cause of the cultivation of the habitable earth."

If the cultivator ceased to be a tenant, would the land be worse cared for?

"The guarantee and the morality of labor."

Under the *régime* of property, labor is not a condition, but a privilege.

"The application of justice."

What is justice without equality of fortunes? A balance with false weights.

"All morality,— "

A famished stomach knows no morality,—

"All public order,—"

Certainly, the preservation of property,—

"Rest on the right of property."[4]

Corner-stone of all which is, stumbling-block of all which ought to be,—such is property.

To sum up and conclude:—

Not only does occupation lead to equality, it *prevents* property. For, since every man, from the fact of his existence, has the right of occupation, and, in order to live, must have material for cultivation on which he may labor; and since, on the other hand, the number of occupants varies continually with the births and deaths,—it follows that the quantity of material which each laborer may claim varies with the number of occupants; consequently, that occupation is always subordinate to population. Finally, that, inasmuch as possession, in right, can never remain fixed, it is impossible, in fact, that it can ever become property.

Every occupant is, then, necessarily a possessor or usufructuary,—a function which excludes proprietorship. Now, this is the right of the usufructuary: he is responsible for the thing entrusted to him; he must use it in conformity with general utility, with a view to its preservation and development; he has no power to transform it, to diminish it, or to change its nature; he cannot so divide the usufruct that another shall perform the labor while he receives the product. In a word, the usufructuary is under the supervision of society, submitted to the condition of labor and the law of equality.

Thus is annihilated the Roman definition of property—*the right of use and abuse*—an immorality born of violence, the most monstrous pretension that the civil laws ever sanctioned. Man receives his usufruct from the hands of society, which alone is the permanent possessor. The individual passes away, society is deathless.

What a profound disgust fills my soul while discussing such simple truths! Do we doubt these things to-day? Will it be necessary to again take arms for their triumph? And can force, in default of reason, alone introduce them into our laws?

All have an equal right of occupancy.

The amount occupied being measured, not by the will, but by the variable conditions of space and number, property cannot exist.

This no code has ever expressed; this no constitution can admit!

4   Giraud, "Investigations into the Right of Property among the Romans."

These are axioms which the civil law and the law of nations deny! ...

But I hear the exclamations of the partisans of another system: "Labor, labor! that is the basis of property!"

Reader, do not be deceived. This new basis of property is worse than the first, and I shall soon have to ask your pardon for having demonstrated things clearer, and refuted pretensions more unjust, than any which we have yet considered.

PART THREE

MIKHAIL BAKUNIN
(1814–1876)

Mikhail Bakunin stands as perhaps the most striking social figure in classical anarchism. His assessment of the negative role of state capture in revolutionary movements and his sharp criticism of Marx's notion of the dictatorship of the proletariat played out in history in ways stunningly close to what Bakunin warned about. The Bolshevik revolution and the creation of the Soviet Union stand as important political statements in their own right and validate Bakunin's insight. So intense were the debates between Bakunin and Marx, and the proponents of each within the First International, that Marx infamously undermined the International by moving its offices to New York rather than have the Bakuninist (that is, anarchist) wing win out.

A figure of the barricades himself imprisoned and driven into exile by various states across Europe, Bakunin set the stage for the anarchist focus on the state and its criminal justice systems as forces of imposed morality of ruling groups rather than as upholders of the right and the just. The legitimacy of the state, state violence, and its social acceptance are refuted and rejected in the following essays.

Chapter 3 was written in 1869 and translated by Sam Dolgoff, ed., *Bakunin on Anarchy* (New York: Vintage Books, 1971). Chapter 4 was written in 1870 and translated by G. P. Maximoff, ed., *The Political Philosophy of Bakunin: Scientific Anarchism* (New York: Free Press, 1953).

CHAPTER 3

The Program
of the International Brotherhood
Mikhail Bakunin

All the evidence indicates that the secret "International Brother-hood," also called "Secret Alliance," was formally dissolved early in 1869. In reply to accusations made by the General Council of the International, both Bakunin and Guillaume denied its existence. There was undoubtedly an informal group of adherents to Bakunin's ideas, but as a formal organization, says Guillaume, "[the Interna-tional Brothers] existed only theoretically in Bakunin's brain as a kind of dream indulged in with delight...." But this does not lessen the importance of the ideas formulated in the program which Bakunin wrote for it.

While the Program does not cover all the subjects discussed in the *Revolutionary Catechism*, it contains a more precise and advanced formulation of Bakunin's ideas about revolutionary strategy; about the expropriation of private, Church, and State property, and its transfer into the collective property of federated workers' industri-al and agricultural associations; faith in the creative capacity of the masses; revolutionary violence and terrorism; revolution by a central-ized "socialist" state; and above all, the tasks of the anarchist vanguard movement (International Brotherhood) in the Social Revolution.

* * *

The association of the International Brothers desires a revolution that shall be at the same time universal, social, philosophical, and econom-ic, so that no stone may remain unturned, in all of Europe first, and then in the rest of the world, to change the present order of things founded on property, on exploitation, domination, and the princi-ple of authority, be it religious, metaphysical, and doctrinaire in the bourgeois manner or even revolutionary in the Jacobin manner. Call-ing for peace for the workers and liberty for all, we want to destroy all the states and all the churches, with all their institutions and their religious, political, financial, juridical, police, educational, economic, and social laws, so that all these millions of wretched human beings, deceived, enslaved, tormented, exploited, may be released from all their official and officious directors and benefactors—both associations and individuals—and at last breathe in complete freedom.

Convinced as we are that individual and social evil resides much less in individuals than in the organization of material things and in social conditions, we will be humane in our actions, as much for the sake of justice as for practical considerations, and we will ruthlessly destroy what is in our way without endangering the revolution. We deny society's free will and its alleged right to punish. Justice itself, taken in its widest, most humane sense, is but an idea, so to say, which is not an absolute dogma; it poses the social problem but it does not think it out. It merely indicates the only possible road to human emancipation, that is the humanization of society by liberty in equality. The positive solution can be achieved only by an increasingly rational organization of society. This solution, which is so greatly desired, our ideal for all, is liberty, morality, intelligence, and the welfare of each through the solidarity of all: human fraternity, in short.

Every human individual is the involuntary product of a natural and social environment within which he is born, and to the influence of which he continues to submit as he develops. The three great causes of all human immorality are: political, economic, and social inequality; the ignorance resulting naturally from all this; and the necessary consequence of these, *slavery*.

Since the social organization is always and everywhere the only cause of crimes committed by men, the punishing by society of criminals who can never be guilty is an act of hypocrisy or a patent absurdity. The theory of guilt and punishment is the offspring of theology, that is, of the union of absurdity and religious hypocrisy. The only right one can grant to society in its present transitional state is the natural right to kill in self-defense the criminals it has itself produced, but not the right to judge and condemn them. This cannot, strictly speaking, be a right, it can only be a natural, painful, but inevitable act, itself the indication and outcome of the impotence and stupidity of present-day society. The less society makes use of it, the closer it will come to its real emancipation. All the revolutionaries, the oppressed, the sufferers, victims of the existing social organization, whose hearts are naturally filled with hatred and a desire for vengeance, should bear in mind that the kings, the oppressors, exploiters of all kinds, are as guilty as the criminals who have emerged from the masses; like them, they are evildoers who are not guilty, since they, too, are involuntary products of the present social order. It will not be surprising if the rebellious people kill a great many of them at first. This will be a misfortune, as unavoidable as the ravages caused by a sudden tempest, and as quickly over; but this natural act will be neither moral nor even useful.

History has much to teach us on this subject. The dreadful guillotine of 1793, which cannot be reproached with having been idle or slow, nevertheless did not succeed in destroying the French aristocracy. The nobility was indeed shaken to its roots, though not completely destroyed, but this was not the work of the guillotine; it was achieved by the confiscation of its properties. In general, we can say that carnage was never an effective means to exterminate political parties; it was proved particularly ineffective against the privileged classes, since power resides less in men themselves than in the circumstances created for men of privilege by the organization of material goods, that is, the institution of the State and its natural basis, *individual property*.

Therefore, to make a successful revolution, it is necessary to attack conditions and material goods; to destroy property and the State. It will then become unnecessary to destroy men and be condemned to suffer the sure and inevitable reaction which no massacre has ever failed and ever will fail to produce in every society.

It is not surprising that the Jacobins and the Blanquists—who became socialists by necessity rather than by conviction, who view socialism as a means and not as the goal of the revolution, since they desire dictatorship and the centralization of the State, hoping that the State will lead them necessarily to the reinstatement of property— dream of a bloody revolution against men, inasmuch as they do not desire the revolution against property. But such a bloody revolution, based on the construction of a powerfully centralized revolutionary State, would inevitably result in military dictatorship and a new master. Hence the triumph of the Jacobins or the Blanquists would be the death of the revolution.

We are the natural enemies of such revolutionaries—the would-be dictators, regulators, and trustees of the revolution—who even before the existing monarchical, aristocratic, and bourgeois states have been destroyed, already dream of creating new revolutionary states, as fully centralized and even more despotic than the states we now have. These men are so accustomed to the order created by an authority, and feel so great a horror of what seems to them to be disorder but is simply the frank and natural expression of the life of the people, that even before a good, salutary disorder has been produced by the revolution they dream of muzzling it by the act of some authority that will be revolutionary in name only, and will only be a new reaction in that it will again condemn the masses to being governed by decrees, to obedience, to immobility, to death; in other words, to slavery and exploitation by a new pseudo-revolutionary aristocracy.

What we mean by revolution is an outburst of what today is called "evil passions" and the destruction of the so-called public order.

We do not fear anarchy, we invoke it. For we are convinced that anarchy, meaning the unrestricted manifestation of the liberated life of the people, must spring from liberty, equality, the new social order, and the force of the revolution itself against the reaction. There is no doubt that this new life—the popular revolution—will in good time organize itself, but it will create its revolutionary organization from the bottom up, from the circumference to the center, in accordance with the principle of liberty, and not from the top down or from the center to the circumference in the manner of all authority. It matters little to us if that authority is called Church, Monarchy, constitutional State, bourgeois Republic, or even revolutionary Dictatorship. We detest and reject all of them equally as the unfailing sources of exploitation and despotism.

The revolution as we understand it will have to destroy the State and all the institutions of the State, radically and completely, from its very first day. The natural and necessary consequences of such destruction will be:

a. the bankruptcy of the State
b. the discontinuance of payments of private debts through the intervention of the State, leaving to each debtor the right to pay his own debts if he so desires

c. the discontinuance of payments of all taxes and of the levy of any contributions, direct or indirect

d. the dissolution of the arms, the judicial system, the bureaucracy, the police, and the clergy

e. the abolition of official justice, the suspension of everything called juridically the law, and the carrying out of these laws; consequently, the abolition and burning of all titles to property, deeds of inheritance, deeds of sale, grants, of all lawsuits—in a word, all the judicial and civil red tape; everywhere and in all things, the revolutionary fact replacing the right created and guaranteed by the State

f. the confiscation of all productive capital and of the tools of production for the benefit of workers' associations, who will have to have them produced collectively

g. the confiscation of all the property owned by the Church and the State as well as the precious metals owned by individuals, for the benefit of the federative Alliance of all the workers' associations, which will constitute the commune. (In return for the goods which have been confiscated, the commune will give the strict necessities of life to all the individuals so dispossessed, and they will later gain more by their own labor if they can and if they wish.)

h. for the purpose of effecting the organization of the revolutionary commune by permanent barricades, and the office of a council of the revolutionary commune by the delegation of one or two deputies for each barricade, one per street or per district, there will be provided deputies invested with imperative, always responsible, and always revocable mandates. The communal council thus organized will be able to choose, from its own members, executive committees, one for each branch of the revolutionary administration of the commune

i. declaration by the capital city, rebellious and organized as a commune, to the effect that, having destroyed the authoritarian, controlled State, which it had the right to do, having been enslaved just like all the other localities, it therefore renounces the right, or rather any claim, to govern the provinces

j. an appeal to all the provinces, communes, and associations to let everything go and follow the example set by the capital: first, to reorganize themselves on a revolutionary basis, then to delegate their deputies, likewise invested with imperative, responsible, and revocable mandates, to a set meeting place, for the purpose of constituting the federation of associations, communes, and provinces which have rebelled in the name of the same principles, and in order to organize a revolutionary force capable of overcoming the reaction. There will be no dispatching of official revolutionary commissars with ribbons decorating their chests but revolutionary propagandists will be sent to all the provinces and communes, particularly to the peasants, who cannot be excited to rebellion by principles or decrees of a dictatorship but solely by the revolutionary fact itself; that is, by the inevitable consequences in all the communes of the complete cessation of the juridical official life of the State. Also, the abolition of the national state in the sense that any foreign country, province, commune, association, or even an isolated individual, that may have rebelled in the name of the same principles will be received into the revolutionary federation regardless of the present frontiers of the states, although they may belong to different political or national systems; and their own provinces, communes, associations, or individuals who defend the reaction will be excluded. It is through the expansion and organization of the revolution for mutual defense of the rebel countries that the universality of the revolution, founded upon the abolition of frontiers and on the ruins of the states, will triumph.

No political or national revolution can ever triumph unless it is transformed into a social revolution, and unless the national revolution, precisely because of its radically socialist character, which is destructive of the State, becomes a universal revolution.

Since the Revolution must everywhere be achieved by the people, and since its supreme direction must always rest in the people, organized in a free federation of agricultural and industrial associations, the new revolutionary State, organized from the bottom up by revolutionary delegations embracing all the rebel countries in the name of the same principles, irrespective of old frontiers and national differences, will have as its chief objective the administration of public services, not the governing of peoples. It will constitute the *new party*, the alliance of the universal revolution, as opposed to the alliance of the reaction.

This revolutionary alliance excludes any idea of dictatorship and of a controlling and directive power. It is, however, necessary for the establishment of this revolutionary alliance and for the triumph of the Revolution over reaction that the unity of ideas and of revolutionary action find an *organ* in the midst of the popular anarchy which will be the life and the energy of the Revolution. This organ should be *the secret and universal association of the International Brothers*.

This association has its origin in the conviction that revolutions are never made by individuals or even by secret societies. They make themselves; they are produced by the force of circumstances, the movement of facts and events. They receive a long preparation in the deep, instinctive consciousness of the masses, then they burst forth, often seemingly triggered by trivial causes. All that a well-organized society can do is, first, to assist at the birth of a revolution by spreading among the masses ideas which give expression to their instincts, and to organize, not the army of the Revolution—the people alone should always be that army—but a sort of revolutionary general staff, composed of dedicated, energetic, intelligent individuals, sincere friends of the people above all, men neither vain nor ambitious, but capable of serving as intermediaries between the revolutionary idea and the instincts of the people.

There need not be a great number of these men. One hundred revolutionaries, strongly and earnestly allied, would suffice for the international organization of all of Europe. Two or three hundred revolutionaries will be enough for the organization of the largest country.

CHAPTER 4

Ethics: Morality of the State
Mikhail Bakunin

THE THEORY OF SOCIAL CONTRACT. Man is not only the most individual being on earth—he is also the most social being. It was a great fallacy on the part of Jean Jacques Rousseau to have assumed that primitive society was established by a free contract entered into by savages. But Rousseau was not the only one to uphold such views. The majority of jurists and modern writers, whether of the Kantian school or of other individualist and liberal schools, who do not accept the theological idea of society being founded upon divine right, nor that of the Hegelian school—of society as the more or less mystic realization of objective morality—nor the primitive animal society of the naturalist school—take *nolens volens*, for lack of any other foundation, the *tacit contract*, as their point of departure.

A tacit contract! That is to say, a wordless, and consequently a thoughtless and will-less contract: a revolting nonsense! An absurd fiction, and what is more, a wicked fiction! An unworthy hoax! For it assumes that while I was in a state of not being able to will, to think, to speak, I bound myself and all my descendants—only by virtue of having let myself be victimized without raising any protest—into perpetual slavery.

LACK OF MORAL DISCERNMENT IN THE STATE PRECEDING THE ORIGINAL SOCIAL CONTRACT. From the point of view of the system which we are now examining the distinction between good and bad did not exist prior to the conclusion of the social contract. At that time every individual remained isolated in his liberty or in his absolute right, paying no attention to the freedom of others except in those cases wherein such attention was dictated by his weakness or his relative strength—in other words, by his own prudence and interest. At that time egoism, according to the same theory, was the supreme law, the only extant right. The good was determined by success, the bad only by failure, and justice was simply the consecration of the accomplished fact, however horrible, cruel, or infamous it might be—as is the rule in the political morality which now prevails in Europe.

THE SOCIAL CONTRACT AS THE CRITERION OF GOOD AND BAD. The distinction between good and bad, according to this system, began only with the conclusion of the social contract. All that which had been recognized as constituting the general interest was declared to be the good, and everything contrary to it, the bad. Members of society who entered into this compact having become citizens, having bound themselves by solemn obligations, assumed thereby the duty of subordinating their private interests to the common weal, to the inseparable interest of all. They also divorced their individual rights from public rights, the only representative of which—the State—was thereby invested with the power to suppress all the revolts of individual egoism, having, however, the duty of protecting every one of its members in the exercise of his rights in so far as they did not run counter to the general rights of the community.

THE STATE FORMED BY THE SOCIAL CONTRACT IS THE MODERN ATHEISTIC STATE. Now we are going to examine the nature of the relations which the State, thus constituted, is bound to enter into with other similar States, and also its relations to the population which it governs. Such an analysis appears to us to be the more interesting and useful inasmuch as the State, as defined here, is precisely the modern State in so far as it is divorced from the religious idea: it is the lay State or the atheist State proclaimed by modern writers.

Let us then see wherein this morality consists. The modern State, as we have said, has freed itself from the yoke of the Church and consequently has shaken off the yoke of universal or cosmopolitan morality of the Christian religion, but it has not yet become permeated with the humanitarian idea or ethics—which it cannot do without destroying itself, for in its detached existence and isolated concentration the State is much too narrow to embrace, to contain the interests and consequently the morality of, humanity as a whole.

ETHICS IDENTIFIED WITH STATE INTERESTS. Modern States have arrived precisely at that point. Christianity serves them only as a pretext and a phrase, only as a means to fool the simpletons, for the aims pursued by them have nothing in common with religious goals. And the eminent statesmen of our times—the Palmerstons, the Muravievs, the Cavours, the Bismarcks, the Napoleons, would laugh a great deal if their openly professed religious convictions were taken seriously. They would laugh even more if anyone attributed to them humanitarian sentiments, considerations, and intentions, which they have always treated publicly as mere silliness. Then what constitutes their morality? Only State interests. From this point of view, which, with very few exceptions, has been the point of view of statesmen, of *strong men* of all times and all countries, all that is instrumental in conserving, exalting, and consolidating the power of the State is good—sacrilegious though it might be from a religious point of view and revolting as it might appear from the point of view of human morality—and vice versa, whatever militates against the interests of the State is bad, even if it be in other respects the most holy and humanely just thing. Such is the true morality and secular practice of all States.

THE COLLECTIVE EGOISM OF PARTICULAR ASSOCIATIONS RAISED INTO ETHICAL CATEGORIES. Such also is the morality of the State founded upon the theory of a social contract. According to this system, the good and the just, since they begin only with the social contract, are in fact nothing but the content and the end purpose of the contract—that is to say, *the common interest and the public right of all individuals who formed this contract, with the exception of those who remained outside of it.* Consequently, by good in this system is meant only the greatest satisfaction given to the collective egoism of a particular and limited association, which, being founded upon the partial sacrifice of the individual egoism of every one of its members, excludes from its midst, as strangers and natural enemies, the vast majority of the human species whether or not it is formed into similar associations.

MORALITY IS CO-EXTENSIVE ONLY WITH THE BOUNDARIES OF PARTICULAR STATES. The existence of a single limited State necessarily presupposes the existence, and if necessary provokes the formation of several States, it being quite natural that the individuals who find themselves outside of this State and who are menaced by it in their existence and liberty, should in turn league themselves against it. Here we have humanity broken up into an indefinite number of States which are foreign, hostile, and menacing toward one another.

There is no common right, and no social contract among them, for if such a contract and right existed, the various States would cease to be absolutely independent of one another, becoming federated members of one great State. Unless this great State embraces humanity as a whole, it will necessarily have against it the hostility of other great States, federated internally. Thus war would always be the supreme law and the inherent necessity of the very existence of humanity.

JUNGLE LAW GOVERNS INTERRELATIONS OF STATES. Every State, whether it is of a federative or a non-federative character, must seek, under the penalty of utter ruin, to become the most powerful of States. It has to devour others in order not to be devoured in turn, to conquer in order not to be conquered, to enslave in order not to be enslaved—for two similar and at the same time alien powers, cannot co-exist without destroying each other.

THE UNIVERSAL SOLIDARITY OF HUMANITY DISRUPTED BY THE STATE. *The state then is the most flagrant negation, the most cynical and complete negation of humanity.* It rends apart the universal solidarity of all men upon earth, and it unites some of them only in order to destroy, conquer, and enslave all the rest. It takes under its protection only its own citizens, and it recognizes human right, humanity, and civilization only within the confines of its own boundaries. And since it does not recognize any right outside of its own confines, it quite logically arrogates to itself the right to treat with the most ferocious inhumanity all the foreign populations whom it can pillage, exterminate, or subordinate to its will. If it displays generosity or humanity toward them, it does it in no case out of any sense of duty: and that is because it has no duty but to itself, and toward those of its members who formed it by an act of free agreement, who continue constituting it on the same free basis, or, as it happens in the long run, have become its subjects.

Since international law does not exist, and since it never can exist in a serious and real manner without undermining the very foundations of the principle of absolute State sovereignty, the State cannot have any duties toward foreign populations. If then it treats humanely a conquered people, if it does not go to the full length in pillaging and exterminating it, and does not reduce it to the last degree of slavery, it does so perhaps because of considerations of political expediency and prudence, or even because of pure magnanimity, but never because of duty—for it has an absolute right to dispose of them in any way it deems fit.

PATRIOTISM RUNS COUNTER TO ORDINARY HUMAN MORALITY. This flagrant negation of humanity, which constitutes the very essence of the State, is from the point of view of the latter the supreme duty and the greatest virtue: it is called *patriotism* and it constitutes the *transcendent morality* of the State. We call it the transcendent morality because ordinarily it transcends the level of human morality and justice, whether private or common, and thereby it often sets itself in sharp contradiction to them. Thus, for instance, to offend, oppress, rob, plunder, assassinate, or enslave one's fellow man is, to the ordinary morality of man, to commit a serious crime.

In public life, on the contrary, from the point of view of patriotism, when it is done for the greater glory of the State in order to conserve or to enlarge its power, all that becomes a duty and a virtue. And this duty, this virtue, are obligatory upon every patriotic citizen. Everyone is expected to discharge those duties not only in respect to strangers but in respect to his fellow-citizens, members and subjects of the same State, whenever the welfare of the State demands it from him.

THE SUPREME LAW OF THE STATE. The supreme law of the State is self-preservation at any cost. And since all States, ever since they came to exist upon the earth, have been condemned to perpetual struggle—a struggle against their own populations, whom they oppress and ruin, a struggle against all foreign States, every one of which can be strong only if the others are weak—and since the States cannot hold their own in this struggle unless they constantly keep on augmenting their power against their own subjects as well as against the neighbor States—it follows that the supreme law of the State is the augmentation of its power to the detriment of internal liberty and external justice.

THE STATE AIMS TO TAKE THE PLACE OF HUMANITY. Such is in its stark reality the sole morality, the sole aim of the State. It worships God himself only because he is its own exclusive God, the sanction of its power and of that which it calls its right, that is, the right to exist at any cost and always to expand at the cost of other States. Whatever serves to promote this end is worthwhile, legitimate, and virtuous. Whatever harms it is criminal. The morality of the State then is the reversal of human justice and human morality.

This transcendent, super-human, and therefore anti-human morality of States is not only the result of the corruption of men who are charged with carrying on State functions. One might say with greater right that corruption of men is the natural and necessary sequel of the State institution. This morality is only the development of the fundamental principle of the State, the inevitable expression of its inherent necessity. The State is nothing else but the negation of humanity; it is a limited collectivity which aims to take the place of humanity and which wants to impose itself upon the latter as a supreme goal, while everything else is to submit and minister to it.

THE IDEA OF HUMANITY, ABSENT IN ANCIENT TIMES, HAS BECOME A POWER IN OUR PRESENT LIFE. That was natural and easily understood in ancient times when the very idea of humanity was unknown, and when every people worshiped its exclusively national gods, who gave it the right of life and death over all other nations. Human right existed only in relation to the citizens of the State. Whatever remained outside of the State was doomed to pillage, massacre, and slavery.

Now things have changed. The idea of humanity becomes more and more of a power in the civilized world, and, owing to the expansion and increasing speed of means of communication, and also owing to the influence, still more material than moral, of civilization upon barbarous peoples, this idea of humanity begins to take hold even of the minds of uncivilized nations. This idea is the invisible power of our century, with which the present powers—the States—must reckon. They cannot submit to it of their own free will because such submission on their part would be equivalent to suicide, since the triumph of humanity can be realized only through the destruction of the States. But the States can no longer deny this idea nor openly rebel against it, for having now grown too strong, it may finally destroy them.

THE STATE HAS TO RECOGNIZE IN ITS OWN HYPOCRITICAL MANNER THE POWERFUL SENTIMENT OF HUMANITY. In the face of this painful alternative there remains only one way out: and that it hypocrisy. The States pay their outward respects to this idea of humanity; they speak and apparently act only in the name of it, but they violate it every day. This, however, should not be held against the States. They cannot act otherwise, their position having become such that they can hold their own only by lying. Diplomacy has no other mission.

Therefore what do we see? Every time a State wants to declare war upon another State, it starts off by launching a manifesto addressed not only to its own subjects but to the whole world. In this manifesto it declares that right and justice are on its side, and it endeavors to prove that it is actuated only by love of peace and humanity and that, imbued with generous and peaceful sentiments, it suffered for a long time in silence until the mounting iniquity of its enemy forced it to bare its sword. At the same time it vows that, disdainful of all material conquest and not seeking any increase in territory, it will put an end to this war as soon as justice is re-established. And its antagonist answers with a similar manifesto, in which naturally right, justice, humanity, and all the generous sentiments are to be found respectively on its side.

Those mutually opposed manifestoes are written with the same eloquence, they breathe the same virtuous indignation, and one is just as sincere as the other; that is to say both of them are equally brazen in their lies, and it is only fools who are deceived by them. Sensible persons, all those who have had some political experience, do not even take the trouble of reading such manifestoes. On the contrary, they seek ways to uncover the interests driving both adversaries into this war, and to weigh the respective power of each of them in order to guess the outcome of the struggle. Which only goes to prove that moral issues are not at stake in such wars.

PERPETUAL WAR IS THE PRICE OF THE STATE'S EXISTENCE. The rights of peoples, as well as the treaties regulating the relations of the States, lack any moral sanction. In every definite historic epoch they are the material expression of the equilibrium resulting from the mutual antagonism of States. So long as States exist, there will be no peace. There will be only more or less prolonged respites, armistices concluded by the perpetually belligerent States; but as soon as a State feels sufficiently strong to destroy this equilibrium to its advantage, it will never fail to do so. The history of humanity fully bears out this point.

CRIMES ARE THE MORAL CLIMATE OF THE STATES. This explains to us why ever since history began, that is, ever since States came into existence, the political world has always been and still continues to be the stage for high knavery and unsurpassed brigandage—brigandage and knavery which are held in high honor, since they are ordained by patriotism, transcendent morality, and by the supreme interest of the State. This explains to us why all the history of ancient and modern States is nothing more than a series of revolting crimes; why present and past kings and ministers of all times and of all countries—statesmen, diplomats, bureaucrats, and warriors—if judged from the point of view of simple morality and human justice, deserve a thousand times the gallows or penal servitude.

For there is no terror, cruelty, sacrilege, perjury, imposture, infamous transaction, cynical theft, brazen robbery, or foul treason which has not been committed and all are still being committed daily by representatives of the State, with no other excuse than this elastic, at times so convenient and terrible phrase *reason of State*. A terrible phrase indeed! For it has corrupted and dishonored more people in official circles and in the governing classes of society than Christianity itself. As soon as it is uttered everything becomes silent and drops out of sight: honesty, honor, justice, right, pity itself vanishes and with it logic and sound sense; black becomes white and white becomes black, the horrible becomes humane, and the most dastardly felonies and most atrocious crimes become meritorious acts.

CRIME—THE PRIVILEGE OF THE STATE. What is permitted to the State is forbidden to the individual. Such is the maxim of all governments. Machiavelli said it, and history as well as the practice of all contemporary governments bear him out on that point. Crime is the necessary condition of the very existence of the State, and it therefore constitutes its exclusive monopoly, from which it follows that the individual who dares commit a crime is guilty in a two-fold sense: first, he is guilty against human conscience, and, above all, he is guilty against the State in arrogating to himself one of its most precious privileges.

STATE MORALITY ACCORDING TO MACHIAVELLI. The great Italian political philosopher, Machiavelli, was the first who gave currency to this phrase (*reason of State*), or at least he gave it its true meaning and the immense popularity which it has enjoyed ever since in governmental circles. Realistic and positive thinker that he was, he came to understand—and he was the first one in this respect—that the great and powerful States could be founded and maintained only by crime—by many great crimes—and by a thorough contempt for anything called honesty.

He wrote, explained, and argued his case with terrible frankness. And since the idea of humanity was wholly ignored in his time; since the idea of fraternity—not human, but religious—preached by the Catholic Church had been, as it always is, nothing but a ghastly irony belied at every instant by the acts of the Church itself; since in his time no one believed that there was such a thing as popular rights—the people having been considered an inert and inept mass, a sort of cannon-fodder for the State, to be taxed impressed into forced labor and kept in a state of eternal obedience; in view of all this Machiavelli arrived quite logically at the idea that the State was the supreme goal of human existence, that it had to be served at any cost, and that since the interest of the State stood above everything else, a good patriot should not recoil from any crime in order to serve the State.

Machiavelli counsels recourse to crime, urges it, and makes it the sine qua non of political intelligence as well as of true patriotism. Whether the State is called monarchy or republic, crime will always be necessary to maintain and assure its triumph. This crime will no doubt change its direction and object, but its nature will remain the same. It will always be the forced and abiding violation of justice and of honesty—for the good of the State.

WHEREIN MACHIAVELLI WAS WRONG. Yes, Machiavelli was right: we cannot doubt it now that we have the experience of three and a half centuries added to his own experience. Yes, History tells us that while small States are virtuous because of their feebleness, powerful States sustain themselves only through crime. But our conclusion will differ radically from that of Machiavelli, and the reason thereof is quite simple: we are the sons of the Revolution and we have inherited from it the Religion of Humanity which we have to found upon the ruins of the Religion of Divinity. We believe in the rights of man, in the dignity and necessary emancipation of the human species. We believe in human liberty and human fraternity based upon human justice.

PATRIOTISM DECIPHERED. We have already seen that by excluding the vast majority of humanity from its midst, by placing it outside of the obligations and reciprocal duties of morality, of justice, and of right, the State denies humanity with this high-sounding word, *Patriotism*, and imposes injustice and cruelty upon all of its subjects as their supreme duty.

MAN'S ORIGINAL WICKEDNESS — THE THEORETICAL PREMISE OF
THE STATE. Every State, like every theology, assumes that man is
essentially wicked and bad. In the State which we are going to examine now, *the good*, as we have already seen, begins with the conclusion of the social contract, and therefore is only the product of this
contract—its very content. It is not the product of liberty. On the
contrary, so long as men remain isolated in their absolute individuality, enjoying all their natural liberty, recognizing no limits to this
liberty but those imposed by fact and not by right, they follow only
one law—the law of natural egoism.

They insult, maltreat, rob, murder, and devour one another,
everyone according to the measure of his intelligence, of his cunning,
and of his material forces, as is now being done by the States. Hence
human liberty produces not good but evil, man being *bad* by nature.
How did he become bad? That is for theology to explain. The fact is
that the State, when it came into existence, found man already in that
state and it set for itself the task of making him good; that is to say, of
transforming the natural man into a citizen.

One might say to this that inasmuch as the State is the product
of a contract freely concluded by men and since good is the product
of the State, it follows that it is the product of liberty. This, however, would be an utterly wrong conclusion. The State, even according to this theory, is not the product of liberty, but, on the contrary,
the product of the voluntary negation and sacrifice of liberty. Natural men, absolutely free from the point of view of *right*, but *in fact*
exposed to all the dangers which at every instant of their lives menace their security, in order to assure and safeguard the latter sacrifice,
abdicate a greater or lesser portion of their liberty, and inasmuch as
they sacrifice it for the sake of their security, insofar as they become
citizens, they also become the *slaves of the State*. Therefore we have
the right to affirm that from the point of view of the State the good
arises not from liberty, but, on the contrary, from the negation of liberty.

THEOLOGY AND POLITICS. Is it not remarkable, this similitude
between theology (the science of the Church) and politics (the theory of the State), this convergence of two apparently contrary orders
of thoughts and facts upon one and the same conviction: that of the
necessity of sacrificing human liberty in order to make men into
moral beings and transform them into saints, according to some,

and virtuous citizens, according to others? As for us, we are hardly surprised at it, for we are convinced that politics and theology are both closely related, stemming from the same origin and pursuing the same aim under two different names; we are convinced that every State is a terrestrial Church, just as every Church with its Heaven— the abode of the blessed and the immortal gods—is nothing but a celestial State.

THE SIMILARITY OF THE ETHICAL PREMISES OF THEOLOGY AND POLITICS. The State then, like the Church, starts with this fundamental assumption that all men are essentially bad and that when left to their natural liberty they will tear one another apart and will offer the spectacle of the most frightful anarchy wherein the strongest will kill or exploit the weaker ones. And is not this just the contrary of what is now taking place in our exemplary States?

Likewise the State posits as a principle the following tenet: In order to establish public order it is necessary to have a superior authority; in order to guide men and repress their wicked passions, it is necessary to have a leader, and also to impose a curb upon the people, but this authority must be vested in a man of virtuous genius,[1] a legislator for his people, like Moses, Lycurgus, or Solon—and that leader and that curb will embody the wisdom and the repressive power of the State.

SOCIETY NOT A PRODUCT OF A CONTRACT. The State is a transitory historic form, a passing form of society—like the Church, of which it is a younger brother—but it lacks the necessary and immutable character of society which is anterior to all development of humanity and which, partaking fully of the almighty power of natural laws, acts, and manifestations, constitutes the very basis of human existence. Man is born into society just as an ant is born into its ant-hill or a bee into its hive; man is born into society from the very moment that he takes his first step toward humanity, from the moment that he becomes a human being, that is, a being possessing to a greater or lesser extent the power of thought and speech. Man does not choose society; on the contrary, he is the product of the latter, and he is just as inevitably subject to the natural laws governing his essential development as to all the other natural laws which he must obey.

1   The ideal of Mazzini.

REVOLT AGAINST SOCIETY INCONCEIVABLE. Society antedates and at the same time survives every human individual, being in this respect like Nature itself. It is eternal like Nature, or rather, having been born upon our earth, it will last as long as the earth. A radical revolt against society would therefore be just as impossible for man as a revolt against Nature, human society being nothing else but the last great manifestation or creation of Nature upon this earth. And an individual who would want to rebel against society that is, against Nature in general and his own nature in particular—would place himself beyond the pale of real existence, would plunge into nothingness, into an absolute void, into lifeless abstraction, into God.

So it follows that it is just as impossible to ask whether society is good or evil as it is to ask whether Nature—the universal, material, real, absolute, sole and supreme being—is good or evil. It is much more than that: it is an immense, positive, and primitive fact, having had existence prior to all consciousness, to all ideas, to all intellectual and moral discernment; it is the very basis, it is the world in which, inevitably and at a much later stage, there began to develop that which we call good and evil.

THE STATE A HISTORICALLY NECESSARY EVIL. It is not so with the State. And I do not hesitate to say that the State is an evil but a historically necessary evil, as necessary in the past as its complete extinction will be necessary sooner or later, just as necessary as primitive bestiality and theological divagations were necessary in the past. The State is not society; it is only one of its historical forms, as brutal as it is abstract in character. Historically, it arose in all countries out of the marriage of violence, rapine, and pillage—in a word, of war and conquest—with the Gods created in succession by the theological fancies of the nations. From its very beginning it has been—and still remains—the divine sanction of brutal force and triumphant iniquity. Even in the most democratic countries, like the United States of America and Switzerland, it is simply the consecration of the privileges of some minority and the actual enslavement of the vast majority.

REVOLT AGAINST THE STATE. Revolt against the State is much easier because there is something in the nature of the State which provokes rebellion. The State is authority, it is force, it is the ostentatious display of and infatuation with power. It does not seek to ingratiate itself, to win over, to convert. Every time it intervenes, it does so with particularly bad grace. For by its very nature it cannot persuade but must impose and exert force. However hard it may try to disguise this nature, it will still remain the legal violator of man's will and the permanent denial of his liberty.

MORALITY PRESUPPOSES FREEDOM. And even when the State enjoins something good, it undoes and spoils it precisely because the latter comes in the form of a command, and because every command provokes and arouses the legitimate revolt of freedom; and also because, from the point of view of true morality, of human and not divine morality, the good which is done by command from above ceases to be good and thereby becomes evil. Liberty, morality, and the humane dignity of man consist precisely in that man does good not because he is ordered to do so, but because he conceives it, wants it, and loves it.

PART FOUR

AUGUST SPIES
(1855–1887)

August Spies offers an anarchist criminological perspective, writing and speaking from an experiential perspective on the criminal justice system. His speech to the court in the context of the Haymarket Affair clearly demonstrates the inhumanity of the capitalist criminal justice system with respect to the privileging of class domination and exploitation. Spies, one of the targets of Lombroso's ideological diatribes, offers an incisive analysis of the socially rooted nature of crime and the injustice reproduced by criminal justice systems. He offers this analysis while facing his own execution by the state.

Chapter 5, "Address of August Spies" was delivered on October 7, 1886 and published in *The Accused [and] the Accusers: The Famous Speeches of the Eight Chicago Anarchists in Court: When Asked If They Had Anything to Say Why Sentence Should Not Be Passed Upon Them: On October 7th, 8th, and 9th, 1886* (Chicago: Socialistic Publishing Society, 1886?), 1–23.

CHAPTER 5

Address of August Spies
August Spies

YOUR HONOR: In addressing this court I speak as the representative of one class to the representative of another. I will begin with the words uttered five hundred years ago on a similar occasion, by the Venetian Doge Faheri, who, addressing the court, said: "My defense is your accusation; the causes of my alleged crime your history!" I have been indicted on a charge of murder, as an accomplice or accessory. Upon this indictment I have been convicted. There was no evidence produced by the State to show or even indicate that I had any knowledge of the man who threw the bomb, or that I myself had anything to do with the throwing of the missile, unless, of course, you weigh the testimony of the accomplices of the State's Attorney and Bonfield, the testimony of Thompson and Gilmer, by the price they were paid for it. If there was no evidence to show that I was legally responsible for the deed, then my conviction and the execution of the sentence is nothing less than willful, malicious, and deliberate murder, as foul a murder as may be found in the annals of religious, political, or any other sort of persecution. There have been many judicial murders committed where the representatives of the State were acting in good faith, believing their victims to be guilty of the charge accused of. In this case the representatives of the State cannot shield themselves with a similar excuse. For they themselves have fabricated most of the testimony which was used as a *pretense* to convict us; to convict us by a jury picked out to convict! Before this court, and before the public, which is supposed to be the State, I charge the State's Attorney and Bonfield with the heinous conspiracy to commit murder.

I will state a little incident which may throw light upon this charge. On the evening on which the Praetorian Guards of the Citizen's Association, the Bankers' Association, the Association of the Board of Trade men, and the railroad princes, attacked the meeting of workingmen on the Haymarket, with murderous intent—on that evening, about 8 o'clock, I met a young man, Legner by name, who is a member of the Aurora Turn-Verein. He accompanied me, and never left me on that evening until I jumped from the wagon, a few seconds before the explosion occurred. He knew that I had not seen Schwab on that evening. He knew that I had no such conversation with anybody as Mr. Marshall Field's protege, Thompson, testified to. He knew that I did not jump from the wagon to strike the match and hand it to the man who threw the bomb. He is not a Socialist. Why did we not bring him on the stand? Because the honorable representatives of the State, Grinnell and Bonfield, spirited him away. These honorable gentlemen knew everything about Legner. They knew that his testimony would prove the perjury of Thompson and Gilmer beyond any reasonable doubt. Legner's name was on the list of witnesses for the State.— He was not called, however, for obvious reasons. Aye, he stated to a number of friends that he had been offered $500 if he would leave the city, and threatened with direful things if he remained here and appeared as a witness for the defense. He replied that he could neither be bought nor bulldozed to serve such a damnable and dastardly plot. When we wanted Legner, he could not be found; Mr. Grinnell said—and Mr. Grinnell is an honorable man!—that he had himself been searching for the young man, but had not been able to find him. About three weeks later I learned that the very same young man had been kidnapped and taken to Buffalo, N.Y., by two of the illustrious guardians of "Law and Order," two Chicago detectives. Let Mr. Grinnell, let the Citizens' Association, his employer, let them answer for this! And let the public sit in judgment upon the would-be assassins!

No, I repeat, the prosecution has not established our legal guilt. Notwithstanding the purchased and perjured testimony of some, and notwithstanding the *originality* (sarcastically) of the proceedings of this trial. And as long as this has not been done, and you pronounce upon us the sentence of an appointed vigilance committee, acting as a jury, I say, you, the alleged representatives and high priests of "Law and Order," are the real and only law breakers, and in this case to the extent of murder. It is well that the people know this. And when I speak of the people I don't mean the few co-conspirators of Grinnell, the noble politicians who thrive upon the misery of the multitudes. These drones may constitute the State, they may control the State, they may have their Grinnells, their Bonfields and other hirelings! No, when I speak of the people I speak of the great mass of human bees, the working people, who unfortunately are not yet conscious of the rascalities that are perpetrated in the "name of the people,"—in their name.

The contemplated murder of eight men, whose only crime is that they have dared to speak the truth, may open the eyes of these suffering millions; may wake them up. Indeed, I have noticed that our conviction has worked miracles in this direction already. The class that clamors for our lives, the good, devout Christians, have attempted in every way, through their newspapers and otherwise, to conceal the true and only issue in this case. By simply designating the defendants as *"Anarchists,"* and picturing them as a newly discovered tribe or species of cannibals, and by inventing shocking and horrifying stories of dark conspiracies said to be planned by them—these good Christians zealously sought to keep the naked fact from the working people and other righteous parties, namely: *That on the evening of May 4, 200 armed men, under the command of a notorious ruffian, attacked a meeting of peaceable citizens!* With what intention? With the intention of murdering them, or as many of them as they could. I refer to the testimony given by two of our witnesses. The wage-workers of this city began to object to being fleeced too much—they began to say some very true things, but they were highly disagreeable to our patrician class; they put forth—well, some very modest demands. They thought eight hours hard toil a day for scarcely two hours' pay was enough. This lawless rabble had to be silenced! The only way to silence them was to frighten them, and murder those whom they looked up to as their "leaders." Yes, these foreign dogs had to be taught a lesson, so that they might never again interfere with the high-handed exploitation of their benevolent and Christian masters. Bonfield, the man who would bring a blush of shame to the managers of the Bartholomew night—Bonfield, the illustrious gentleman with a visage that would have done excellent service to Doré in portraying Dante's fiends of hell—Bonfield was the man best fitted to consummate the conspiracy of the Citizens' Association, of our patricians. If I had thrown that bomb, or had caused it to be thrown, or had known of it, I would not hesitate a moment to say so. It is true that a number of lives were lost—many were wounded. But hundreds of lives were thereby saved! But for that bomb, there would have been a hundred widows and hundreds of orphans where now there are a few. These facts have been carefully suppressed, and *we were accused and convicted of conspiracy by the real conspirators and their agents*. This, your honor, is one reason why sentence should not be passed by a court of justice—if that name has any significance at all.

"But," says the State, "you have published articles on the manufacture of dynamite and bombs." Show me a daily paper in this city that has not published similar articles! I remember very distinctly a long article in the Chicago Tribune of February 23, 1885. The paper contained a description and drawings of different kinds of infernal machines and bombs. I remember this one especially, because I bought the paper on a railroad train, and had ample time to read it. But since that time the *Times* has often published similar articles on the subject, and some of the dynamite articles found in the *Arbeiter-Zeitung* were translated articles from the *Times*, written by Generals Molineux and Fitz John Porter, in which the use of dynamite bombs against striking workingmen is advocated as the most effective weapon against them. May I learn why the editors of these papers have not been indicted and convicted for murder? Is it because they have advocated the use of this destructive agent only against the common rabble? I seek information. Why was Mr. Stone of the *News* not made a defendant in this case? In his possession was found a bomb. Besides that Mr. Stone published an article in January which gave full information regarding the manufacture of bombs. Upon this information any man could prepare a bomb ready for use at the expense of not more than ten cents. The *News* probably has ten times the circulation of the *Arbeiter-Zeitung*. Is it not likely that the bomb used on May 4th was one made after the *News'* pattern? As long as these men are not charged with murder and convicted, I insist, your honor, that such discrimination in favor of capital is incompatible with justice, and sentence should therefore not be passed.

Grinnell's main argument against the defendants was—"They were foreigners; they are not citizens." I cannot speak for the others. I will only speak for myself. I have been a resident of this State fully as long as Grinnell, and probably have been as good a citizen—at least, I should not wish to be compared with him.

Grinnell has incessantly appealed to the patriotism of the jury. To that I reply in the language of Johnson, the English literateur, "patriotism is the last resort of a scoundrel." My efforts in behalf of the disinherited and disfranchised millions, my agitation in this direction, the popularization of economic teachings—in short, the education of the wage-workers, is declared "a conspiracy against society." The word "society" is here wisely substituted for "the State," as represented by the patricians of today. It has always been the opinion of the ruling classes that the people must be kept in ignorance, for they lose their servility, their modesty and their obedience to the powers that be, as their intelligence increases. The education of a black slave a quarter of a century ago was a criminal offense. Why? Because the intelligent slave would throw off his shackles at whatever cost. Why is the education of the working people of today looked upon by a certain class as an offense against the State? For the same reason! The State, however, wisely avoided this point in the prosecution of this case. From their testimony one is forced to conclude that we had, in our speeches and publications, preached nothing else but destruction and dynamite. The court has this morning stated that there is no case in history like this. I have noticed, during this trial, that the gentlemen of the legal profession are not well versed in history. In all historical cases of this kind truth had to be perverted by the priests of the established power that was nearing its end.

What have we said in our speeches and publications?

We have interpreted to the people their conditions and relations in society. We have explained to them the different social phenomena and the social laws and circumstances under which they occur. We have, by way of scientific investigation, incontrovertibly proved and brought to their knowledge that the system of wages is the root of the present social iniquities—iniquities so monstrous that they cry to Heaven. We have further said that the wage system, as a specific form of social development, would, by the necessity of logic, have to give way to higher forms of civilization; that the wage system must furnish the foundation for a social system of co-operation—that is, *Socialism*. That whether this or that theory, this or that scheme regarding future arrangements were accepted was not a matter of choice, but one of historical necessity, and that to us the tendency of progress seemed to be *Anarchism*—that is, a free society without kings or classes—a society of sovereigns in which liberty and economic equality of all would furnish an unshakable equilibrium as a foundation and condition of natural order.

It is not likely that the honorable Bonfield and Grinnell can conceive of a social order not held intact by the policeman's club and pistol, nor of a free society without prisons, gallows, and State's attorneys. In such a society they probably fail to find a place for themselves. And is this the reason why Anarchism is such a "pernicious and damnable doctrine?"

Grinnell has intimated to us that Anarchism was on trial. The theory of Anarchism belongs to the realm of speculative philosophy. There was not a syllable said about Anarchism at the Haymarket meeting. At that meeting the very popular theme of reducing the hours of toil was discussed. But, "Anarchism is on trial!" foams Mr. Grinnell. If that is the case, your honor, very well; you may sentence me, for I am an Anarchist. I believe with Buckle, with Paine, Jefferson, Emerson, and Spencer, and many other great thinkers of this century, that the state of castes and classes—the state where one class dominates over and lives upon the labor of another class, and calls this *order*—yes; I believe that this barbaric form of social organization, with its legalized plunder and murder, is doomed to die, and make room for a free society, voluntary association, or universal brotherhood, if you like. You may pronounce the sentence upon me, honorable judge, but let the world know that in A. D. 1886, in the State of Illinois, eight men were sentenced to death, because they believed in a better future; because they had not lost their faith in the ultimate victory of liberty and justice! "You have taught the destruction of society and civilization," says the tool and agent of the Bankers' and Citizens' Association, Grinnell. That man has yet to learn what civilization is. It is the old, old argument against human progress. Read the history of Greece, of Rome; read that of Venice; look over the dark pages of the church, and follow the thorny path of science. "No change! No change! You would destroy society and civilization!" has ever been the cry of the ruling classes. They are so comfortably situated under the prevailing system that they naturally abhor and fear even the slightest change. Their privileges are as dear to them as life itself, and every change threatens these privileges. But civilization is a ladder whose steps are monuments of such changes! Without these social changes—all brought about against the will and the force of the ruling classes—there would be no civilization. As to the destruction of society which we have been accused of seeking, sounds this not like one of Æsop's fables—like the cunning of the fox? We, who have jeopardized our lives to save society from the fiend—the fiend who has grasped her by the throat; who sucks her life-blood, who devours her children—we, who would heal her bleeding wounds, who would free her from the fetters you have wrought around her; from the misery you have brought upon her—we her enemies!!

Honorable judge, the demons of hell will join in the laughter this irony provokes!

We have preached dynamite! Yes, we have predicted from the lessons history teaches, that the ruling classes of today would no more listen to the voice of reason than their predecessors; that they would attempt by brute force to stay the wheels of progress. Is it a lie, or was it the truth we told? Are not the large industries of this once free country already conducted under the surveillance of the police, the detectives, the military, and the sheriffs—and is this return to militancy not developing from day to day? American sovereigns— think of it—working like galley convicts under military guards! We have predicted this, and predict that soon these conditions will grow unbearable. What then? The mandate of the feudal lords of our time is slavery, starvation, and death! This has been their programme for the past years. We have said to the toilers, that science had penetrated the mystery of nature—that from Jove's head once more has sprung a Minerva—dynamite! If this declaration is synonymous with murder, why not charge those with the crime to whom we owe the invention? To charge us with an attempt to overthrow the present system on or about May 4th by force, and then establish Anarchy, is too absurd a statement, I think, even for a political office-holder to make. If Grinnell believed that we attempted such a thing, why did he not have Dr. Bluthardt make an inquiry as to our sanity? Only mad men could have planned such a brilliant scheme, and mad people cannot be indicted or convicted of murder. If there had existed anything like a conspiracy or a pre-arrangement, does your honor believe that events would not have taken a different course than they did on that evening and later? This "conspiracy" nonsense is based upon an oration I delivered on the anniversary of Washington's birthday at Grand Rapids, Mich., more than a year and a half ago. I had been invited by the Knights of

Labor for that purpose. I dwelt upon the fact that our country was far from being what the great revolutionists of the last century intended it to be. I said that those men, if they lived today, would clean the Augean stables with iron brooms, and that they, too, would undoubtedly be characterized as "wild Socialists." It is not unlikely that I said Washington would have been hanged for treason if the revolution had failed. Grinnell made this "sacrilegious remark" his main arrow against me. Why? Because he intended to inveigh the know-nothing spirit against us. But who will deny the correctness of the statement? That I should have compared myself with Washington, is a base lie. But if I had, would that be murder? I may have told that individual who appeared here as a witness that the workingmen should procure arms, as force would in all probability be the *ultima ratio*; and that in Chicago there were so and so many armed, but I certainly did not say that we proposed to "inaugurate the social revolution." And let me say here: Revolutions are no more made than earthquakes and cyclones. Revolutions are the effect of certain causes and conditions. I have made social philosophy a specific study for more than ten years, and I could not have given vent to such nonsense! I do believe, however, that the revolution is near at hand—in fact, that it is upon us. But is the physician responsible for the death of the patient because he foretold that death? If any one is to be blamed for the coming revolution it is the ruling class who steadily refused to make concessions as reforms became necessary; who maintain that they can call a halt to progress, and dictate a stand still to the eternal forces, of which they themselves are but the whimsical creation.

The position generally taken in this case is that we are morally responsible for the police riot on May 4th. Four or five years ago I sat in this very court room as a witness. The working men had been trying to obtain redress in a lawful manner. They had voted and, among others, had elected their Aldermanic candidate from the Fourteenth Ward. But the street car company did not like that man. And two of the three election judges of one precinct, knowing this, took the ballot box to their home and "corrected" the election returns, so as to cheat the constituents of the elected candidate of their rightful representative and give the representation to the benevolent street car monopoly. The workingmen spent $1,500 in the prosecution of the perpetrators of this crime. The proof against them was so overwhelming that they confessed to having falsified the returns and forged the official documents. Judge Gardner, who was presiding in this court, acquitted them, stating that "that act had apparently not been prompted by criminal intent." I will make no comment. But when we approach the field of moral responsibility, it has an immense scope! Every man who has in the past assisted in thwarting the efforts of those seeking reform is responsible for the existence of the revolutionists in this city today! Those, however, who have sought to bring about reforms must be exempted from the responsibility—and to these *I* belong.

If the verdict is based upon the assumption of moral responsibility, your honor, I give this as a reason why sentence should not be passed.

If the opinion of the court given this morning is good law, then there is no person in this country who could not lawfully be hanged. I vouch that, upon the very laws you have read, there is no person in this courtroom now who could not be "fairly, impartially and lawfully" hanged! Fouché, Napoleon's right bower, once said to his master: "Give me a line that any one man has ever written, and I will bring him to the scaffold." And this court has done essentially the same. Upon that law every person in this country can be indicted for conspiracy, and, as the case may be, for murder. Every member of a trade union, Knights of Labor, or any other labor organization, can be convicted of conspiracy, and in cases of violence, for which they may not be responsible at all, of murder, as we have been. This precedent once established, and you force the masses who are now agitating in a peaceable way into open rebellion! You thereby shut off the last safety valve—and the blood which will be shed, the blood of the innocent— it will come upon your heads!

"Seven policemen have died," said Grinnell, suggestively winking at the jury. You want a life for a life, and have convicted an equal number of men, of whom it cannot be truthfully said that they had anything whatever to do with the killing of Bonfield's victims. The very same principle of jurisprudence we find among various savage tribes. Injuries among them are equalized, so to speak. The Chinooks and the Arabs, for instance, would demand the life of an enemy for every death that they had suffered at their enemy's hands. They were not particular in regard to the persons, just so long as they had a life for a life. This principle also prevails today among the natives of the Sandwich Islands. If we are to be hanged on this principle, then let us know it, and let the world know what a civilized and Christian country it is in which the Goulds, the Vanderbilts, the Stanfords, the Fields, Armours, and other local money *hamsters* have come to the rescue of liberty and justice!

Grinnell has repeatedly stated that our country is an enlightened country (Sarcastically). The verdict fully corroborates the assertion! This verdict against us is the anathema of the wealthy classes over their despoiled victims—the vast army of wage workers and farmers. If your honor would not have these people believe this; if you would not have them believe that we have once more arrived at the Spartan Senate, the Athenian Areopagus, the Venetian Council of Ten, etc., then sentence should not be pronounced. But, if you think that by hanging us you can stamp out the labor movement—the movement from which the downtrodden millions, the millions who toil and live in want and misery—the wage slaves—expect salvation—if this is your opinion, then hang us! Here you will tread upon a spark, but there, and there, and behind you and in front of you, and everywhere, flames will blaze up. It is a subterranean fire. You cannot put it out. The ground is on fire upon which you stand. You can't understand it. You don't believe in magical arts, as your grandfathers did, who burned witches at the stake, but you do believe in conspiracies; you believe that all these occurrences of late are the work of conspirators! You resemble the child that is looking for his picture behind the mirror. What you see, and what you try to grasp is nothing but the deceptive reflex of the stings of your bad conscience. You want to "stamp out the conspirators"—the "agitators?" Ah, stamp out every factory lord who has grown wealthy upon the unpaid labor of his employés. Stamp out every landlord who has amassed fortunes from the rent of over-burdened workingmen and farmers. Stamp out every machine that is revolutionizing industry and agriculture, that intensifies the production, ruins the producer, that increases the national wealth, while the creator of all these things stands amidst them tantalized with hunger! Stamp out the railroads, the telegraph, the telephone, steam and yourselves—for everything breathes the revolutionary spirit.

You, gentlemen, are the revolutionists! You rebel against the effects of social conditions which have tossed you, by the fair hand of

Fortune, into a magnificent paradise. Without inquiring, you imagine that no one else has a right in that place. You insist that you are the chosen ones, the sole proprietors. The forces that tossed you into the paradise, the industrial forces, are still at work. They are growing more active and intense from day to day. Their tendency is to elevate all mankind to the same level, to have all humanity share in the paradise you now monopolize. You, in your blindness, think you can stop the tidal wave of civilization and human emancipation by placing a few policemen, a few gatling guns, and some regiments of militia on the shore—you think you can frighten the rising waves back into the unfathomable depths, whence they have arisen, by erecting a few gallows in the perspective. You, who oppose the natural course of things, *you* are the real revolutionists. *You* and *you* alone are the conspirators and destructionists!

Said the court yesterday, in referring to the Board of Trade demonstration: "These men started out with the express purpose of sacking the Board of Trade building." While I can't see what sense there would have been in such an undertaking, and while I know that the said demonstration was arranged simply as a means of propaganda against the system that legalizes the respectable business carried on there, I will assume that the three thousand workingmen who marched in that procession really intended to sack the building. In this case they would have differed from the respectable Board of Trade men only in this—that they sought to recover property in an unlawful way, while the others sack the entire country lawfully and unlawfully—this being their highly respectable profession. This court of "justice and equity" proclaims the principle that when two persons do the same thing, it is not the same thing. I thank the court for this confession. It contains all that we have taught and for which we are to be hanged, in a nutshell! Theft is a respectable profession when practiced by the privileged class. It is a felony when resorted to in selfpreservation by the other class. Rapine and pillage are the order of a certain class of gentlemen who find this mode of earning a livelihood easier and preferable to honest labor—this is the kind of order we have attempted, and are now trying, and will try as long as we live to do away with. Look upon the economic battlefields! Behold the carnage and plunder of the Christian patricians! Accompany me to the quarters of the wealth-creators in this city. Go with me to the half-starved miners of the Hocking Valley. Look at the pariahs in the Monongahela Valley, and many other mining districts in this country, or pass along the railroads of that great and most orderly and law-abiding citizen, Jay Gould. And then tell me whether this order has in it any moral principle for which it should be preserved. I say that the preservation of such an order is criminal—is murderous. It means the preservation of the systematic destruction of children and women in factories. It means the preservation of enforced idleness of large armies of men, and their degradation. It means the preservation of intemperance, and sexual as well as intellectual prostitution. It means the preservation of misery, want, and servility on the one hand, and the dangerous accumulation of spoils, idleness, voluptuousness, and tyranny on the other. It means the preservation of vice in every form.

And last but not least, it means the preservation of the class struggle, of strikes, riots and bloodshed. That is *your* "order," gentlemen; Yes, and it is worthy of you to be the champions of such an order. You are eminently fitted for that role. You have my compliments!

Grinnell spoke of Victor Hugo. I need not repeat what he said, but will answer him in the language of one of our German philosophers: "Our bourgeoise erect monuments in honor of the memory of the classics. If they had read them they would burn them!" Why, amongst the articles read here from the *Arbeiter-Zeitung*, put in evidence by the State, by which they intend to convince the jury of the dangerous character of the accused Anarchists, is an extract from Goethe's Faust,

"Es erben sich Gesetz und Rechte,
Wie eine ew'ge Krankheit fort," etc.

"Laws and class privileges are transmitted like an hereditary disease." And Mr. Ingham in his speech told the Christian jurors that our comrades, the Paris communists, had in 1871, dethroned God, the Almighty, and had put up in his place a low prostitute. The effect was marvelous! The good Christians were shocked.

I wish your honor would inform the learned gentlemen that the episode related occurred in Paris nearly a century ago, and that the sacrilegious perpetrators were the cotemporaries of the founders of the Republic—and among them was Thomas Paine. Nor was the woman a prostitute, but a good *citoyenne de Paris*, who served on that occasion simply as an allegory of the goddess of reason.

Referring to Most's letter, read here, Mr. Ingham said: "They," meaning Most and myself, "They might have destroyed thousands of innocent lives in the Hocking Valley with that dynamite." I have said all I know about the letter on the witness stand, but will add that two years ago I went through the Hocking Valley as a correspondent. While there I saw hundreds of lives in the process of slow destruction, gradual destruction. There was no dynamite, nor were they Anarchists who did that diabolical work. It was the work of a party of highly respectable monopolists, law-abiding citizens, if you please. It is needless to say the murderers were never indicted. The press had little to say, and the State of Ohio assisted them. What a terror it would have created if the victims of this diabolical plot had resented and blown some of those respectable cut-throats to atoms! When, in East St. Louis, Jay Gould's hirelings, "the men of grit," shot down in cold blood and killed six inoffensive workingmen and women, there was very little said, and the grand jury refused to indict the gentlemen. It was the same way in Chicago, Milwaukee and other places. A Chicago furniture manufacturer shot down and seriously wounded two striking workingmen last spring. He was held over to the grand jury. The grand jury refused to indict the gentleman.

But when, on one occasion, a workingman in self-defense resisted the murderous attempt of the police and threw a bomb, and for once blood flowed on the other side, then a terrific howl went up all over the land: "Conspiracy has attacked vested rights!" And eight victims are demanded for it. There has been much said about the public sentiment. There has been much said about the public clamor. Why, it is a fact that no citizen dared express another opinion than that prescribed by the authorities of the State, for if one had done otherwise, he would have been locked up; he might have been sent to the gallows to swing, as they will have the pleasure of doing with us, if the decree of our "honorable court" is consummated.

"These men," Grinnell said repeatedly, "have no principles; they are common murderers, assassins, robbers," etc. I admit that our aspirations and objects are incomprehensible to unprincipled ruffians, but surely for this we are not to be blamed. The assertion, if I mistake not, was based upon the ground that we sought to destroy property. Whether this perversion of facts was intentional, I know not. But in justification of our doctrines I will say that the assertion is an infamous falsehood. Articles have been read here from the *Arbeiter-Zeitung* and *Alarm* to show the dangerous characters of the defendants. The files of the *Arbeiter-Zeitung* and *Alarm* have been searched for the past years. Those articles which generally commented upon some atrocity committed by the authorities upon striking workingmen were picked out and read to you. Other articles were not read to the court. Other articles were not what was wanted. The State's Attorney upon those articles (who well knows that he tells a falsehood when he says it), asserts that "these men have no principle."

A few weeks before I was arrested and charged with the crime for which I have been convicted, I was invited by the clergymen of the Congregational Church to lecture upon the subject of Socialism, and debate with them. This took place at the Grand Pacific Hotel. And so that it cannot be said that after I have been arrested, after I have been indicted, and after I have been convicted, I have put together some principles to justify my action, I will read what I said then—

Capt. Black: "Give the date of the paper."

Mr. Spies: "January 9, 1886."

Capt. Black: "What paper, the *Alarm*?"

Mr. Spies: "The *Alarm*. When I was asked upon that occasion what Socialism was, I said this:"

"Socialism is simply a resumé of the phenomena of the social life of the past and present traced to their fundamental causes, and brought into logical connection with one another. It rests upon the established fact that the economic conditions and institutions of a people from the ground work of all their social conditions, of their ideas—aye, even of their religion, and further, that all changes of economic conditions, every step in advance, arises from the struggles between the dominating and dominated class in different ages. You, gentlemen, cannot place yourselves at this standpoint of speculative science; your profession demands that you occupy the opposite position, that which professes acquaintance with things as they actually exist, but which presumes a thorough understanding of matters which to ordinary mortals are entirely incomprehensible. It is for this reason that you cannot become Socialists. (Cries of "Oh! oh!") Lest you should be unable to exactly grasp my meaning, however, I will now state the matter a little more plainly. It cannot be unknown to you that in the course of this century there have appeared an infinite number of inventions and discoveries, which have brought about great, aye, astonishing changes in the production of the necessities and comforts of life. The work of machines has, to a great extent, replaced that of men.

"Machinery involves a great accumulation of power, and always a greater division of labor in consequence.

"The advantages resulting from this centralization of production were of such a nature as to cause its still further extension, and from this concentration of the means of labor and of the operations of laborers, while the old system of distribution was (and is) retained, arose those improper conditions which ails society today.

"The means of production thus came into the hands of an ever decreasing number, while the actual producers, through the introduction of machinery, deprived of the opportunity to toil, and being at the same time disinherited of the bounties of nature, were consigned to pauperism, vagabondage—the so-called crime and prostitution—all these evils which you, gentlemen, would like to exorcise with your little prayer-book.

"The Socialists award your efforts a jocular rather than a serious attention—[symptoms of uneasiness]—otherwise, pray, let us know how much you have accomplished so far by your moral lecturing toward ameliorating the condition of those wretched beings who through bitter want have been driven to crime and desperation? [Here several gentlemen sprang to their feet, exclaiming, 'We have done a great deal in some directions!'] Aye, in some cases you have perhaps given a few alms; but what influence has this, if I may ask, had upon societary conditions, or in effecting any change in the same? Nothing; absolutely nothing. You may as well admit it, gentlemen, for you cannot point me out a single instance.

"Very well. The proletarians doomed to misery and hunger through the labor-saving of our centralized production, whose number in this country we estimate at about a million and a half, is it likely that they and the thousands who are daily joining their ranks, and the millions who are toiling for a miserable pittance, will suffer peacefully and with Christian resignation their destruction at the hands of their thievish and murderous, albeit very Christian, wage masters? They will defend themselves. It will come to a fight.

"The necessity of common ownership in the means of toil will be realized, and the era of socialism, of universal co-operation, begins. The dispossessing of the usurping classes—the socialization of these possessions—and the universal co-operation of toil, not for speculative purposes, but for the satisfaction of the demands which we make upon life; in short co-operative labor for the purpose of continuing life and of enjoying it—this in general outlines, *is Socialism*. This is not, however, as you might suppose, a mere 'beautifully conceived plan,' the realization of which would be well worth striving for if it could only be brought about. No; this socialization of the means of production, of the machinery of commerce, of the land and earth, etc., is not only something desirable, but has become an imperative necessity, and wherever we find in history that something has once become a necessity, there we always find that the next step was the doing away with that necessity by the supplying of the logical want.

"Our large factories and mines, and the machinery of exchange and transportation, apart from every other consideration, have become too vast for private control. Individuals can no longer monopolize them.

"Everywhere, wherever we cast our eyes, we find forced upon our attention the unnatural and injurious effects of unregulated private production. We see how one man, or a number of men, have not only brought into the embrace of their private ownership a few inventions in technical lines, but have also confiscated for their exclusive advantage all natural powers, such as water, steam, and electricity. Every fresh invention, every discovery belongs to them. The world exists for them only. That they destroy their fellow beings right and left they little care. That, by their machinery, they even work the bodies of little children into gold pieces, they hold to be an especially good work and a genuine Christian act. They murder, as we have said, little children and women by hard labor, while they let strong men go hungry for lack of work.

"People ask themselves how such things are possible, and the answer is that the competitive system is the cause of it. The thought of a co-operative, social, rational, and well regulated system of management irresistibly impresses the observer. The advantages of such a system are of such a convincing kind, so patent to observation—and where could there be any other way out of it? According to physical laws a body always moves itself, consciously or unconsciously, along the line of least resistance. So does society as a whole. The path of co-operative labor and distribution is leveled by the concentration of the means of labor under the private capitalistic system. We are already moving right in that track. We cannot retreat even if we would. The force of circumstances drives us on to Socialism.

"'And now, Mr. Spies, won't you tell' us how you are going to carry out the expropriation of the possessing classes?' asked Rev. Dr. Scudder.

"'The answer is the thing itself. The key is furnished by the storms raging through the industrial life of the present. You see how penuriously the owners of the factories, of the mines, cling to their privileges, and will not yield the breadth of an inch. On the other hand, you see the half-starved proletarians driven to the verge of violence.'

"'So your remedy would be violence?'

"'Remedy? Well, I should like it better if it could be done without violence, but you, gentlemen, and the class you represent, take care that it cannot be accomplished otherwise. Let us suppose that the workingmen of today go to their employers, and say to them: "Listen! Your administration of affairs doesn't suit us any more; it leads to disastrous consequences. While one part of us are worked to death, the others, out of employment, are starved to death; little children are ground to death in the factories, while strong, vigorous men remain idle; the masses live in misery while a small class of respectables enjoy luxury and wealth; all this is the result of your maladministration, which will bring misfortune even to yourselves; step down and out now: let us have your property, which is nothing but unpaid labor; we shall take this thing in our own hands; we shall administrate matters satisfactorily, and regulate the institutions of society; voluntarily we shall pay you a life-long pension." Now, do you think the "bosses" would accept this proposition? You certainly don't believe it. Therefore force will have to decide—or do you know of any other way?'

"'So you are organizing a revolution?'

"It was shortly before my arrest, and I answered: 'Such things are hard to organize. A revolution is a sudden upswelling—a convulsion of the fevered masses of society.'

"We are preparing society for that, and insist upon it that workingmen should arm themselves and keep ready for the struggle. The better they are armed the easier will the battle be, and the less the bloodshed.

"'What would be the order of things in the new society?'

"'I must decline to answer this question, as it is, till now, a mere matter of speculation. The organization of labor on a co-operative basis offers no difficulties. The large establishments of today might be used as patterns. Those who will have to solve these questions will expediently do it, instead of working according to our prescriptions—if we should make anything of the kind; they will be directed by the circumstances and conditions of the time, and these are beyond our horizon. About this you needn't trouble yourselves.'

"'But, friend, don't you think that about a week after the division, the provident will have all, while the spendthrift will have nothing?'

"'The question is out of order,' interfered the chairman; 'there was nothing said about division.'

"Prof. Wilcox: 'Don't you think the introduction of Socialism would destroy all individuality?'

"'How can anything be destroyed which does not exist? In our times there is no individuality; that only can be developed under Socialism, when mankind will be independent economically. Where do you meet today with real individuality? Look at yourselves, gentlemen! You don't dare to give utterance to any subjective opinion which might not suit the feelings of your bread givers and customers. You are hypocrites (murmurs of indignation); every business man is a hypocrite. Everywhere is mockery, servility, lies and fraud. And the laborers! You feign anxiety about their individuality; about the individuality of a class that has been degraded to machines—used each day for ten or twelve hours as appendages of the lifeless machines! About their individuality you are anxious!'"

Does that sound as though I had at that time, as has been imputed to me, organized a revolution—a so-called social revolution, which was to occur on or about the first of May to establish Anarchy in place of our present "ideal order?" I guess not.

So Socialism does not mean the destruction of society. Socialism is a constructive and not a destructive science. While capitalism expropriates the masses for the benefit of the privileged class; while capitalism is that school of economics which teaches how one can live upon the labor (i.e., property) of others; Socialism teaches how all may possess property, and further teaches that every man must work honestly for his own living, and not be playing the "respectable board of trade man," or any other highly (?) respectable business man or banker, such as appeared here as talesmen in the jurors' box, with the fixed opinion that we ought to be hanged. Indeed, I believe they have that opinion! Socialism, in short, seeks to establish a universal system of co-operation, and to render accessible to each and every member of the human family the achievements and benefits of civilization, which, under capitalism, are being monopolized by a privileged class, and employed, not as they should be, for the common good of all, but for the brutish gratification of an avaricious class. Under capitalism the great inventions of the past, far from being a blessing for mankind, have been turned into a curse! Under Socialism the prophecy of the Greek poet, Antiporas, would be fulfilled, who, at the invention of the first water mill, exclaimed: "This is the emancipator of male and female slaves;" and likewise the prediction of Aristotle, who said: "When, at some future age, every tool, upon command or predestination, will perform its work as the art works of Daedalus did, which moved by themselves, or like the three feet of Hephaestos which went to their sacred work instinctively, when thus the weaver shuttles will weave by themselves, then we shall no longer have masters and slaves."

Socialism says this time has come, and can you deny it? You say: "Oh, these heathens, what did they know?" True! They knew nothing of political economy, they knew nothing of Christendom. They failed to conceive how nicely these men-emancipating machines could be employed to lengthen the hours of toil and to intensify the burdens of the slaves. These heathens, yes, they excused the slavery of the one on the ground that thereby another would be afforded the opportunity of human development. But to preach the slavery of the masses in order that a few rude and arrogant parvenues might become "eminent manufacturers," "extensive packing house owners," or "influential shoe black dealers"—to do this they lacked that specific Christian organ.

Socialism teaches that the machines, the means of transportation and communication are the result of the combined efforts of society, past and present, and that they are therefore rightfully the indivisible property of society, just the same as the soil and the mines and all natural gifts should be. This declaration implies that those who have appropriated this wealth wrongfully, though lawfully, shall be expropriated by society. The expropriation of the masses by the monopolists has reached such a degree that the expropriation of the expropriators has become an imperative necessity, an act of social self-preservation. Society will reclaim its own, even though you erect a gibbet on every street corner. And Anarchism, this terrible "ism," deduces that under a co-operative organization of society, under economic equality and individual independence, the State—the political State—will pass into barbaric antiquity. And we will be where all are free, where there are no longer masters and servants, where intellect stands for brute force; there will no longer be any use for the policemen and militia to preserve the so-called "peace and order"— the order that the Russian general spoke of when he telegraphed to the Czar after he had massacred half of Warsaw, "Peace reigns in Warsaw!"

Anarchism does not mean bloodshed; does not mean robbery, arson, etc. These monstrosities are, on the contrary, the characteristic features of capitalism. Anarchism means peace and tranquility to all. Anarchism, or Socialism, means the re-organization of society upon scientific principles and the abolition of causes which produce vice and crime. Capitalism first produces these social diseases and then seeks to cure them by punishment.

The court has had a great deal to say about the incendiary character of the articles read from the *Arbeiter-Zeitung*. Let me read to you an editorial which appeared in the Fond du Lac *Commonwealth*, in October, 1886, a Republican paper. If I am not mistaken the court is Republican, too.

"To arms, Republicans! Work in every town in Wisconsin for men not afraid of firearms, blood or dead bodies, to preserve peace (that is the 'peace' I have been speaking of) and quiet; avoid a conflict of parties to prevent the administration of public affairs from falling into the hands of such obnoxious men as James G. Jenkins. Every Republican in Wisconsin should go armed to the polls next election day. The grain stacks, houses and barns of active Democrats should be burned; their children burned and their wives outraged, that they may understand that the Republican party is the one which is bound to rule, and the one which they should vote for, or keep their vile carcasses away from the polls. If they still persist in going to the polls, and persist in voting for Jenkins, meet them on the road, in the bush, on the hill, or anywhere, and shoot every one of these base cowards and agitators. If they are too strong in any locality, and succeed in putting their opposition votes in the ballot box, break open the box and tear in shreds their discord-breathing ballots. Burn them. This is the time for effective work. Yellow fever will not catch among Morrison Democrats; so we must use less noisy and more effective means. The agitators must be put down, and whoever opposes us does so at his peril. Republicans, be at the polls in accordance with the above directions, and don't stop for a little blood. That which made the solid South will make a solid North!" What does your honor say to these utterances of a "law and order" organ—a Republican organ? How does the *Arbeiter-Zeitung* compare with this?

The book of John Most, which was introduced in court, I have never read, and I admit that passages were read here that are repulsive—that must be repulsive to any person who has a heart. But I call your attention to the fact that these passages have been translated from a publication of Andrieux, the ex-prefect of police, Paris, by an exponent of *your order*! Have the representatives of your order ever stopped at the sacrifice of human blood? Never!

It has been charged that we (the eight here) constituted a conspiracy. I would reply to that that my friend Lingg I had seen but twice at meetings of the Central Labor Union, where I went as a reporter, before I was arrested. I had never spoken to him. With Engel, I have not been on speaking terms for at least a year. And Fischer, my lieutenant (?), used to go around and make speeches against me. So much for that.

Your honor has said this morning, "we must learn their objects from what they have said and written," and in pursuance thereof the court has read a number of articles.

Now, if I had as much power as the court, and were a law abiding citizen, I would certainly have the court indicted for some remarks made during this trial. I will say that if I had not been an Anarchist at the beginning of this trial I would be one now. I quote the exact language of the court on one occasion : "It does not necessarily follow that all laws are foolish and bad because a good many of them are so." That is treason, sir! if we are to believe the court and the State's attorney. But, aside from that, I cannot see how we shall distinguish the good from the bad laws. Am I to judge of that? No; I am not. But if I disobey a bad law, and am brought before a bad judge, I undoubtedly would be convicted.

In regard to a report in the *Arbeiter-Zeitung*, also read this morning, the report of the Board of Trade demonstration, I would say (and this is the only defense, the only word I have to say in my own defense) that I did not know of that article until I saw it in the paper, and the man who wrote it, wrote it rather as a reply to some slurs in the morning papers. He was discharged. The language used in that article would never have been tolerated if I had seen it.

Now, if we cannot be directly implicated with this affair, connected with the throwing of the bomb, where is the law that says, these men shall be picked out to suffer? Show me that law if you have it! If the position of the court is correct, then half of the population of this city ought to be hanged, because they are responsible the same as we are for that act on May 4. And if half of the population of Chicago is not hanged, then show me the law that says, "eight men shall be picked out and hanged as scapegoats!" You have no good law. Your decision, your verdict, our conviction is nothing but an arbitrary will of this lawless court. It is true there is no precedent in jurisprudence in this case! It is true we have called upon the people to arm themselves. It is true that we told them time and again that the great day of change was coming. It was not our desire to have bloodshed. We are not beasts. We would not be Socialists if we were beasts. It is because of our sensitiveness that we have gone into this movement for the emancipation of the oppressed and suffering. It is true we have called upon the people to arm and prepare for the stormy times before us.

This seems to be the ground upon which the verdict is to be sustained. "But when a long train of abuses and usurpations pursuing invariably the same object evinces a design to reduce the people under absolute despotism, it is their right, it is their duty to throw off such government and provide new guards for their future safety." This is a quotation from the Declaration of Independence. Have we broken any laws by showing to the people how these abuses, that have occurred for the last twenty years, are invariably pursuing one object, viz: to establish an oligarchy in this country so strong and powerful and monstrous as never before has existed in any country? I can well understand why that man Grinnell did not urge upon the grand jury to charge us with treason. I can well understand it. You cannot try and convict a man for treason who has upheld the constitution against those who trample it under their feet. It would not have been as easy a job to do that, Mr. Grinnell, as to charge these men with murder.

Now, these are my ideas. They constitute a part of myself. I cannot divest myself of them, nor would I, if I could. And if you think that you can crush out these ideas that are gaining ground more and more every day; if you think you can crush them out by sending us to the gallows; if you would once more have people suffer the penalty of death because they have dared to tell the truth—and I defy you to show us where we have told a lie—I say, if death is the penalty for proclaiming the truth, then I will proudly and defiantly pay the costly price! Call your hangman! Truth crucified in Socrates, in Christ, in Giordano Bruno, in Huss, in Galileo, still lives—they and others whose number is legion have preceded us on this path. We are ready to follow!

PART FIVE

PETER KROPOTKIN
(1842–1921)

Peter Kropotkin is almost certainly the most influential classical anarchist theorist within formal social sciences. His works have informed thinking in a range of disciplines from geography through political science, economics, and sociology. Beyond social sciences his works inform perspectives in biology, especially understandings of evolution. Kropotkin's writings have also been influential in literary criticism and, of course, philosophy. And his influence continues in the present period, as new generations of scholars turn more and more to anarchism in areas like geography and sociology.

Kropotkin's work should be recognized for his insights regarding the antecedants of crime and for offering a framework for critical criminological analysis. Some of Kropotkin's contributions to critical criminology include, but are not limited to, abolitionism, restorative justice, and critical legal studies. In addition, Kropotkin offered some of the early, pointed criticisms of Cesare Lombroso's criminology, his research and analysis, offering instead, and against Lombroso, a *social* analysis of crime and punishment. Kropotkin's analysis was experiential, he himself having been held for years in Russian and French prisons and having faced deportation multiple times.

Kropotkin offered a searing criticism of the brutality of prisons, and offered alternatives to punitive approaches to social ills. He also did much to analyze the social nature of laws as aspects, not of deliberation, justice, and order, but of class rule. Kropotkin reminds the reader that rule of law is rule of the specific order in which the law is created and the dominant ones who make it. These analyses are exemplified in the chapters by Kropotkin included here.

Chapter 6, pamphlet, *Law and Authority* (London: International Publishing Co., 1886). Chapter 7 from *In Russian and French Prisons* (London: Ward and Downey, 1887).

CHAPTER 6

Law and Authority: An Anarchist Essay
Peter Kropotkin

Chapter 1

"When ignorance reigns in society and disorder in the minds of men, laws are multiplied, legislation is expected to do everything, and each fresh law being a fresh miscalculation, men are continually led to demand from it what can proceed only from themselves, from their own education and their own morality." It is no revolutionist who says this, nor even a reformer. It is the jurist, Dalloy, author of the Collection of French law known as "Repertoire de la Legislation." And yet, though these lines were written by a man who was himself a maker and admirer of law, they perfectly represent the abnormal condition of our society.

In existing States a fresh law is looked upon as a remedy for evil. Instead of themselves altering what is bad, people begin by demanding a *law* to alter it. If the road between two villages is impassable, the peasant says:—"There should be a law about parish roads." If a park-keeper takes advantage of the want of spirit in those who follow him with servile observance and insults one of them, the insulted man says, "There should be a law to enjoin more politeness upon park-keepers." If there is stagnation in agriculture or commerce, the husbandman, cattle-breeder, or corn speculator argues, "It is protective legislation that we require." Down to the old clothesman there is not one who does not demand a law to protect his own little trade. If the employer lowers wages or increases the hours of labour, the politician in embryo exclaims, "We must have a law to put all that to rights," instead of telling the workers that there are other, and much more effectual means of settling these things straight; namely, recovering from the employer the wealth of which he has been despoiling the workmen for generations. In short, a law everywhere and for everything! A law about fashions, a law about mad dogs, a law about virtue, a law to put a stop to all the vices and all the evils which result from human indolence and cowardice.

We are so perverted by an education which from infancy seeks to kill in us the spirit of revolt, and to develop that of submission to authority; we are so perverted by this existence under the ferule of a law, which regulates every event in life—our birth, our education, our development, our love, our friendship—that, if this state of things continues, we shall lose all initiative, all habit of thinking for ourselves. Our society seems no longer able to understand that it is possible to exist otherwise than under the reign of Law, elaborated by a representative government and administered by a handful of rulers; and even when it has gone so far as to emancipate itself from the thraldom, its first care had been to reconstitute it immediately. "The Year I. of Liberty" has never lasted more than a day, for after proclaiming it men put themselves the very next morning under the yoke of Law and Authority.

Indeed, for some thousands of years, those who govern us have done nothing but ring the changes upon "Respect for law, obedience to authority." This is the moral atmosphere in which parents bring up their children, and school only serves to confirm the impression. Cleverly assorted scraps of spurious science are inculcated upon the children to prove necessity of law; obedience to the law is made a religion; moral goodness and the law of the masters are fused into one and the same divinity. The historical hero of the schoolroom is the man who obeys the law, and defends it against rebels.

Later, when we enter upon public life, society and literature, impressing us day by day and hour by hour, as the waterdrop hollows the stone, continue to inculcate the same prejudice. Books of history, of political science, of social economy, are stuffed with this respect for law; even the physical sciences have been pressed into the service by introducing artificial modes of expression, borrowed from theology and arbitrary power, into knowledge which is purely the result of observation. Thus our intelligence is successfully befogged, and always to maintain our respect for law. The same work is done by newspapers. They have not an article which does not preach respect for law, even where the third page proves every day to demonstrate the imbecility of that law, and shows how it is dragged through every variety of mud and filth by those charged with its administration. Servility before the law has become a virtue, and I doubt if there was ever even a revolutionist who did not begin in his youth as the defender of law against what are generally called "abuses," although these last are inevitable consequences of the law itself.

Art pipes in unison with would-be science. The hero of the sculptor, the painter, the musician shields Law beneath his buckler, and, with flashing eyes and distended nostrils stands ever ready to strike down the man who would lay hands upon her. Temples are raised to her; revolutionists themselves hesitate to touch the high priests consecrated to her service, and when revolution is about to sweep away some ancient institution, it is still by law that it endeavors to sanctify the deed.

The confused mass of rules of conduct called Law, which has been bequeathed to us by slavery, serfdom, feudalism, and royalty, has taken the place of those stone monsters before whom human victims used to be immolated, and whom slavish savages dared not even touch lest they should be slain by the thunder-bolts of heaven.

This new worship has been established with especial success since the rise to supreme power of the middle class—since the great French Revolution. Under the ancient *regime*, men spoke little of laws; unless, indeed, it were, with Montesquieu, Rousseau, and Voltaire, to oppose them to royal caprice; obedience to the good pleasure of the king and his lackeys was compulsory on pain of hanging or imprisonment. But during and after the Revolution, when the lawyers rose to power, they did their best to strengthen the principle upon which their ascendancy depended. The middle-class at once accepted it as a dyke to dam up the popular torrent. The priestly crew hastened to sanctify it, to save their bark from foundering amid the breakers. Finally, the people received it as an improvement upon the arbitrary authority and violence of the past.

To understand this, we must transport ourselves in imagination into the eighteenth century. Our hearts must have ached at the story of the atrocities committed by the all-powerful nobles of that time upon the men and women of the people, before we can understand what must have been the magic influence upon the peasant's mind of the words, "Equality before the law, obedience to the law without distinction of birth or fortune." He, who until then, had been treated more cruelly than a beast, he who had never had any rights, he who had never obtained justice against the most revolting actions on the part of a noble, unless in revenge he killed him and was hanged—he saw himself recognised by this maxim, at least in theory, at least with regard to his personal rights, as the equal of his lord. Whatever this law might be, it promised to affect lord and peasant alike ; it proclaimed the equality of rich and poor before the judge. The promise was a lie, and to-day we know it ; but at that period it was an advance, a homage to justice, as hypocrisy is a homage rendered to truth. This is the reason that when the saviours of the menaced middle-class (the Robespierres and the Dantons) took their stand upon the writings of the Rousseaus and the Voltaires, and proclaimed "Respect for law, the same for every man," the people accepted the compromise; for their revolutionary impetus had already spent its force in the contest with a foe whose ranks drew closer day by day. They bowed the neck beneath the yoke of law to save themselves from the arbitrary power of their lords.

The Middle-Class has even since continued to make the most of this maxim, which, with another principle, that of representative government, sums up the whole philosophy of the bourgeois age, the XIX century. It has preached this doctrine in its schools, it has propagated it in its writings, it has moulded its art and science to the same purpose, it has thrust its beliefs into every hole and corner—like a pious Englishwoman, who slips tracts under the door,—and it has done all this so successfully, that to-day we behold the issue in the detestable fact, that, at the very moment when the spirit of turbulent criticism is re-awakening, men who long for freedom begin the attempt to obtain it by entreating their masters to be kind enough to protect them by modifying the laws which these masters themselves have created!

But times and tempers are changed since a hundred years ago. Rebels are everywhere to be found, who no longer wish to obey the law without knowing whence it comes, what are its uses, and whither arises the obligation to submit to it, and the reverence with which it is encompassed. The rebels of our day are criticizing the very foundations of Society, which have hitherto been held sacred, and first and foremost amongst them that fetish, law. Just for this reason the upheaval which is at hand, is no mere insurrection, it is a *Revolution*.

The critics analise the sources of law, and find there, either a god, product of the terrors of the savage, and stupid, paltry and malicious as the priests who vouch for its supernatural origin, or else, bloodshed, conquest by fire and sword. They study the characteristics of law, and instead of perpetual growth corresponding to that of the human race, they find its distinctive trait to be immobility, a tendency to crystalise what should be modified and developed day by day. They ask how law has been maintained, and in its service they see the atrocities of Byzantinism, the cruelties of the Inquisition, the tortures of the Middle Ages, living flesh torn by the lash of the executioner, chains, clubs, axes, the gloomy dungeons of prisons, agony, curses and tears. In our own days they see, as before, the axe, the cord, the rifle, the prison; on the one hand, the brutalised prisoner, reduced to the condition of a caged beast by the debasement of his whole moral being, and on the other, the judge, stripped of every feeling which does honor to human nature, living like a visionary in a world of legal fictions, revelling in the inflection of imprisonment and death, without even suspecting, in the cold malignity of his madness, the abyss of degradation into which he has himself fallen before the eyes of those whom he condemns.

They see a race of law-makers legislating without knowing what their laws are about; to-day voting a law on the sanitation of towns, without the faintest notion of hygiene, tomorrow making regulations for the armament of troops, without so much as understanding a gun; making laws about teaching and education without ever having given a lesson of any sort, or even an honest education to their own children; legislating at random in all directions, but never forgetting the penalties to be meted out to ragamuffins, the prison and the galleys, which are to be the portion of men a thousand times less immoral than these legislators themselves.

Finally, they see the gaoler on the way to lose all human feeling, the detective trained as a blood-hound, the police spy despising himself; "informing," metamorphosed into a virtue; corruption, erected into a system; all the vices, all the evil qualities of mankind countenanced and cultivated to insure the triumph of law.

All this we see, and, therefore, instead of inanely repeating the old formula, "Respect the law," we say, "Despite law and all its attributes!" In place of the cowardly phrase, "Obey the law," our cry is "Revolt against all laws!"

Only compare the misdeeds accomplished in the name of each law, with the good it has been able to effect, and weigh carefully both good and evil, and you will see if we are right.

Chapter II

Relatively speaking, law is a product of modern times. For ages and ages mankind lived without any written law, even that graved in symbols upon the entrance stones of a temple. During that period, human relations were simply regulated by customs, habits and usages, made sacred by constant repetition, and acquired by each person in childhood, exactly as he learned how to obtain his food by hunting, cattle-rearing, or agriculture.

All human societies have passed through this primitive phase, and to this day a large proportion of mankind have no written law. Every tribe has its own manners and customs; customary law, as the jurists say. It has social habits, and that suffices to maintain cordial relations between the inhabitants of the village, the members of the tribe or community. Even amongst ourselves—the "civilised" nations—when we leave large towns, and go into the country, we see that there the mutual relations of the inhabitants are still regulated according to ancient and generally accepted customs, and not according to the written law of the legislators. The peasants of Russia, Italy, and Spain, and even of a large part of France and England, have no conception of written law. It only meddles with their lives to regulate their relations with the State. As to relations between themselves, though these are sometimes very complex, they are simply regulated according to ancient custom. Formerly, this was the case with mankind in general.

Two distinctly marked currents of custom are revealed by analysis of the usages of primitive people.

As man does not live in a solitary state, habits and feelings develop within him which are useful for the preservation of society and the propagation of the race. Without social feelings and usages, life in common would have been absolutely impossible. It is not law which has established them; they are anterior to all law. Neither is it religion which has ordained them; they are anterior to all religions. They are found amongst all animals living in society. They are spontaneously developed by the very nature of things, like those habits in animals which men call instinct. They spring from a process of evolution, which is useful, and, indeed, necessary, to keep society together in the struggle it is forced to maintain for existence. Savages end by no longer eating one another, because they find it in the long-run more advantageous to devote themselves to some sort of cultivation, than to enjoy the pleasure of feasting upon the flesh of an aged relative once a year. Many travellers have depicted the manners of absolutely independent tribes, where laws and chiefs are unknown, but where the members of the tribe have given up stabbing one another in every dispute, because the habit of living in society has ended by developing certain feelings of fraternity and oneness of interest, and they prefer appealing to a third person to settle their differences. The hospitality of primitive peoples, respect for human life, the sense of reciprocal obligation, compassion for the weak, courage, extending even to the sacrifice of self for others, which is first learnt for the sake of children and friends, and later, for that of members of the same community—all these qualities are developed in man anterior to all law, independently of all religion, as in the case of the social animals. Such feelings and practices are the inevitable results of social life. Without being, as say priests and metaphysicians, inherent in man, such qualities are the consequence of life in common.

But side by side with these customs, necessary to the life of societies and the preservation of the race, other desires, other passions, and therefore other habits and customs, are evolved in human association. The desire to dominate others and impose one's own will upon them; the desire to seize upon the products of the labour of a neighbouring tribe; the desire to surround oneself with comforts without producing anything, whilst slaves provide their master with the means of procuring every sort of pleasure and luxury—these selfish, personal desires give rise to another current of habits and customs. The priest and the warrior, the charlatan who makes a profit out of superstition, and after freeing himself from the fear of the devil, cultivates it in others; and the bully, who procures the invasion and pillage of his neighbours, that he may return laden with booty, and followed by slaves; these two, hand in hand, have succeeded in imposing upon primitive society customs advantageous to both of them, but tending to perpetuate their domination of the masses. Profit, gin by the indolence, the fears, the inertia of the crowd, and thanks to the continual repetition of the same acts, they have permanently established customs which have become a solid basis for their own domination.

For this purpose, they would have made use, in the first place, of that tendency to run in a groove, so highly developed in mankind. In children and all savages it attains striking proportions, and it may also be observed in animals. Man, when he is at all superstitious, is always afraid to introduce any sort of change into existing conditions; he generally venerates what is ancient. "Our fathers did so and so; they got on pretty well; they brought you up; they were not unhappy; do the same!" the old say to the young, every time the latter wish to alter things. The unknown frightens them, they prefer to cling to the past, even when that past represents poverty, oppression, and slavery. It may even be said that the more miserable a man is, the more he dreads every sort of change, lest it may make him more wretched still. Some ray of hope, a few scraps of comfort, must penetrate his gloomy abode before he can begin to desire better things, to criticise the old ways of living, and prepare to imperil them for the sake of bringing about a change. So long as he is not imbued with hope, so long as he is not freed from the tutelage of those who utilise his superstition and his fears, he prefers remaining in his former position. If the young desire any change, the old raise a cry of alarm against the innovators. Some savages would rather die than transgress the customs of their country, because they have been told from childhood that the least infraction of established routine would bring ill-luck, and ruin the whole tribe. Even in the present day, what numbers of politicians, economists, and would-be revolutionists act under the same impression, and cling to a vanishing past. How many care only to seek for precedents. How many fiery innovators are mere copyists of bygone revolutions.

The spirit of routine, originating in superstition, indolence, and cowardice, has in all times been the mainstay of oppression. In primitive human societies, it was cleverly turned to account by priests and military chiefs. They perpetuated customs useful only to themselves, and succeeded in imposing them on the whole tribe. So long as this conservative spirit could be exploited so as to assure the chief in his encroachments upon individual liberty, so long as the only inequalities between men were the work of nature, and these were not increased a hundred-fold by the concentration of power and wealth, there was no need for law, and the formidable paraphernalia of tribunals and ever-augmenting penalties to enforce it.

But as society became more and more divided into two hostile classes, one seeking to establish its domination, the other struggling to escape, the strife began. Now the conqueror was in a hurry to secure the results of his actions in a permanent form, he tried to place them beyond question, to make them holy and venerable by every means in his power. Law made its appearance under the sanction of the priest, and the warrior's club was placed at its service. Its office was to render immutable such customs as were to the advantage of the dominant minority. Military authority undertook to ensure obedience. This new function was a fresh guarantee to the power of the warrior; now he had not only mere brute force at his service; he was the defender of law.

If law, however, presented nothing but a collection of prescriptions serviceable to rulers, it would find some difficulty in insuring acceptance and obedience. Well, the legislators confounded in one code the two currents of custom, of which we have just been speaking, the maxims which represent principles of morality and social union wrought out as a result of life in common, and the mandates, which are meant to ensure external existence to inequality. Customs, absolutely essential to the very being of society, are, in the code, cleverly intermingled with usages imposed by the ruling caste, and both claim equal respect from the crowd. "Do not kill," says the code, and hastens to add, "And pay tithes to the priest." "Do not steal," says the code, and immediately after, "He who refuses to pay taxes, shall have his hand struck off."

Such was law; and it has maintained its twofold character to this day. Its origin is the desire of the ruling class to give permanence to customs imposed by themselves for their own advantage. Its character is the skilful co-mingling of customs useful to society, customs which have no need of law to insure respect, with other customs useful only to rulers, injurious to the mass of the people, and maintained only by the fear of punishment.

Like individual capital, which was born of fraud and violence, and developed under the auspices of authority, law has no title to the respect of men. Born of violence and superstition, and established in the interests of consumer, priest and rich exploiter, it must be utterly destroyed on the day when the people desire to break their chains.

We shall be still better convinced of this when, in the next chapter, we have analysed the ulterior development of law, under the auspices of religion, authority and the existing parliamentary system.

Chapter III

We have seen in the previous chapter how law originated in established usage and custom, and how from the beginning it has represented a skilful mixture of social habits, necessary to the preservation of the human race, with other customs, imposed by those who used popular superstition, as well as the right of the strongest, for their own advantage. This double character of law has determined its own later development during the growth of political organization. Whilst in the course of ages the nucleus of social custom inscribed in law has been subjected to but slight and gradual modifications, the other portion has been largely developed in directions indicated by the interests of the dominant classes, and to the injury of the classes they oppress. From time to time these dominant classes have allowed a law to be extorted from them which presented, or appeared to present, some guarantee for the disinherited. But then such laws have but repealed a previous law, made for the advantage of the ruling caste. "The best laws," says Buckle, "were those which repealed the preceding ones." But what terrible efforts have been needed, what rivers of blood have been spilt, every time there has been a question of the repeal of one of these fundamental enactments serving to hold the people in fetters. Before she could abolish the vestiges of serfdom and feudal rights, and break up the power of the royal court, France was forced to pass through four years of revolution and twenty years of war. Decades of conflict are needful to repeal the least of the iniquitous laws, bequeathed us by the past, and even then they scarcely disappear except in periods of revolution.

The history of the genesis of capital has already been told by Socialists many times. They have described how it was born of war and pillage, of slavery and serfdom, of modern fraud and exploitation. They have shown how it is nourished by the blood of the worker, and how little by little it has conquered the whole world. The same story, concerning the genesis and development of law has yet to be told. As usual, the popular intelligence has stolen a march upon men of books. It has already put together the philosophy of this history, and is busy laying down its essential landmarks.

Law, in its quality of guarantee of the results of pillage, slavery and exploitation, has followed the same phrases of development as capital; twin brother and sister, they have advanced hand in hand, sustaining one another with the suffering of mankind. In every country in Europe their history is approximately the same. It has differed only in detail; the main facts are alike; and to glance at the development of law in France or Germany is to know its essential traits, its phases of development, in most of the European nations.

In the first instance, law was a national pact or contract. Such a contract was agreed upon between the legions and people at the Champs de Mars,[1] a relic of the same period is preserved even yet in the Field of May of the primitive Swiss cantons despite the alterations effected by the interference of centralising and middle-class civilisation. It is true that this contract was not always freely accepted. Even in those early days the rich and strong were imposing their will upon the rest. But at all events they encountered an obstacle to their encroachments in the mass of the people, who often made them feel their power in return.

But as the Church on one side and the nobles on the other, succeeded in enthralling the people, the right of law-making escaped from the hands of the nation and passed into those of the privileged orders. Fortified by the wealth accumulating in her coffers, the Church extended her authority; she tampered more and more with private life, and under pretext of saving souls, she seized upon the labour of her serfs, she gathered taxes from every class, she increased her jurisdiction, she multiplied penalties, and enriched herself in proportion to the number of offences committed, for the produce of every fine poured into her coffers. Laws had no longer any connection with the interests of the nation. "They might have been supposed to emanate rather from a council of religious fanatics than from legislators," observes an historian of French law.

---

1   The annual assembly of the early Franks, originally held in March, there the first month of the year.

At the same time, as the Baron likewise extended his authority over labourers in the fields and artizans in the towns, he too became legislator and judge. The few relics of national law dating from the tenth century are merely agreements regulating service, statute labour, and tribute due from serf and vassals to their lord. The legislators of that period were a handful of brigands, organised for the plunder of a people daily becoming more peaceful, as they applied themselves to agricultural pursuits. These robbers exploited the feelings for justice inherent in the people—they posed as the administrators of that justice, made a source of revenue for themselves out of its fundamental principles and concocted laws to maintain their own domination.

Later on, these laws, collected and classified by jurists, formed the foundation of our modern codes. And are we to talk about respecting these codes, the legacy of baron and priest?

The first revolution, the revolt of the townships, was successful in abolishing a portion only of these laws; the charters of enfranchised towns are, for the most part, a mere compromise between baronial and episcopal legislation, and the new relations created within the free borough itself. Yet what a difference between these laws, and the laws we have now! The town did not take upon itself to imprison and execute citizens for reasons of State; it was content to expel anyone who plotted with the enemies of the city, and to raze his house to the ground. It confined itself to imposing fines for so-called "crimes and misdemeanours;" and in the townships of the twelfth century may even be discerned the just principle, today forgotten, which holds the whole community responsible for the misdoing of each of its members. The societies of that time looked upon crime as an accident or a misfortune; a conception common amongst the Russian peasantry at this moment. Therefore, they did not admit of the principle of personal vengeance as preached by the Bible, but considered that the blame for each misdeed reverted to the whole society. It needed all the influence of the Byzantine Church, which imported into the West the refined cruelties of Eastern despotism, to introduce into the manners of Gauls and Germans the penalty of death, and the horrible tortures afterwards inflicted on those regarded as criminals. Just in the same way, it needed all the influence of the Roman code, the product of the corruption of Imperial Rome, to introduce the notions as to absolute property in land, which have overthrown the communistic customs of primitive people.

As we know, the free townships were not able to hold their own. Torn by intestine dissensions between rich and poor, burgher and serf, they fell an easy prey to royalty. And as royalty acquired fresh strength, the right of legislation passed more and more into the hands of a clique of courtiers. Appeal to the nation was made only to sanction the taxes demanded by the King. Parliament summoned at intervals of two centuries, according to the good pleasure or caprice of the Court, "Councils Extraordinary," Assemblies of Notables, Ministers, scarce heeding the "grievances of the King's subjects"—these are the legislators of France. Later still, when all power is concentrated in a single man, who can say "I am the State," edicts are concocted in the "secret counsels of the Prince," according to the whim of a minister, or of an imbecile King; and subjects must obey on pain of death. All judicial guarantees are abolished; the nation is the serf of royalty, and of a handful of courtiers. And at this period the most horrible penalties startle our gaze—the wheel, the stake, flaying alive, tortures of every description, invented by the sick fancy of monks and madmen, seeking delight in the sufferings of executed criminals.

The great Revolution began the demolition of this framework of law, bequeathed to us by feudalism and royalty. But after having demolished some portions of the ancient edifice, the Revolution delivered over the power of law-making to the bourgeoisie, who, in their turn, began to raise a fresh framework of laws, intended to maintain and perpetuate middle-class domination amongst the masses. Their Parliament makes laws right and left, and mountains of law accumulate with frightful rapidity. But what *are* all these laws at bottom?

The major portion have but one object—to protect private property, *i.e.*, wealth acquired by the exploitation of man by man. Their aim is to open out to capital fresh fields for exploitation, and to sanction the new forms which that exploitation continually assumes, as capital swallows up another branch of human activity, railways, telegraphs, electric light, chemical industries, the expression of man's thought in literature and science, &c. The object of the rest of these laws is fundamentally the same. They exist to keep up the machinery of government, which serves to secure to capital the exploitation and monopoly of the wealth produced. Magistrature, police, army, public instruction, finance, all serve one God—capital; all have but one object—to facilitate the exploitation of the worker by the capitalist. Analyse all the laws passed for the last eighty years and you will find nothing but this. The protection of the person, which is put forward as the true mission of law, occupies an imperceptible space amongst them, for, in existing society, assaults upon the person, directly dictated by hatred and brutality, tend to disappear. Now-a-days, if anyone is murdered, it is generally for the sake of robbing him; rarely from personal vengeance. But if this class of crimes and misdemeanours is continually diminishing, we certainly do not owe the change to legislation. It is due to the growth of humanitarianism in our societies, to our increasingly social habits rather than to the prescriptions of our laws. Repeal to-morrow every law dealing with the protection of the person, and to-morrow stop all proceedings for assault, and the number of attempts, dictated by personal vengeance and by brutality, would not be augmented by one single instance.

It will, perhaps, be objected that, during the last fifty years, a good many liberal laws have been enacted. But, if these laws are analysed, it will be discovered that this liberal legislation consists in the repeal of the laws bequeathed to us by the barbarism of preceding centuries. Every liberal law, every radical programme, may be summed up in these words, abolition of laws grown irksome to the middle-class itself, and return and extension to all citizens of liberties enjoyed by the townships of the twelfth century. The abolition of capital punishment, trial by jury for all "crimes" (there was a more liberal jury in the twelfth century), the election of magistrates, the right of bringing public officials to trial, the abolition of standing armies, free instruction, &c., everything that is pointed out as an invention of modern liberalism, is but a return to the freedom which existed before Church and King had laid hands upon every manifestation of human life.

Thus the protection of exploitation, directly by laws on property, and indirectly by the maintenance of the State, is both the spirit and the substance of our modern codes, and the one function of our costly legislative machinery. But it is time we gave up being satisfied with mere phrases, and learned to appreciate their real signification. The law, which on its first appearance presented itself as a compendium of customs useful for the preservation of society, is now perceived to be nothing but an instrument for the maintenance of exploitation, and the domination of the toiling masses by rich idlers. At the present day its civilising mission is *nil*; it has but one object, to bolster up exploitation.

This is what is told us by history as to the development of law. Is it in virtue of this history that we are called upon to respect it? Certainly not. It has no more title to respect than capital, the fruit of pillage; and the first duty of the revolutionists of the nineteenth century will be to make a bonfire of all existing laws, as they will of all titles to property.

Chapter IV

The millions of laws which exist for the regulation of humanity, appear upon investigation to be divided into three principal categories—protection of property, protection of persons, protection of government. And by analysing each of these three categories, we arrive at the same logical and necessary conclusion: *the uselessness and hurtfulness of law*.

Socialists know what is meant by protection of property. Laws on property are not made to guarantee either to the individual or to society the enjoyment of the produce of their own labour. On the contrary, they are made to rob the producer of a part of what he has created, and to secure to certain other people that portion of the produce which they have stolen either from the producer or from society as a whole. When, for example, the law establishes Mr. So-and-So's right to a house, it is not establishing his right to a cottage he has built for himself, or to a house he has erected with the help of some of his friends. In that case no one would have disputed his right. On the contrary, the law is establishing his right to a house which is *not* the product of his labor; first of all, because he has had it built for him by others to whom he has not paid the full value of their work; and next, because that house represents a social value, which he could not have produced for himself. The law is establishing his right to what belongs to everybody in general and to nobody in particular. The same house built in the midst of Siberia would not have the value it possesses in a large town, and, as we know, that value arises from the labour of something like fifty generations of men who have built the town, beautified it, supplied it with water and gas, fine promenades, colleges, theatres, shops, railways, and roads leading in all directions. Thus, by recognising the right of Mr. So-and-So to a particular house in Paris, London, or Rouen, the law is unjustly appropriating to him a certain portion of the produce of the labour of mankind in general. And it is precisely because this appropriation and all other forms of property, bearing the same character, are a crying injustice, that a whole arsenal of laws, and a whole army of soldiers, policemen, and judges are needed to maintain it against the good sense and just feeling inherent in humanity.

Well, half our laws, the civil code in each country, serves no other purpose than to maintain this appropriation, this monopoly for the benefit of certain individuals, against the whole of mankind. Three-fourths of the causes decided by the tribunals are nothing but quarrels between monopolists—two robbers disputing over their booty. And a great many of our criminal laws have the same object in view, their end being to keep the workman in a subordinate position towards his employer, and thus afford security for exploitation.

As for guaranteeing the product of his labour to the producer, there are no laws which even attempt such a thing. It is so simple and natural, so much a part of the manners and customs of mankind, that law has not given it so much as a thought. Open brigandage, sword in hand, is no feature of our age. Neither does one workman ever come and dispute the produce of his labour with another. If they have a misunderstanding they settle it by calling in a third person, without having recourse to law. The only person who exacts from another what the other has produced, is the proprietor, who comes in and deducts the lion's share. As for humanity in general, it everywhere respects the right of each to what he has created, without the interposition of any special laws.

As all the laws about property, which make up thick volumes of codes, and are the delight of our lawyers, have no other object than to protect the unjust appropriation of human labour by certain monopolists, there is no reason for their existence, and, on the day of the Revolution, social revolutionists are thoroughly determined to put an end to them. Indeed, a bonfire might be made with perfect justice of all laws bearing upon the so-called "rights of property," all title-deeds, all registers, in a word, of all that is in any way connected with an institution which will soon be looked upon as a blot in the history of humanity, as humiliating as the slavery and serfdom of past ages.

The remarks just made upon laws concerning property are quite as applicable to the second category of laws; those for the maintenance of government *i.e.* Constitutional Law.

It again is a complete arsenal of laws, decrees, ordinances, orders in council, and what not, all serving to protect the diverse forms of representative government, delegated or usurped, beneath which humanity is writhing. We know very well—Anarchists have often enough pointed out in their perpetual criticism of the various forms of government—that the mission of all governments, monarchical, constitutional, or republican, is to protect and maintain by force the privileges of the classes in possession, the aristocracy, clergy, and traders. A good third of our laws—and each country possesses some tens of thousands of them—the fundamental laws on taxes, excise duties, the organisation of ministerial departments and their offices, of the army, the police, the Church, &c., have no other end than to maintain, patch up, and develop the administrative machine. And this machine in its turn serves almost entirely to protect the privileges of the possessing classes. Analyse all these laws, observe them in action day by day, and you will discover that not one is worth preserving.

About such laws there can be no two opinions. Not only Anarchists, but more or less revolutionary radicals also, are agreed that the only use to be made of laws concerning the organisation of government is to fling them into the fire.

The third category of law still remains to be considered, that relating to the protection of the person and the detection and prevention of "crime." This is the most important, because most prejudices attach to it; because, if law enjoys a certain amount of consideration, it is in consequence of the belief that this species of law is absolutely indispensable to the maintenance of security in our societies. These are laws developed from the nucleus of customs useful to human communities, which have been turned to account by rulers to sanctify their own domination. The authority of the chiefs of tribes, of rich families in towns, and of the king, depended upon their judicial functions, and even down to the present day, whenever the necessity of government is spoken of, its function as supreme judge is the thing implied. "Without a government men would tear one another to pieces," argues the village orator. "The ultimate end of all government is to secure twelve honest jurymen to every accused person," said Burke.

Well, in spite of all the prejudices existing on this subject, it is quite time that anarchists should boldly declare this category of laws as useless and injurious as the preceding ones.

First of all, as to so-called "crimes"—assaults upon persons—it is well-known that two-thirds, and often as many as three-fourths, of such "crimes" are instigated by the desire to obtain possession of someone's wealth. This immense class of so-called "crimes and misdemeanours" will disappear on the day on which private property ceases to exist. "But," it will be said, "there will always be brutes who will attempt the lives of their fellow-citizens, who will lay their hands to a knife in every quarrel, and revenge the slightest offence by murder, if there are no laws to restrain and punishments to withhold them." This refrain is repeated ever time the right of society *to punish* is called in question.

Yet there is one fact upon this head which at the present time, is thoroughly established; the severity of punishment does not diminish the amount of crime. Hang, and, if you like, quarter murderers, and the number of murders will not decrease by one. On the other hand, abolish the penalty of death, and there will not be one murder more; there will be fewer. Statistics prove it. But if the harvest is good, and bread cheap, and the weather fine, the number of murders immediately decreases. This again is proved by statistics. The amount of crime always augments and diminishes in proportion to the price of provisions and the state of the weather. Not that all murders are actuated by hunger. That is not the case. But when the harvest is good and provisions are at an obtainable price, and when the sun shines, men, lighter hearted and less miserable than usual, do not give way to gloomy passions, do not from trivial motives, plunge a knife into the bosom of a fellow creature.

Moreover, it is also a well-known fact that the fear of punishment has never stopped a single murderer. He who kills his neighbour from revenge or misery does not reason much about consequence; and there have been few murderers who were not firmly convinced that they should escape prosecution.

Without speaking of a society in which a man will receive a better education, in which the development of all his faculties, and the possibility of exercising them, will procure him so many enjoyments, that he will not seek to poison them by remorse—without speaking of the society of the future—even in our society, even with those sad products of misery, whom we see to-day in the public-houses of great cities—on the day when no punishment is inflicted upon murderers, the number of murders will not augment by a single case; and it is extremely probable that it will be, on the contrary, diminished by all those cases which are due at present to habitual criminals, who have been brutalised in prison.

We are continually being told of the benefits conferred by law, and the beneficial effect of penalties, but have the speakers ever attempted to strike a balance between the benefits attributed to laws and penalties, and the degrading effect of these penalties upon humanity? Only calculate all the evil passions awakened in mankind by the atrocious punishments formerly inflicted in our streets! Man is the cruellest animal upon earth; and who has pampered and developed the cruel instincts unknown, even amongst monkeys, if it is not the king, the judge, and the priests, armed with law, who caused flesh to be torn off in strips, boiling pitch to be poured into wounds, limbs to be dislocated, bones to be crushed, men to be sawn asunder to maintain their authority? Only estimate the torrent of depravity let loose in human society by the "informing" which is countenanced by judges, and paid in hard cash by governments, under pretext of assisting in the discovery of "crime." Only go into the gaols and study what man becomes when he is deprived of freedom and shut up with other depraved beings, steeped in the vice and corruption which oozes from the very walls of our existing prisons. Only remember that the more these prisons are reformed, the more detestable they become; our model modern penitentiaries are a hundred-fold more abominable than the dungeons of the middle ages. Finally, consider what corruption, depravity of mind, is kept up amongst men by the idea of obedience, the very essence of law; of chastisement; of authority having the right to punish, to judge irrespective of our conscience and the esteem of our friends; of the necessity for executioners, gaolers and informers—in a word, by all the attributes of law and authority. Consider all this, and you will assuredly agree with us in saying that a law inflicting penalties is an abomination which should cease to exist.

Peoples without political organisation, and therefore less depraved than ourselves, have perfectly understood that the man who is called "criminal" is simply unfortunate; that the remedy is not to flog him, to chain him up, or to kill him on the scaffold or in prison, but to relieve him by the most brotherly care, by treatment based on equality, by the usages of life amongst honest men. In the next revolution we hope that this cry will go forth:

"Burn the guillotines; demolish the prisons; drive away the judges, policemen, and informers—the impurest race upon the face of the earth; treat as a brother the man who has been led by passion to do ill to his fellow; above all, take from the ignoble products of middle-class idleness the possibility of displaying their vices in attractive colours; and be sure that but few crimes will mar our society."

The main supports of crime are idleness, law and authority; laws about property, about government, laws about penalties and misdemeanours; and authority, which takes upon itself to manufacture these laws and to apply them.

No more laws! No more judges! Liberty, equality, and practical human sympathy are the only effectual barriers we can oppose to the anti-social instincts of certain amongst us.

CHAPTER 7

Are Prisons Necessary?
Peter Kropotkin

If we take into consideration all the influences indicated in the above rapid sketch, we are bound to recognize that all of them, separately and combined together, act in the direction of rendering men who have been detained for several years in prisons less and less adapted for life in society; and that none of them, not a single one, acts in the direction of raising the intellectual and moral faculties, of lifting man to a higher conception of life and its duties, of rendering him a better, a more human creature than he was.

Prisons do *not* moralize their inmates; they do *not* deter them from crime. And the question arises: What shall we do with those who break, not only the written law—that sad growth of a sad past—but also those very principles of morality which every man feels his own heart? That is the question which now preoccupies the best minds of our century.

There was a time when Medicine consisted in administering some empirically-discovered drugs. The patients who fell into the hands of the doctor might be killed by his drugs, or they might rise up notwithstanding them, the doctor had the excuse of doing what all his fellows did; he could not outgrow his contemporaries.

But our century which has boldly taken up so many questions, but faintly forecast by its predecessors, has taken up this question too, and approached it from the other end. Instead of merely curing diseases, medicine tries now to prevent them; and we all know the immense progress achieved, thanks to the modern view of disease. Hygiene is the best of medicines.

The same has to be done with the great social phenomenon which has been called Crime until now, but will be called Social Disease by our children. Prevention of the disease is the best of cures: such is the watchword of a whole younger school of writers which grew up of late, especially in Italy, represented by Poletti,[1] Ferri,[2] Cola-janni,[3] and, to some limited extent, by Lombroso; of the great school of psychologists represented by Griesinger,[4] Krafft-Ebing,[5] Despine[6] on the Continent, and Maudsley[7] in this country; of the sociologists like Quételet and his unhappily too scanty followers; and finally, in the modern school of Psychology with regard to the individual, and of the social reformers with regard to society. In their works we have already the elements of a new position to be taken with regard to those unhappy people whom we have hanged, or decapitated, or sent to jail until now.

Three great causes are at work to produce what is called crime: the social causes, the anthropological, and, to use Ferri's expression, the cosmical.

The influence of these last is but insufficiently known, and yet it cannot be denied. We know from the Postmaster-General's Reports that the number of letters containing money which are thrown into the pillar-boxes without any address is very much the same from year to year. If so capricious an element in our life as oblivion of a certain given kind is subject to laws almost as strict as those which govern the motion of the heavenly bodies, it is still more true with regard to breaches of law. We can predict with a great approximation the num-ber of murders which will be committed next year in each country of Europe. And if we should take into account the disturbing influences which will increase, or diminish, next year, the number of murders committed, we might predict the figures with a still greater accuracy.

There was, some time ago, in *Nature*, an essay on the number of assaults and suicides committed in India with relation to tempera-ture and the moisture of the air. Everybody knows that an excessively

1   *Il Delinquente*; Udine, 1865.
2   *Nuovi orizzonti del Dirritto e della Procedure penale*; *Socialismo e Criminalità*, and several others.
3   *L'alcoolismo, sue consequena morali e sue cause*; Catania, 1887. A study I cannot but warmly recommend to those writers on the subject who so often mistake the effects for causes.
4   *Gesammelte Abhandlungen*, Berlin 1882. *Pathologie der Psychischen Krankheiten*.
5   *Zweifehafte Geistzustände*, Erlangen, 1873; *Grundzüge der Criminal-Psychologie*, 1872; *Lehrbuch der gerichtlichen Psychopatie*, Stuttgart, 1875.
6   *Psychologie Naturelle, Paris 1868*; *Congrès Pénitentiaire de Stockholm* in 1878, vol. ii.
7   "Insanity in Relation to Crime," London, 1880.

hot and moist temperature renders men more nervous than they are when the temperature is moderate and a dry wind blows over our fields. In India, where the temperature grows sometimes exceedingly hot, and the air at the same time grows exceedingly moist, the enervating influence of the atmosphere is obviously felt still more strongly than in our latitudes. Mr. S. A. Hill, therefore, calculates from figures extending over several years, a formula which enables you, when you know the average temperature and humidity of each month, to say, with an astonishing approximation to exactitude, the number of suicides and wounds due to violence which have been registered during the month.[8] Like calculations may seem very strange to minds unaccustomed to treat psychological phenomena as dependent upon physical causes, but the facts point to this dependence so clearly as to leave no room for doubt. And persons who have experienced the effects of tropical heat accompanied by tropical moisture on their own nervous system, will not wonder that precisely during such days Hindoos are inclined to seize a knife to settle a dispute, or the men disgusted with life are more inclined to put an end to it by suicide.[9]

The influence of cosmical causes on our actions has not yet been fully analyzed; but several facts are well established. It is known, for instance, that attempts against persons (violence, murders, and so on) are on the increase during the summer, and that during the winter the number of attempts against property reaches its maximum. We cannot go through the curves drawn by Professor E. Ferri,[10] and see

8   S. A. Hill, "The Effects of the Weather upon the Death-Rate and Crime in India," *Nature*, vol. 29, 1884, p. 338. The formula shows that the number of suicides and acts of violence committed each month is equal to the excess of the average monthly temperature over 48° Fahr. Multiplied by 7·2, *plus* the average moistness, multiplied by 2. The author adds:—"Crimes of violence in India may therefore be said to be proportional in frequency to the tendency to *prickly heat*, that excruciating condition of the skin induced by a high temperature combined with moisture. Any one who has suffered from this ailment, and knows how it affected his temper will really understand how the conditions which produce it may sometimes lead to homicide and other crimes." Under cold weather the influence is the reverse.

9   See also Mayr, *Gesetzmässigkeit in Gesellschaftsleben*, as also E. Ferri in *Archico di Psychiatria, fasc. 2nd*; *La Teoria dell' imputabilatà e la Negazione del libero arbitrio*, Bologna, 1881; and many others.

10   *Das Verbrechen in seiner Abhängigkeit von Temperatur*, Berlin 1882. Also, Colajanni's *Oscillations thermométriques et délits contre les personnes*, in *Bibl. d'Anthropologie Criminelle*, Lyons, 1886.

on the same sheet the curves of temperature and those showing the number of attempts against persons, without being deeply impressed with their likeness: one easily mistakes them for one another. Unhappily this kind of research has not been prosecuted with the eagerness it deserves, so that few of the cosmical causes have been analyzed as to their influence on human actions.

It must be acknowledged also that the inquiry offers many difficulties, because most cosmical causes exercise their influence only in an indirect way; thus, for instance, when we see that the number of breaches of law fluctuates with the crops of cereals, or with the wine-crops, the influence of cosmical agents appears only through the medium of a series of influences of a social character. Still, nobody will deny that when weather is fine, the crops good, and the villagers cheerful, they are far less inclined to settle their small disputes by violence than during stormy or gloomy weather, when a spoiled crop spreads moreover general discontent. I suppose that women who have constant opportunities of closely watching the good and bad temper of their husbands could tell us plenty about the influence of weather on peace in their homes.

The so-called 'anthropological causes' to which much attention has been given of late, are certainly much more important than the preceding. The influence of inherited faculties and of the bodily organization on the inclination towards crime has been illustrated of late by so many highly interesting investigations, that we surely can form a nearly complete idea about this category of causes which bring men and women within our penal jurisdiction. Of course, we cannot endorse in full the conclusions of one of the most prominent representatives of this school, Dr. Lombroso,[11] especially those he arrives at in one of his writings.[12] When he shows us that so many inmates of our prisons have some defect in the organization of their brains, we must accept this statement as a mere fact. We may even admit with him that the majority of convicts and prisoners have longer arms than people at liberty. Again, when he shows us that the most brutal murders have been committed by men who had some serious defect in their bodily structure, we have only to incline before this statement and recognize its accuracy. It is a statement—not more.

11   *L' Uomo delinquente*, 3rd edition, Torino, 1884.
12   *Sull'Incremento del Delitto*, Roma, 1879.

But we cannot follow Mr. Lombroso when he infers too much from this and like facts, and considers society entitled to take any measures against people who have like defects of organization. We cannot consider society as entitled to exterminate all people having defective structure of brain and still less to imprison those who have long arms. We may admit that most of the perpetrators of the cruel deeds which from time to time stir public indignation have not fallen very far short of being sad idiots. The head of Frey, for instance, an engraving of which has made of late the tour of the Press, is an instance in point. But *all* idiots do not become assassins, and still less all feeble-minded men and women; so that the most impetuous criminalist of the anthropological school would recoil before a wholesale assassination of all idiots if he only remembered how many of them are free—some of them under care, and very many of them having other people under their care—the difference between these last and those who are handed over to the hangman being only a difference of the circumstances under which they were born and have grown up. In how many otherwise respectable homes, and palaces, too, not to speak of lunatic asylums, shall we not find the very same features which Dr. Lombroso considers characteristic of "criminal madness"? Brain diseases may favour the growth of criminal propensities; but they may *not*, when under proper care. The good sense, and still more the good heart of Charles Dickens have perfectly well understood this plain truth.

Certainly we cannot follow Dr. Lombroso in all his conclusions, still less those of his followers; but we must be grateful to the Italian writer for having devoted his attention to and popularized his researches into, the medical aspects of the question. Because, for an unprejudiced mind, the only conclusions that can be drawn from his varied and most interesting researches is, that most of those whom we treat as criminals are people affected by bodily diseases, and that their illness ought to be submitted to some treatment, instead of being aggravated by imprisonment.

Mr. Maudsley's researches into insanity with relation to crime are well known in this country.[13] But none of those who have seriously read his works can leave them without being struck by the

13   "Responsibility in Mental Disease," London, 1872; "Body and Will," London, 1883.

circumstance that most of those inmates of our jails who have been imprisoned for attempts against persons are people affected with some disease of the mind; that the "ideal madman whom the law creates," and the only one whom the law is ready to recognize as irresponsible for his acts, is as rare as the ideal "criminal" whom the law insists upon punishing. Surely there is, as Mr. Maudsley says, a wide "borderland between crime and insanity, near one boundary of which we meet with something of madness but more of sin (of conscious desire of doing some harm, we prefer to say), and near the other boundary of which something of sin but more of madness." But, "a just estimate of the moral responsibility of the unhappy people inhabiting this borderland" will never be made as long as the idea of "sin," or of "bad will," is not got rid of.[14]

Unhappily, hitherto our penal institutions have been nothing but a compromise between the old ideas of revenge, of punishment of the "bad will" and "sin," and the modern ideas of "deterring from crime," both softened to a very slight extent by some notions of philanthropy. But the time, we hope, is not far distant when the noble ideas which have inspired Griesinger, Krafft-Ebing, Despine, and some of the modern Italian criminalists, like Colajanni and Ferri, will become the property of the general public, and make us ashamed of having continued so long to hand over those whom we call criminals to hangmen and jailers. If the conscientious and extensive labours of the writers just named were more widely known, we should all easily understand that most of those who are kept now in jails, or put to death, are merely people in need of the most careful fraternal treatment. I do not mean, of course, that we ought to substitute lunatic asylums for prisons. Far be it from me to entertain this abhorrent idea. Lunatic

14   Maudsley's "Responsibility in Mental Disease." On page 27, Mr. Maudsley says: "In like manner, though a criminal might be compassionated it would still be necessary to deprive him of the power of doing further mischief; society has clearly the right to insist on that being done; and though he might be kindly cared for, the truest kindness to him and others would still be *the enforcement of that kind of discipline which is best fitted to bring him, if possible, to a healthy state of mind, even if it were hard labour within the measure of his strength.*" Leaving aside the "right" of society to enforce hard labour, which might be doubted upon, because Mr. Maudsley recognizes himself that society has "manufactured its criminals," we wonder that so open a mind admits, even for a moment, that imprisonment with hard labour *may be* best fitted to bring anybody to a healthy state of mind.

asylums are nothing else but prisons; and those whom we keep in prisons are not lunatics, nor even people approaching the sad boundary of the borderland where man loses control over his actions. Far be from me the idea which is sometimes brought forward as to maintaining prisons by placing them under pedagogists and medical men. What most of those who are now sent to jail are in need of is merely a fraternal help from those who surround them, to aid them in developing more and more the higher instincts of human nature which have been checked in their growth either by some bodily disease—anemia of the brain, disease of the heart, the liver, or the stomach—or, still more, by the abominable conditions under which thousands and thousands of children grow up, and millions of adults are living, in what we call our centres of civilization. But these higher faculties cannot be exercised when man is deprived of liberty, of the free guidance of his actions, of the multifarious influences of the human world. Let us carefully analyze each breach of the moral unwritten law, and we shall always find—as good old Griesinger said—that it is not due to something which has suddenly sprung up in the man who accomplished it: it is the result of effects which, for years past, have deeply stirred within him.[15] Take, for instance, a man who has committed an act of violence. The blind judge of our days comes forward and sends him to prison. But the human being who is not overpowered by the kind of mania which is inculcated by the study of Roman jurisprudence—who analyzes instead of merely sentencing—would say, with Griesinger, that although in this case the man has not suppressed his affections, but has left them to betray themselves by an act of violence, this act has been prepared long since. Before this time, probably throughout his life, the same person has often manifested some anomaly of mind by noisy expression of his feelings, by crying loudly after some trifling disagreeable circumstance, by easily venting his bad temper in those who stood by him; and, unhappily, he has not from his childhood found anybody who was able to give a better direction to his nervous impressibility. The causes of the violence which has brought him into the prisoners' dock must be sought long years before. And if we push our analysis still deeper, we discover that this state of mind is itself a consequence of some physical disease

15   *Vierteljahrsschrift für gerichtliche und öffentliche Medicin*, 1867.

either inherited or developed by an abnormal life; some disease of the heart, the brain, or the digestive system. For many years these causes have been at work before resulting in some deed which falls within the reach of the law.

More than that. If we analyse ourselves, if everybody would frankly acknowledge the thoughts which have sometimes passed through his mind, we should see that all of us have had—be it as an imperceptible wave traversing the brain, like a flash of light—some feelings and thoughts such as constitute the motive of all acts considered as criminal. We have repudiated them at once; but if they had had the opportunity of recurring again and again; if they were nurtured by circumstances, or by a want of exercise of the best passions—love, compassion, and all those which result from living in the joys and sufferings of those who surround us; then these passing influences, so brief that we hardly noticed them, would have degenerated into some morbid element in our character.

That is what we ought to teach our children from the earliest childhood, while now we imbue them from their tenderest years with ideas of justice identified with revenge, of judges and tribunals. And if we did this, instead of doing as we do now, we should no longer have the shame of avowing that we hire assassins to execute our sentences, and pay warders for performing a function for which no educated man would like to prepare his own children. Functions which we consider so degrading cannot be an element of moralization.

Fraternal treatment to check the development of the anti-social feelings which grow up in some of us—not imprisonment—is the only means that we are authorized in applying, and can apply, with some effect to those in whom these feelings have developed in consequence of bodily disease or social influences. And that is not a Utopia; while to fancy that punishment is able to check the growth of anti-social feelings is a Utopia—a wicked Utopia; the Utopia of "leave me in peace, and let the world go as it likes."

Many of the anti-social feelings, we are told by Dr. J. Bruce Thompson[16] and many others, are inherited; and facts amply support this conclusion. But what is inherited? Is it a certain bump of criminality, or something else? What is inherited is insufficient

16   *Journal of Mental Science*, January, 1870, p. 488 sq.

self-control, or a want of firm will, or a desire for risk and excitement,[17] or disproportionate vanity. Vanity, for instance, coupled with a desire for risk and excitement, is one of the most striking features amidst the population of our prisons. But vanity finds many fields for its exercise. It may produce a maniac like Napoleon the First, or a Frey; but it produces also, under some circumstances—especially when instigated and guided by a sound intellect—men who pierce tunnels and isthmuses, or devote all their energies towards pushing through some great scheme for what they consider the benefit of humanity; and then it may be checked, and even reduced almost to nothingness, by the parallel growth of intelligence. If it is a want of firmness of will which has been inherited, we know also that this feature of character may lead to the most varied consequences according to the circumstances of life. How many of our "good fellows" suffer precisely from this defect? It is a sufficient reason for sending them to prison?

Humanity has seldom ventured to treat its prisoners like human beings; but each time it has done so it has been rewarded for its boldness. I was sometimes struck at Clairvaux with the kindness bestowed on sick people by several assistants in the hospital; I was touched by several manifestations of a refined feeling of delicacy. Dr. Campbell, who has had much more opportunity of learning this trait of human nature during his thirty years' experience as prison-surgeon, goes much farther. By mild treatment, he says, "with as much consideration as if they had been delicate ladies [I quote his own words], the greatest order was generally maintained in the hospital." He was struck with that "esteemable trait in the character of prisoners—observable even among the roughest criminals; I mean the great attention they bestow on the sick." "The most hardened criminals," he adds, "are not exempt from this feeling." And he says elsewhere: "Although many of these men, from their former reckless life and habits of depredation might be supposed to be hardened and

17   The importance of this factor, well pointed out by Ed. Du Cane, is proved by the circumstance that what they call "the criminal age" is the age between twenty-five and thirty-four. After that age, a desire for a quieter life makes the breaches of law suddenly decrease. The proposal of Ed. Du Cane ("if those persons whose career evidences in them marked criminal tendencies could either be locked up or kept under supervision until they passed, say, the age of forty") is typical of the peculiar logics developed in those people who have been for some time superintendents of prisons.

indifferent, they have a keen sense of what is right or wrong." All honest men who have had to do with prisoners, can but confirm the experience of Dr. Campbell.

What is the secret of this feature, which surely cannot fail to strike people accustomed to consider the convict as very little short of a wild beast? *The assistants in hospitals have an opportunity of exercising their good feelings.* They have opportunities of feeling compassion for somebody, and of acting accordingly. Moreover, they enjoy within the hospital much more freedom than the other convicts; and those of whom Dr. Campbell speaks were under the direct moral influence of a doctor like himself—not of a soldier.

In short, anthropological causes—that is, defects of organization—play a most important part in bringing men to jail; but these causes are not causes of "criminality," properly speaking. The same causes are at work amidst millions and millions of our modern psychopathic generation; but they lead to anti-social deeds only under certain unfavourable circumstances. Prisons do not cure these pathological deformities, they only reinforce them; and when a psychopate leaves a prison, after having been subjected for several years to its deteriorating influence, he is without comparison less fit for life in society than he was before. If he is prevented from committing fresh anti-social deeds, that can only been attained by undoing the work of the prison, by obliterating the features with which it inculcates those who have passed through its ordeal—a task which certainly is performed by some friends of humanity, but a task utterly hopeless in so many cases.

There is something to say also with regard to those whom criminalists describe as qualified assassins, and who in so many countries imbued with the old Biblical principle of a tooth for a tooth, are sent to the gallows. It may seem strange in this country, but the fact is that throughout Siberia—where there is ample opportunity to judge different categories of exiles—the "murderers" are considered as the best class of the convict population; and I was very happy to see that Mr. Davitt, who has so acutely analyzed crime and its causes, has also been able to make a like observation.[18] It is not known as

18   He says: "Murders occasionally occur in connection with robbery, it is true; but they are as a rule accidental to the perpetuation of the latter crime, and scarcely ever premeditated. The most heinous of all offenses—murder deliberately intended and

generally as it ought to be that the Russian law has not recognized capital punishment for more than a century. However freely political offenders have been sent to the gallows under Alexander II. and III., so that 31 men have been put to death during the preceding reign[19] and about 25 since 1881, capital punishment does not exist in Russia for common-law offences. It was abolished in 1753, and since that time murderers are merely condemned to hard-labour from eight to twenty years (parricides for life), after the expiration of which term they are settled free for life in Siberia. Therefore, Eastern Siberia is full of liberated assassins; and, nevertheless, there is hardly another country where you could travel and stay with greater security. During my very extensive journeys in Siberia I never carried with me a defensive weapon of any kind, and the same was the case with my friends, each of whom every year travelled something like ten thousand miles across this immense territory. As mentioned in a preceding chapter the number of murders which are committed in East Siberia by liberated assassins, or by the numberless runaways, is exceedingly small; while the unceasing robberies and murders of which Siberia complains now, take place precisely in Tomsk and throughout Western Siberia, whereto no murderers, and only minor offenders are exiled. In the earlier parts of this century it was not uncommon to find at an official's house that the coachman was a liberated murderer, or that the nurse who bestowed such motherly care upon the children bore imperfectly obliterated marks of the branding-iron. As to those who would suggest that probably the Russians are a milder sort of men than those of Western Europe, they have only to remember the scenes which have accompanied the outbreaks of peasants; and they might be asked also, how far the absence of executions and of all that abominable talk which is fed by descriptions of executions—the talk in which English prisoners delight most—has contributed to foster a cold contempt for human life.

planned before its commission—is ordinarily the offspring of the passions of revenge and jealousy, or the outcome of social or political wrongs; and is more frequently the result of some derangement of the nobler instincts of human nature than traceable to its more debased orders or appetites."—*Leaves from a Prison Diary*, vol. I, 17.

19   Nobody knows exactly how many scores, or hundreds, of Poles were executed in 1863–65.

The shameful practice of legal assassination which is still carried on in Western Europe, the shameful practice of hiring for a guinea an assassin[20] to accomplish a sentence which the judge would not have the courage to carry out himself—this shameful practice and all that hardly-imaginable amount of corruption it continues to pour into society, has not even the excuse of preventing murder. Nowhere has the abolition of capital punishment increased the number of murders. If the practice of putting men to death is still in use, it is merely a result of craven fear, coupled with reminiscences of a lower degree of civilization when the tooth-for-tooth principle was preached by religion.

But if the cosmical causes—either directly or indirectly—exercise so powerful an influence on the yearly amount of anti-social acts; if psychological causes, deeply rooted in the intimate structure of the body, are also a powerful factor in bringing men to commit breaches of the law, what will remain of the theories of the writers on the criminal law after we have also taken into account the social causes of what we call crime?

There was a custom of old by which each commune (clan, Mark, Gemeinde) was considered responsible as a whole for any anti-social act committed by any of its members. This old custom has disappeared like so many good remnants of the communal organization of old. But we are returning to it; and again, after having passed through a period of the most unbridled individualism, the feeling is growing amongst us that society is responsible for the anti-social deeds committed in its midst. If we have our share of glory in the achievement of the geniuses of our century, we have our part of shame in the deeds of our assassins.

From year to year thousands of children grow-up in the filth—material and moral—of our great cities, completely abandoned amidst a population demoralized by a life from hand to mouth, the incertitude of to-morrow, and a misery of which no former epoch has had even an apprehension. Left to themselves and to the worst influences of the street, receiving but little care from their parents ground down by a terrible struggle for existence, they hardly know what a happy home is; but they learn from earliest childhood what the vices of our great cities are. They enter life without even knowing

20   Du Cane's "Punishment and Prevention of Crime," 23.

a handicraft which might help them to earn their living. The son of a savage learns hunting from his father; his sister learns how to manage their simple household. The children whose father and mother leave the den they inhabit, early in the morning, in search of any job which may help them to get through the next week, enter life not even with that knowledge. They know no handicraft; their home has been the muddy street; and the teachings they received in the street were of the kind known by those who have visited the whereabouts of the gin-palaces of the poor, and of the places of amusement of the richer classes.

It is all very well to thunder denunciations about the drunken habits of this class of the population, but if those who denounce them had grown up in the same conditions as the children of the labourer who every morning conquers by means of his own fists the right of being admitted at the gate of a London dockyard,—how many of them would not have become the continual guests of the gin-palaces?—the only palaces with which the rich have endowed the real producers of all riches.

When we see this population growing up in all our big manufacturing centres we cannot wonder that our big cities chiefly supply prisons with inmates. I never cease to wonder, on the contrary, that relatively so small a proportion of these children become thieves or highway robbers. I never cease to wonder at the deep-rootedness of social feelings in the humanity of the nineteenth century, at the goodness of heart which still prevails in the dirty streets, which are the causes that relatively so few of those who grow up in absolute neglect declare open war against our social institutions. These good feelings, this aversion to violence, this resignation which makes them accept their fate without hatred growing in their hearts, are the only real barrier which prevents them from openly breaking all social bonds,— not the deterring influence of prisons. Stone would not remain upon stone in our modern palaces, were it not for these feelings.

And at the other end of the social scale, money that is representative signs of human work, is squandered in unheard-of luxury, very often with no other purpose than to satisfy a stupid vanity. While old and young have no bread, and are really starving at the very doors of our luxurious shops,—these know no limits to their lavish expenditures.

When everything round about us—the shops and the people we see in the streets, the literature we read, the money-worship we meet with every day—tends to develop an unsatiable thirst for unlimited wealth, a love for sparkish luxury, a tendency towards spending money foolishly for every avowable and unavowable purpose; when there are whole quarters in our cities each house of which reminds us that man has too often remained a beast, whatever the decorum under which he conceals his bestiality; when the watchword of our civilized world is: "Enrich yourselves! Crush down everything you meet in your way, by all means short of those which might bring you before a court!" When apart from a few exceptions, all—from the landlord down to the artisan—are taught every day in a thousand ways that the *beau-ideal* of life is to manage affairs so as to make others work for you; when manual work is so despised that those who perish from want of bodily exercise prefer to resort to gymnastics, imitating the movements of sawing and digging, instead of sawing wood and hoeing the soil; when hard and blackened hands are considered a sign of inferiority, and a silk dress and the knowledge of how to keep servants under strict discipline is a token of superiority; when literature expends its art in maintaining the worship of richness and treats the "impractical idealist" with contempt—what need is there to talk about inherited criminality when so many factors of our life work in one direction—that of manufacturing beings unsuited for a honest existence, permeated with anti-social feelings!

Let us organize our society so as to assure to everybody the possibility of regular work for the benefit of the commonwealth—and that means of course a through transformation of the present relations between work and capital; let us assure to every child a sound education and instruction, both in manual labour and science, so as to permit him to acquire, during the first twenty years of his life, the knowledge and habits of earnest work—and we shall be in no more need of dungeons and jails, of judges and hangmen. Man is a result of those conditions in which he has grown up. Let him grow in habits of useful work: let him be brought by his earlier life to consider humanity as one great family, no member of which can be injured without the injury being felt by a wide circle of his fellows, and ultimately by the whole of society; let him acquire a taste for the highest enjoyment of science and art—much more lofty and durable than those given by the satisfaction of lower passions,—and we may be sure that we shall not have many breaches of those laws of morality which are an unconscious affirmation of the best conditions for life in society.

Two-third of all breaches of law being so-called "crimes against property," these cases will disappear, or be limited to a quite trifling amount, when property, which is now the privilege of the few, shall return to its real source—the community. As to "crimes against persons," already their numbers are rapidly decreasing, owing to the growth of moral and social habits which necessarily develop in each society and can only grow when common interests contribute more and more to tighten the bonds which induce men to live a common life.

Of course, whatever be the economical bases of society, there will always be in its midst a certain number of beings with passions more strongly developed and less easily controlled than the rest; and there always will be men whose passions may occasionally lead them to commit acts of an anti-social character. But these passions can receive another direction, and most of them can be rendered almost or quite harmless by the combined efforts of those who surround us. We live now in too much isolation. Everybody cares only for himself, or his nearest relatives. Egotistic—that is, unintelligent—individualism in material life has necessarily brought about an individualism as egotistic and as harmful in the mutual relations of human beings. But we have known in history, and we see still, communities where men are more closely connected together than in our Western European cities. China is an instance in point. The great "compound family" is there still the basis of the social organization: the members of the compound family know one another perfectly; they support one another, they help one another, not merely in material life, but also in moral troubles; and the number of "crimes" both against property and persons, stands at an astonishingly low level (in the central provinces, of course, not on the sea-shore). The Slavonian and Swiss agrarian communes are another instance. Men know one another in these smaller aggregations: they mutually support one another; while in our cities all bond between the inhabitants have disappeared. The old family, based on a common origin, is disintegrating. But men cannot live in this isolation, and the elements of new social groups—those ties arising between the inhabitants of the same spot having many interests in common, and those of people united by the prosecution of common aims—is growing. Their growth can only be accelerated by such changes as would bring about a closer mutual dependency and a greater equality between the members of our communities.

And yet, notwithstanding all this, there surely will remain a limited number of persons whose anti-social passions—the result of bodily diseases—may still be a danger for the community. Shall humanity send these to the gallows, or lock them up in prisons? Surely it will not resort to this wicked solution of the difficulty.

There was a time when lunatics, considered as possessed by the devil, were treated in the most abominable manner. Chained in stalls like animals, they were dreaded even by their keepers. To break their chains, to set them free, would have been considered then as a folly. But a man came—Pinel—who dared to take off their chains, and to offer them brotherly words, brotherly treatment. And those who were looked upon as ready to devour the human being who dared to approach them, gathered round their liberator, and proved that he was right in his belief in the best features of human nature, even in those whose intelligence was darkened by disease. From that time the cause of humanity was won. The lunatic was no longer treated like a wild beast. Men recognized in him a brother.

The chains disappeared, but asylums—another name for prisons—remained, and within their walls a system as bad as that of the chains grew up by-and-by. But then the peasants of a Belgian village, moved by their simple good sense and kindness of heart, showed the way towards a new departure which learned students of mental disease did not perceive. They set the lunatics quite free. They took them into their families, offered them a bed in their poor houses, a chair at their plain tables, a place in their ranks to cultivate the soil, a place in their dancing-parties. And the fame spread wide of "miraculous cures" effected by the saint to whose name the church of Gheel was consecrated. The remedy applied by the peasants was so plain, so old—it was liberty—that the learned people preferred to trace the result to Divine influences instead of taking things as they were. But there was no lack of honest and good-hearted men who understood the force of the treatment invented by the Gheel peasants, advocated it, and gave all their energies to overcome the inertia of mind, the cowardice, and the indifference of their surroundings.[21]

Liberty and fraternal care have proved the best cure on our side of the above-mentioned wide borderland "between insanity and crime." They will prove also the best cure on the other boundary of the same borderland. Progress is in that direction. All that tends that way will bring us nearer to the solution of the great question which has not ceased to preoccupy human societies since the remotest antiquity, and which cannot be solved by prisons.

21   One of them, Dr. Arthur Mitchell, is well known in Scotland. Compare his "Insane in private Dwellings," Edinburgh, 1864; as also "Care and Treatment of Insane Poor," in *Edinb. Med. Journal* for 1868.

Left: Michael Schwab, Right: Joseph E. Gary

PART SIX

MICHAEL SCHWAB AND
JOSEPH E. GARY
(Schwab: 1853–1898; Gary: 1821–1906)

Michael Schwab's piece here shows that anarchist criminology has always been experiential and includes engaged contributions from social activists criminalized for their organizing work and that these contributions come from prominent figures. He wrote this piece while imprisoned, a part of the US state's efforts to break working-class resistance and labor organizing during and after the Haymarket Affair, which offers a polite corrective to the self-serving and distorted fantasies offered by Lombroso in describing Schwab's working-class colleagues, some of whom were targeted for execution by the state. Schwab's article stands strong in the history of anarchist analysis written by prisoners while imprisoned.

Joseph E. Gary was the judge who tried the Haymarket anarchists for the political riot that took place in Haymarket Square in Chicago. Schwab included this letter by Judge Gary to Richard J. Oglesby, Governor of Illinois, to demonstrate the ambiguities and contradictions tainting this trial.

Chapter 8 was originally published in The Monist, no. IV (1891).

CHAPTER 8

A Convicted Anarchist's Reply to Professor Lombroso
Michael Schwab and Joseph E. Gary

I have read with much interest Professor Lombroso's article about the anarchists, and I found many things in it that are true, but also many errors. Even should we admit Professor Lombroso's theory to be correct, it would in the present case avail but little, because the portraits from which he made his deductions are not sufficiently truthful for his purpose. 'Schaak's' book is said to be a fictitious 'robber story' and I am informed that it contains many untruths absolutely invented for ornament and decoration. It is in the highest degree improbable that such a book should not have caricatured the portraits of the anarchists. In books designed for sale to the masses, the illustrations are not, as a rule, of any value as works of art, even if the persons pictured in them enjoy the author's favor. The only true to life pictures are the photographs which Dr. Carus sent to Professor Lombroso, and these were taken in the county jail; but it appears that the Professor thought little of them, for he says, 'Perhaps these photographs were taken some years before the crime, when they were very young,' and the pictures in the *Vorbote* were drawn after the photographs, and are therefore of no account so long as the photographs themselves are accessible.

Certain as it is that vice, crime, and brutality very often find a characteristic expression of face, so equally certain is it also that prominent physiognomists very often judge inaccurately and falsely. There are many instances of this. In Mantegazza's work are found examples. Now, if it is difficult to arrive at a correct opinion under favorable circumstances, it is almost impossible to do so if such pictures as those of Schaak's, with Schaak's explanations, form the basis and starting point of the inquiry.

Johann Most has an unsymmetric face; this however, is not the fault of nature, but of an unskilful surgeon. Of Engel I know nothing, except that he joined the socialists at an advanced age. In his earlier years he advocated anti-Socialistic ideas. After his first arrest he was set free upon the good word of Coroner Herz, who declared that he knew Engel for years as a quiet and well-behaved citizen.

With Lingg I was not on friendly terms, and therefore propriety demands that I keep silent about him.

Spies was born in the house of a forester, which had formerly been a *Raubschloss*. The connection between this fact and the other one that Spies twenty years later was converted to socialism by an American, is not very clear to me. He was undoubtedly the most gifted of all the indicted anarchists, and he had a most intelligent appearance; his forehead was well developed. Temperance in eating and drinking was one of his qualities, but as regards his intellectual activity, I regret to say that this was not the case. Many of his articles betrayed nervous over-excitement. In the beginning of the year 1886, all intellectual work was forbidden him by his physician, and for a few weeks he followed his advice. He was full of compassion for the poor and wretched, and he helped them wherever he could. Concerning his charities he observed strict silence. Any reference to them was disagreeable to him, and made him angry. A man who had once rudely offended him without cause, being in distress Spies obtained work for him. I came to the knowledge of this by accident. One of the employees of the *Arbeiter Zeitung* who received but a small salary told me that Spies out of his own pocket gave him for some months $2.00 a week to pay a doctor and procure medicine. The salary of Spies was only $19.00 a week, and from this he supported his mother. Spies was of a very tender nature, and what his comrades thought of his blood thirstiness maybe gathered from the following anecdote. A certain man by the name of Matzinger had translated an article from the French, "The Day After the Revolution," and Spies asked an acquaintance of mine, "What would you do the day after the revolution?" The answer was, "I should imprison you till all was over, for your sentimentality would prevent us from any energetic methods." The bystanders laughed; Spies flushed and said nothing.

Fielden has been treated worst by Professor Lombroso. His father has been characterised as a sort of genius, and in closest connection with it, the Professor says, "Almost all the sons of men of genius are lunatics, idiots, or criminals." I hope the Professor, mindful of this, is not married.

If the term genius has so wide a meaning, the above statement is certainly incorrect. Goethe on his mother's side had very talented ancestors, and his father was extremely well gifted. The son of Goethe was a drunkard, but we know that this unfortunate inheritance came from his mother's side. The Darwin family was famous for two hundred years. The sons of Hegel and Schelling were also able men. Many more instances of that kind could be adduced; and whenever a genius or his posterity goes to the wall, there are often external circumstances that cause it. The Fielden who became famous as a Member of Parliament at the time of the Chartist movement in England, was a relative, but not the father of Sam Fielden. Sam Fielden's father was a very intelligent laborer, who also took part in the Chartist movement, without, however, becoming very prominent in it. By the bye, the descendants of the first named Fielden are neither "lunatics, idiots, nor criminals," but wealthy manufacturers. And now to Sam Fielden; no lunatic, idiot, or criminal could make the speech which he made when asked why sentence of death should not be pronounced against him, a speech concerning which Mr. Grinnell, the prosecutor, said that "had it been made to the jury, they would have acquitted him." Mr. Luther Laflin Mills, formerly States Attorney, declared in my presence that it was a masterpiece. That there was any criminal disposition in Sam nobody ever had any idea. He was nearly forty years old when arrested, and his wealthy employers considered him an honest man, and a harmless enthusiast of an amiable nature. He had become entangled in the Anarchist prosecution by a strange concatenation of circumstances.

Professor Lombroso's opinion concerning Fielden, formed by the study of portraits, stands in a strange contrast to the estimate of character made by the judge who tried and sentenced the anarchists. Three days before the execution Judge Gary wrote the following letter to Governor Oglesby:

Chicago, ILL, November 8, 1887.

To the Hon. Richard J. Oglesby, Governor of Illinois.

Sir: In the application of Samuel Fielden for a commutation of his sentence, it is not necessary as to the case itself that I should do more than refer to the decision of the Supreme Court for a history of his crime.

Outside of what is there shown, there is in the nature and private character of the man, a natural love of justice, an impatience at all undeserved suffering, an impulsive temper; and an intense love of and thirst for the applause of his hearers made him an advocate of force as a heroic remedy for the hardships that the poor endure. In his own private life he was the honest, industrious, and peaceable laboring man.

In what he said in court before sentence he was respectful and decorous. His language and conduct since have been irreproachable. As there is no evidence that he knew of any preparation to do the specific act of throwing the bomb that killed Degan he does not understand even now that general advice to large masses to do violence makes him responsible for the violence done by reason of that advice, nor that being joined by others in an effort to subvert law and order by force makes him responsible for the acts of those others tending to make that effort effectual.

In short, he was more a misguided enthusiast than a criminal conscious of the horrible nature and effect of his teachings and of his responsibility therefor. What shall be done in his case is partly a question of humanity, and partly a question of state policy, upon which it seems to me action on the part of your excellency favorable to him is justifiable.

I attach this to a copy of his petition to your excellency and refer to that for what he says of the change that has come upon himself.

Respectfully Yours,
Joseph E. Gary.

Professor Lombroso wrote his article with the best intentions, I fully recognise the fact; and certainly he was governed by the most humane motives. But even conceding the correctness of his theory he necessarily failed from the insufficiency of his materials.

One thing more, Anarchism is a collective term like Liberalism. People understand by it many different and sometimes contradictory theories. That part of it which is not in harmony with human progress will fail, shall fail, and must fail, but that part of it which is good will live in spite of all. The mistake, however, which has been made in our special case will not again be made in America; and that also will be for the general good.

Joliet Penitentiary.
M. Schwab.

PART SEVEN

ERRICO MALATESTA
(1853–1932)

Errico Malatesta notes that everyday social order under capitalism is violence. This renders questions of violence or nonviolence in social struggles moot. The state is already violent. Capital is already violent. In his reflections on his trial Malatesta notes that capitalist rule rests on tyranny. It could not last a day without it. And it raises hatred (tyranny for capital) to a principle of justice. The struggle of the exploited is a struggle of love. Anarchists, unlike authoritarians, do not claim to hold an infallible formula for ending crime as authoritarians propose through laws and force.

Law defends prejudices pervasive at the time they are made. Malatesta is clear that formal armed police corps, even public social defense, is undesirable. That power will always be dangerous and corrupting. No one should be a cop by profession. Police must be replaced by service that protects the public socially (healthcare, teachers, etc.). This is an important critical perspective given contemporary efforts by police forces to diversify into areas like harm reduction and healthcare as means to expand their reach and increase their already bloated budgets.

Chapter 9 was originally published as "Verso l'Anarchia," *La Questione Sociale* (Dec. 9, 1899), first translated into English in *Man!* (April 1933), and appears in Davide Turcato, ed., *The Complete Works of Malatesta*, Vol. IV (Chico: AK Press, 2019). Chapter 10 was originally published in *Umanità Nova* (Sept. 20, 1921). Chapter 11 was originally published in *Umanità Nova* (Sept. 16, 1921).

CHAPTER 9

Towards Anarchy
Errico Malatesta

It is a general opinion that we, because we call ourselves revolutionists, expect Anarchy to come with one stroke—as the immediate
result of an insurrection that violently attacks all that which exists
and which replaces it with institutions that are really new.[1] And to
say the truth this idea is not lacking among some comrades who also
conceive the revolution in such a manner.

This prejudice explains why so many honest opponents believe
Anarchy a thing impossible; and it also explains why some comrades,
disgusted with the present moral condition of the people and seeing that Anarchy cannot come about soon, waver between an extreme
dogmatism which blinds them to the realities of life and an opportun-
ism which practically makes them forget that they are Anarchists and
that for Anarchy they should struggle.

Of course the triumph of Anarchy cannot be the consequence
of a miracle; it cannot come about in contradiction to the laws of
development (an axiom of evolution that nothing occurs without sufficient cause), and nothing can be accomplished without the adequate
means.

If we should want to substitute one government for another, that
is impose our desires upon others, it would only be necessary to com-
bine the material forces needed to resist the actual oppressors and put
ourselves in their place.

But we do not want this; we want Anarchy which is a society based
on free and voluntary accord—a society in which no one can force his
wishes on another and in which everyone can do as he pleases and

1   [Editor's note] The below version was originally published as "Towards Anarchism" though we have used the version preferred by Davide Turcato, editor of the
Complete Works of Malatesta. This improved version uses "Anarchy" in the title and
has some stylistic improvements over the original English translation in *Man!* (1933).
Originally published as "Verso l'anarchia," *La Questione Sociale* (1899).

together all will voluntarily contribute to the well-being of the community. But because of this Anarchy will not have definitively and universally triumphed until all men will not only not want to be commanded but will not want to command; nor will Anarchy have succeeded unless they will have understood the advantages of solidarity and know how to organize a plan of social life wherein there will no longer be traces of violence and imposition.

And as the conscience, determination, and capacity of men continuously develop and find means of expression in the gradual modification of the new environment and in the realization of the desires in proportion to their being formed and becoming imperious, so it is with Anarchy; Anarchy cannot come but little by little—slowly, but surely, growing in intensity and extension.

Therefore, the subject is not whether we accomplish Anarchy today, tomorrow, or within ten centuries, but that we walk toward Anarchy today, tomorrow, and always.

Anarchy is the abolition of exploitation and oppression of man by man, that is the abolition of private property and government; Anarchy is the destruction of misery, of superstitions, of hatred. Therefore, every blow given to the institutions of private property and to the government, every exaltation of the conscience of man, every disruption of the present conditions, every lie unmasked, every part of human activity taken away from the control of the authority, every augmentation of the spirit of solidarity and initiative, is a step towards Anarchy.

The problem lies in knowing how to choose the road that really approaches the realization of the ideal and in not confusing the real progress with hypocritical reforms. For with the pretext of obtaining immediate ameliorations these false reforms tend to distract the masses from the struggle against authority and capitalism; they serve to paralyze their actions and make them hope that something can be attained through the kindness of the exploiters and governments. The problem lies in knowing how to use the little power we have—that we go on achieving, in the most economical way, more prestige for our goal.

There is in every country a government which, with brutal force, imposes its laws on all; it compels all to be subjected to exploitation and to maintain, whether they like it or not, the existing institutions.

It forbids the minority groups to actuate their ideas, and prevents the social organizations in general from modifying themselves according to, and with, the modifications of public opinion. The normal peaceful course of evolution is arrested by violence, and thus with violence it is necessary to reopen that course. It is for this reason that we want a violent revolution today; and we shall want it always—so long as man is subject to the imposition of things contrary to his natural desires. Take away the governmental violence, ours would have no reason to exist.

We cannot as yet overthrow the prevailing government; perhaps tomorrow from the ruins of the present government we cannot prevent the arising of another similar one. But this does not hinder us, nor will it tomorrow, from resisting whatever form of authority— refusing always to submit to its laws whenever possible, and constantly using force to oppose force.

Every weakening of whatever kind of authority, each accession of liberty will be a progress toward Anarchy; always it should be conquered—never asked for; always it should serve to give us greater strength in the struggle; always it should make us consider the state as an enemy with whom we should never make peace; always it should make us remember well that the decrease of the ills produced by the government consists in the decrease of its attributions and powers, not in increasing the number of rulers or in having them chosen by the ruled. By government we mean any person or group of persons in the state, country, community, or association who has the right to make laws and inflict them upon those who do not want them.

We cannot as yet abolish private property; we cannot regulate the means of production that is necessary to work freely; perhaps we shall not be able to do so in the next insurrectional movement. But this does not prevent us now, or will it in the future, from continually opposing capitalism. And each victory, however small, gained by the workers against their exploiters, each decrease of profit, every bit of wealth taken from the individual owners and put to the disposal of all, shall be a progress—a forward step toward Anarchy. Always it should serve to enlarge the claims of the workers and to intensify the struggle; always it should be accepted as a victory over an enemy and not as a concession for which we should be thankful; always we should remain firm in our resolution to take with force, as soon as it will be possible, those means which the private owners, protected by the government, have stolen from the workers.

The right of force having disappeared, the means of production being placed under the management of whomever wants to produce, the rest must be the fruit of a peaceful evolution.

It would not be Anarchy, yet, or it would be only for those few who want it, and only in those things they can accomplish without the cooperation of the non-anarchists. This does not necessarily mean that the ideal of Anarchy will make little or no progress, for little by little its ideas will extend to more men and more things until it will have embraced all mankind and all life's manifestations.

Having overthrown the government and all the existing dangerous institutions which with force it defends, having conquered complete freedom for all and with it the right to the means of production, without which liberty would be a lie, and while we are struggling to arrive to this point, we do not intend to destroy those things which we little by little will reconstruct.

For example, there functions in the present society the service of supplying food. This is being done badly, chaotically, with great waste of energy and material and in view of capitalist interests; but after all, one way or another we must eat. It would be absurd to want to disorganize the system of producing and distributing food unless we could substitute it with something better and more just.

There exists a postal service. We have thousands of criticisms to make, but in the meantime we use it to send our letters, and shall continue to use it, suffering all its faults, until we shall be able to correct or replace it.

There are schools, but how badly they function. But because of this we do not allow our children to remain in ignorance—refusing their learning to read and write. Meanwhile we wait and struggle for a time when we shall be able to organize a system of model schools to accommodate all.

From this we can see that, to arrive at Anarchy, material force is not the only thing to make a revolution; it is essential that the workers, grouped according to the various branches of production, place themselves in a position that will insure the proper functioning of their social life—without the aid or need of capitalists or governments.

And we see also that the Anarchist ideals are far from being in contradiction, as the "scientific socialists" claim, to the laws of evolution as proved by science; they are a conception which fits these laws perfectly; they are the experimental system brought from the field of research to that of social realization.

CHAPTER 10

Class Struggle or Class Hatred?:
"People" and "Proletariat"
Errico Malatesta

I expressed to the jury in Milan some ideas about class struggle and proletariat that raised criticism and amazement. I better come back to those ideas.

I protested indignantly against the accusation of inciting to hatred; I explained that in my propaganda I had always sought to demonstrate that the social wrongs do not depend on the wickedness of one master or the other, one governor or the other, but rather on masters and governments as institutions; therefore, the remedy does not lie in changing the individual rulers, instead it is necessary to demolish the principle itself by which men dominate over men; I also explained that I had always stressed that proletarians are not individually better than bourgeois, as shown by the fact that a worker behaves like an ordinary bourgeois, and even worse, when he gets by some accident to a position of wealth and command.

Such statements were distorted, counterfeited, put in a bad light by the bourgeois press, and the reason is clear. The duty of the press, paid to defend the interests of police and sharks, is to hide the real nature of anarchism from the public, and seek to accredit the tale about anarchists being full of hatred and destroyers; the press does that by duty, but we have to acknowledge that they often do it in good faith, out of pure and simple ignorance. Since journalism, which once was a calling, decayed into mere job and business, journalists have lost not only their ethical sense, but also the intellectual honesty of refraining from talking about what they do not know.

Let us forget about hack writers, then, and let us talk about those who differ from us in their ideas, and often only in their way of expressing ideas, but still remain our friends, because they sincerely aim at the same goal we aim at.

Amazement is completely unmotivated in these people, so much so that I would tend to think it is affected. They cannot ignore that I have been saying and writing those things for fifty years, and that the same things have been said by hundreds and thousands of anarchists, at my same time and before me.

Let us rather talk about the dissent.

There are the "worker-minded" people, who consider having callous hands as being divinely imbued with all merits and all virtues; they protest if you dare talking about people and mankind, failing to swear on the sacred name of proletariat.

Now, it is a truth that history has made the proletariat the main instrument of the next social change, and that those fighting for the establishment of a society where *all* human beings are free and endowed with all the means to exercise their freedom, must rely mainly on the proletariat.

As today the hoarding of natural resources and capital created by the work of past and present generations is the main cause of the subjection of the masses and of all social wrongs, it is natural for those who have nothing, and therefore are more directly and clearly interested in sharing the means of production, to be the main agents of the necessary expropriation. This is why we address our propaganda more particularly to the proletarians, whose conditions of life, on the other hand, make it often impossible for them to rise and conceive a superior ideal. However, this is no reason for turning the poor into a fetish just because he is poor; neither it is a reason for encouraging him to believe that he is intrinsically superior, and that a condition surely not coming from his merit or his will gives him the right to do wrong to the others as the others did wrong to him. The tyranny of callous hands (which in practice is still the tyranny of few who no longer have callous hands, even if they had once), would not be less tough and wicked, and would not bear less lasting evils than the tyranny of gloved hands. Perhaps it would be less enlightened and more brutal: that is all.

Poverty would not be the horrible thing it is, if it did not produce moral brutishness as well as material harm and physical degradation when prolonged from generation to generation. The poor have different faults than those produced in the privileged classes by wealth and power, but not better ones.

If the bourgeoisie produces the likes of Giolitti and Graziani and all the long succession of mankind's torturers, from the great conquerors to the avid and bloodsucking petty bosses, it also produces the likes of Cafiero, Reclus, and Kropotkin, and the many people that in any epoch sacrificed their class privileges to an ideal. If the proletariat gave and gives so many heroes and martyrs of the cause of human redemption, it also gives off the white guards, the slaughterers, the traitors of their own brothers, without which the bourgeois tyranny could not last a single day.

How can hatred be raised to a principle of justice, to an enlightened spirit of demand, when it is clear that evil is everywhere, and it depends upon causes that go beyond individual will and responsibility?

Let there be as much class struggle as one wishes, if by class struggle one means the struggle of the exploited against the exploiters for the abolition of exploitation. That struggle is a way of moral and material elevation, and it is the main revolutionary force that can be relied on.

Let there be no hatred, though, because love and justice cannot arise from hatred. Hatred brings about revenge, desire to be over the enemy, need to consolidate one's superiority. Hatred can only be the foundation of new governments, if one wins, but it cannot be the foundation of anarchy.

Unfortunately, it is easy to understand the hatred of so many wretches whose bodies and sentiments are tormented and rent by society: however, as soon as the hell in which they live is lit up by an ideal, hatred disappears and a burning desire of fighting for the good of all takes over.

For this reason true haters cannot be found among our comrades, although there are many rhetoricians of hatred. They are like the poet, who is a good and peaceful father, but he sings of hatred, because this gives him the opportunity of composing good verses... or perhaps bad ones. They talk about hatred, but their hatred is made of love.

For this reason I love them, even if they call me names.

CHAPTER 11

Further Thoughts on the Question of Crime
Errico Malatesta

Letter from Aldo Venturini

Bologna, September 8, 1921

Dearest Malatesta,

I read with great interest your two articles, recently appeared in *Umanità Nova*, about the important, and always worth discussing, problem of crime.

No doubt your arguments in support of the solution we anarchists give to the question are indisputably clear and effective. However, let me insist on some of your ideas, which solve some aspects of the problem, but do so in a way either too general and abstract or too particular.

For example, you say: "For us the accomplishment of social duties must be voluntary, and one has a right to take a forcible action only against those who voluntary offend others and hinder a peaceful social coexistence. Force and physical constraint can only be used against a materially violent thrust, for sheer necessity of defence".

Going by the second part of your reasoning, it would almost look like only "a materially violent thrust" constitutes a violation of the justice principle that will be fundamental in the future society.

Why force and physical constraint, although limited and inspired by the idea of a sheer necessity of defence, should not be used also in those cases (unfortunately these will be aspects of the moralizing crime of the new social environment) in which a serious damage can be still caused to one's fellow men without exercising a "materially violent" act?

Is not the act of exercising material violence upon a person, to rob him of some belonging, equivalent to the act of succeeding in the same robbing without using any violence whatsoever?

Moreover, what is the difference between, say, someone who violently kills a fellow man and someone who drives him to die by exercising a criminal and shifty persuasion?

The foregoing is just an example, not to say that hundreds of cases could be mentioned in which the offence, the damage to someone else's life can happen without material violence.

On the other hand, there is a right violence and a wrong violence. Therefore, the injustice does not lie so much in the external act that carries it out, as in the fact itself that someone has to suffer anyway by someone else's nastiness and wickedness.

On this topic you say: "We do not see any other solution than leave decisions in the hands of those concerned, in the hands of the people, i.e. the mass of citizens, which will act differently according to the circumstances and to their own varying degree of civilization."

However, "people" is too generic an expression here, hence the question remains unsolved.

This kind of reasoning seems to repeat the error made by Kropotkine, according to whom the people is supposed to do everything, and for him the people is only a generic multitude.

Saverio Merlino criticized very well this and other errors of Kropotkine's idea of anarchism; and, arguing with you, he offers the following solution to the relevant problem of social defence in his book "Collectivist Utopia": "Between the current system and the assumption that crime should cease, I believe there is room for intermediate forms of social defence that differ from a government function. Such social defense would be exercised under the people's eyes and control in every place, as any other public service, like health, transportation, etc. and therefore it could not degenerate into an instrument of oppression and domination."

Why should not we anarchists reach this concept? We want to abolish the present machinery of so called justice, with all its painful and inhuman aspects, but we do not want to replace it with either individual liberty or the crowd's summary judgement.

The sense of justice of men needs to be improved, and the forms of expressing and defending it need to be worked out.

I raised these modest objections to you, mainly to offer you the opportunity to come back to such an important topic, which needs to be discussed.

Consider me always
your loving
Aldo Venturini

Malatesta's Reply:

The criticism of our friend Venturini is quite right: however, I point out to him that I only expressed *some* ideas about the complex question of crime, with no intention to offer a solution valid for all possible cases.

I believe that all that can be said and done to fight crime can only have a relative value, depending on the time, the places, and above all the degree of moral development of the environment where the events take place. The problem of crime will only find an ultimate and completely adequate solution when ... crime will no longer exist.

I know we are usually blamed for the vagueness and indeterminacy of our proposals to solve the most painful social problem. And I know that anarchists, unanimous in the destructive criticism of current morals and institutions, split up in the most diverse schools and tendencies, as soon as it comes to dealing with the problem of reconstruction and practical life in the future society.

However, this does not seem bad to me; on the contrary, it seems to me the main characteristic and merit of anarchism, which does not intend to fix the avenues of the future beforehand, but rather to simply guarantee the conditions of freedom necessary for the social evolution to eventually secure the greatest well-being and the greatest material, spiritual, and intellectual development for all.

The authoritarians, the rulers, either believe they hold an infallible formula, or must pretend to hold it, as they intend to lay down and impose the law. However, all history shows that the law's only use is to defend, strengthen, and perpetuate the interests and prejudices prevailing at the time the law is made, thus forcing mankind to move from revolution to revolution, from violence to violence.

On the contrary, we do not boast that we possess absolute truth; we believe that *social truth* is not a fixed quantity, good for all times, universally applicable, or determinable in advance, but that instead, once freedom has been secured, mankind will go forward discovering and acting gradually with the least number of upheavals and with a minimum of friction. Thus our solutions always leave the door open to different and, one hopes, better solutions.

It is true that in reality one has to take specific action, and cannot live without doing anything particular, always awaiting something better. However, today we can only run after an ideal, even if we know that ideals are not the only factors of history. In life, besides the drawing force of ideals, there are material conditions, habits, contrasts of interest and will, in brief, innumerable necessities which one has to submit to, in the everyday conduct. In practice, one does what one can: in any case, anarchists must stick to the mission of pushing towards their ideal, and preventing, or striving to prevent, that the inevitable flaws and the possible injustices be sanctioned by the law and perpetuated through the State's force, i.e. the force of all placed at the service of some.

Anyway, let us come back to the topic of crime.

As Venturini correctly points out, there are worse ways of offending justice and freedom than those committed by material violence, against which the resort to physical constraint can be necessary and urgent. Therefore I agree that the principle I put forward, i.e. that one has a right to resort to material force only against those who want to violate someone else's right by material force, does not cover all the possible cases and cannot be regarded as absolute. Perhaps we would come closer to a more comprehensive formula by asserting the right to forcible self defense against physical violence as well as against acts equivalent in manner and consequences to physical violence.

We are entering a case by case analysis though, which would require a survey of different cases, leading to a thousand different solutions, without touching the main point, the greatest difficulty of the question yet, i.e. *who would judge and who would carry out the judgements?*

I had claimed the need to *leave decisions in the hands of those concerned, in the hands of the people, i.e. the mass of citizens, etc.*

Venturini points out that "people" is too generic an expression, and I agree with him. I am far from admiring "the people" as Kropotkine did. Although, on the other hand, he fixed up everything by calling the crowd "people" only when it behaved in a way he liked. I know that the people is capable of anything: ferocious today, generous tomorrow, socialist one day, fascist another day, at one time it rises up against the priests and the Inquisition, at some other time it watches Giordano Bruno's stake praying and applauding, at one moment it is ready for any sacrifice and heroism, at some other moment it is subject to the worst influence of fear and greed. What can one do about that? One has to work with the available material, and try to get the best out of it.

Like Venturini, I do not want either individual liberty or the crowd's summary judgement; however, I could not accept the solution proposed by Merlino, who would like to organize the social defence against criminals as any other public service, like health, transportation, etc., because I fear the formation of a body of armed people, which would acquire all the flaws and present all the dangers of a police corps.

In the interest of a service, i.e. of the public, it is useful that railwaymen, for instance, specialize in their job, doctors and teachers entirely devote themselves to their arts; however, it is dangerous and corrupting, although technically advantageous perhaps, to allow someone to be a policeman or a judge by profession.

Everybody should take care of social defence, in the same way in which everybody promptly helps when public calamities occur.

To me a policeman is worse than a criminal, at least than a minor common criminal; a policeman is more dangerous and harmful to society. However, if people do not feel sufficiently protected by the public, no doubt they immediately call for the policeman. Therefore, the only way of preventing the policeman from existing is to make him useless by replacing him in those functions that constitute a real protection for the public.

I conclude with the words of Venturini: "The sense of justice of men needs to be improved, and the forms of expressing and defending it need to be worked out."

PART EIGHT

VOLTAIRINE DE CLEYRE
(1866–1912)

Voltairine de Cleyre distinguishes between social conscience and personal conscience. Every crime is a charge against society and society must honestly confront its own errors. Crime will be ended as much as is possible not by lawyers and judges but by the development of social conscience. And social conscience stands to uproot social institutions.

For de Cleyre, you can teach your neighbor but must not judge or condemn. If one cannot meet your standard, let them alone. Nature knows nothing of crime. Social conscience makes it so. She notes too the "accidental" criminal. De Cleyre prefigures later critical criminologists in shifting attention to anti-social acts, what today would be called social harms. She notes that these can be done by an individual or by the whole nation—as in war. Yet the "cruelest of murderers, the Government" would assume "to correct the individual offender," caging and tormenting them and tying them up in "miles of laws."

Chapter 12 was originally a lecture to the Social Science Club of Philadelphia in 1903 and appears in Alexander Berkman, ed., *Selected Works of Voltairine de Cleyre: Poems, Essays, Sketches and Stories, 1885–1911* (Chico: AK Press, 2016).

CHAPTER 12

Crime and Punishment
Voltairine de Cleyre

Men are of three sorts: the turn backs, the rush-aheads, and the indifferents. The first and second are comparatively few in number. The really conscientious conservative, eternally looking backward for his models and trying hard to preserve that which is, is almost as scarce an article as the genuine radical, who is eternally attacking that which is and looking forward to some indistinct but glowing vision of a purified social life. Between them lies the vast nitrogenous body of the indifferents, who go through life with no large thoughts or intense feelings of any kind, the best that can be said of them being that they serve to dilute the too fierce activities of the other two. Into the callous ears of these indifferents, nevertheless, the opposing voices of conservative and radical are continually shouting; and for years, for centuries, the conservative wins the day, not because he really touches the consciences of the indifferent so much (though in a measure he does that) as because his way causes his hearer the least mental trouble. It is easier to this lazy, inert mentality to nod its head and approve the continuance of things as they are, than to listen to proposals for change, to consider, to question, to make an innovating decision. These require activity, application,—and nothing is so foreign to the hibernating social conscience of your ordinary individual. I say "social" conscience, because I by no means wish to say that these are conscienceless people; they have, for active use, sufficient conscience to go through their daily parts in life, and they think that is all that is required. Of the lives of others, of the effects of their attitude in cursing the existences of thousands whom they do not know, they have no conception; they sleep; and they hear the voices of those who cry aloud about these things, dimly, as in dreams; and they do not wish to awaken. Nevertheless, at the end of the centuries they always awaken. It is the radical who always wins at last. At the end of the centuries institutions are reviewed by this aroused social conscience, are revised, sometimes are utterly rooted out.

Thus it is with the institutions of Crime and Punishment. The conservative holds that these things have been decided from all time; that crime is a thing-in-itself, with no other cause than the viciousness of man; that punishment was decreed from Mt. Sinai, or whatever holy mountain happens to be believed in in his country; that society is best served by strictness and severity of judgment and punishment. And he wishes only to make his indifferent brothers keepers of other men's consciences along these lines. He would have all men be hunters of men, that crime may be tracked down and struck down.

The radical says: All false, all false and wrong. Crime has not been decided from all time: crime, like everything else, has had its evolution according to place, time, and circumstance. "The demons of our sires become the saints that we adore,"—and the saints, the saints and the heroes of our fathers, are criminals according to our codes. Abraham, David, Solomon,—could any respectable member of society admit that he had done the things they did? Crime is not a thing-in-itself, not a plant without roots, not a something proceeding from nothing; and the only true way to deal with it is to seek its causes as earnestly, as painstakingly, as the astronomer seeks the causes of the perturbations in the orbit of the planet he is observing, sure that there must be one, or many, somewhere. And Punishment, too, must be studied. The holy mountain theory is a failure. Punishment is a failure. And it is a failure not because men do not hunt down and strike enough, but because they hunt down and strike at all; because in the chase of those who do ill, they do ill themselves; they brutalize their own characters, and so much the more so because they are convinced that this time the brutal act is done in accord with conscience. The murderous deed of the criminal was *against* conscience, the torture or the murder of the criminal by the official is *with* conscience. Thus the conscience is diseased and perverted, and a new class of imbruted men created. We have punished and punished for untold thousands of years, and we have not gotten rid of crime, we have not diminished it. Let us consider then.

The indifferentist shrugs his shoulders and remarks to the conservative: "What have I to do with it? I will hunt nobody and I will save nobody. Let every one take care of himself. I pay my taxes; let the judges and the lawyers take care of the criminals. And as for you, Mr. Radical, you weary me. Your talk is too heroic. You want to play Atlas and carry the heavens on your shoulders. Well, do it if you like. But don't imagine I am going to act the stupid Hercules and transfer your burden to my shoulders. Rave away until you are tired, but let me alone."

"I will not let you alone. I am no Atlas. I am no more than a fly; but I will annoy you, I will buzz in your ears; I will not let you sleep. You must think about this."

That is about the height and power of my voice, or of any individual voice, in the present state of the question. I do not deceive myself. I do not imagine that the question of crime and punishment will be settled till long, long after the memory of me shall be as completely swallowed up by time as last year's snow is swallowed by the sea. Two thousand years ago a man whose soul revolted at punishment, cried out: "Judge not, that ye be not judged," and yet men and women who have taken his name upon their lips as holy, have for all those two thousand years gone on judging as if their belief in what he said was only lip-belief; and they do it to-day. And judges sit upon benches and send men to their death,—even judges who do not themselves believe in capital punishment; and prosecutors exhaust their eloquence and their tricks to get men convicted; and women and men bear witness against sinners; and then they all meet in church and pray, "Forgive us our trespasses as we forgive those who trespass against us!"

Do they mean anything at all by it?

And I know that just as the voice of Jesus was not heard, and is not heard, save here and there; just as the voice of Tolstoy is not heard, save here and there; and others great and small are lost in the great echoless desert of indifferentism, having produced little perceptible effect, so my voice also will be lost, and barely a slight ripple of thought be propagated over that dry and fruitless expanse; even that the next wind of trial will straighten and leave as unimprinted sand.

Nevertheless, by the continued and unintermitting action of forces infinitesimal compared with the human voice, the greatest effects are at length accomplished. A wave-length of light is but the fifty-thousandth part of an inch, yet by the continuous action of waves like these have been produced all the creations of light, the entire world of sight, out of masses irresponsive, dark, colorless. And doubt not that in time this cold and irresponsive mass of indifference will feel and stir and realize the force of the great sympathies which will change the attitude of the human mind as a whole towards Crime and Punishment, and erase both from the world.

Not by lawyers and not by judges shall the final cause of the criminal be tried; but lawyer and judge and criminal together shall be told by the Social Conscience, "Depart in peace."

A great ethical teacher once wrote words like unto these: "I have within me the capacity for every crime."

Few, reading them, believe that he meant what he said. Most take it as the sententious utterance of one who, in an abandonment of generosity, wished to say something large and leveling. But I think he meant exactly what he said. I think that with all his purity Emerson had within him the turbid stream of passion and desire; for all his hard-cut granite features he knew the instincts of the weakling and the slave; and for all the sweetness, the tenderness, and the nobility of his nature, he had the tiger and the jackal in his soul. I think that within every bit of human flesh and spirit that has ever crossed the enigma bridge of life, from the prehistoric racial morning until now, all crime and all virtue were germinal. Out of one great soul-stuff are we sprung, you and I and all of us; and if in you the virtue has grown and not the vice, do not therefore conclude that you are essentially different from him whom you have helped to put in stripes and behind bars. Your balance may be more even, you may be mixed in smaller proportions altogether, or the outside temptation has not come upon you.

I am no disciple of that school whose doctrine is summed up in the teaching that Man's Will is nothing, his Material Surroundings all. I do not accept that popular socialism which would make saints out of sinners only by filling their stomachs. I am no apologist for characterlessness, and no petitioner for universal moral weakness. I believe in the individual. I believe that the purpose of life (in so far as we can give it a purpose, and it has none save what we give it) is the assertion and the development of strong, self-centered personality. It is therefore that no religion which offers vicarious atonement for the misdoer, and no philosophy which rests on the cornerstone of irresponsibility, makes any appeal to me. I believe that immeasurable mischief has been wrought by the ceaseless repetition for the last two thousand years of the formula: "Not through any merit of mine shall I enter heaven, but through the sacrifice of Christ."—Not through the sacrifice of Christ, nor any other sacrifice, shall any one attain strength, save in so far as he takes the spirit and the purpose of the sacrifice into his own life and lives it. Nor do I see anything as the result of the teaching that all men are the helpless victims of external circumstance and under the same conditions will act precisely alike, than a lot of spineless, nerveless, bloodless crawlers in the tracks of stronger men,—too desirous of ease to be honest, too weak to be successful rascals.

Let this be put as strongly as it can now, that nothing I shall say hereafter may be interpreted as a gospel of shifting and shirking.

But the difference between us, the Anarchists, who preach self-government and none else, and Moralists who in times past and present have asked for individual responsibility, is this, that while they have always framed creeds and codes for the purpose of *holding others to account*, we draw the line upon ourselves. Set the standard as high as you will; live to it as near as you can; and if you fail, try yourself, judge yourself, condemn yourself, if you choose. Teach and persuade your neighbor if you can; consider and compare his conduct if you please; speak your mind if you desire; but if he fails to reach your standard or his own, try him not, judge him not, condemn him not. He lies beyond your sphere; you cannot know the temptation nor the inward battle nor the weight of the circumstances upon him. You do not know how long he fought before he failed. Therefore you cannot be just. Let him alone.

This is the ethical concept at which we have arrived, not by revelation from any superior power, not through the reading of any inspired book, not by special illumination of our inner consciousness; but by the study of the results of social experiment in the past as presented in the works of historians, psychologists, criminologists, sociologists and legalists.

Very likely so many "ists" sound a little oppressive, and there may be those to whom they may even have a savor of pedantry. It sounds much simpler and less ostentatious to say "Thus saith the Lord," or "The Good Book says." But in the meat and marrow these last are the real presumptions, these easy-going claims of familiarity with the will and intent of Omnipotence. It may sound more pedantic to you to say, "I have studied the accumulated wisdom of man, and drawn certain deductions therefrom," than to say "I had a talk with God this morning and he said thus and so"; but to me the first statement is infinitely more modest. Moreover there is some chance of its being true, while the other is highly imaginative fiction.

This is not to impugn the honesty of those who inherit this survival of an earlier mental state of the race, and who accept it as they accept their appetites or anything else they find themselves born with. Nor is it to belittle those past efforts of active and ardent souls who claimed direct divine inspiration as the source of their doctrines. All religions have been, in their great general outlines, the intuitive graspings of the race at truths which it had not yet sufficient knowledge to demonstrate,—rude and imperfect statements of ideas which were yet but germinal, but which, even then, mankind had urgent need to conceive, and upon which it afterwards spent the efforts of generations of lives to correct and perfect. Thus the very ethical concept of which I have been speaking as peculiarly Anarchistic, was preached as a religious doctrine by the fifteenth century Tolstoy, Peter Chilciky; and in the sixteenth century, the fanatical sect of the Anabaptists shook Germany from center to circumference by a doctrine which included the declaration that "pleadings in courts of law, oaths, capital punishment, and all absolute power were incompatible with the Christian faith." It was an imperfect illumination of the intellect, such only as was possible in those less enlightened days, but an illumination that defined certain noble conceptions of justice. They appealed to all they had, the Bible, the inner light, the best that they knew, to justify their faith. We to whom a wider day is given, who can appeal not to one book but to thousands, who have the light of science which is free to all that can command the leisure and the will to know, shining white and open on these great questions, dim and obscure in the days of Peter Chilciky, we should be the last to cast a sneer at them for their heroic struggle with tyranny and cruelty; though to-day the man who would claim their claims on their grounds would justly be rated atavist or charlatan.

Nothing or next to nothing did the Anabaptists know of history. For genuine history, history which records the growth of a whole people, which traces the evolution of its mind as seen in its works of peace,—its literature, its art, its constructions—is the creation of our own age. Only within the last seventy-five years has the purpose of history come to have so much depth as this. Before that it was a mere register of dramatic situations, with no particular connection, a chronicle of the deeds of prominent persons, a list of intrigues, scandals, murders big and little; and the great people, the actual builders and preservers of the race, the immense patient, silent mass who painfully filled up all the waste places these destroyers made, almost ignored. And no man sought to discover the relations of even the recorded acts to any general causes; no man conceived the notion of discovering what is political and moral growth or political and moral suicide. That they did not do so is because writers of history, who are themselves incarnations of their own time spirit, could not get beyond the unscientific attitude of mind, born of ignorance and fostered by the Christian religion, that man is something entirely different from the rest of organized life; that he is a free moral agent, good if he pleases and bad if he pleases, that is, according as he accepts or rejects the will of God; that every act is isolated, having no antecedent, morally, but the will of its doer. Nor until modern science had fought its way past prisons, exilements, stakes, scaffolds, and tortures, to the demonstration that man is no free-will freak thrust by an omnipotent joker upon a world of cause and sequence to play havoc therein, but just a poor differentiated bit of protoplasm as much subject to the general processes of matter and mind as his ancient progenitor in the depths of the Silurian sea, not until then was it possible for any real conception of the scope of history to begin. Not until then was it said: "The actions of men are the effects of large and general causes. Humanity as a whole has a regularity of movement as fixed as the movement of the tides; and given certain physical and social environments, certain developments may be predicted with the certainty of a mathematical calculation." Thus crime, which for so many ages men have gone on punishing more or less light-heartedly, so far from having its final cause in individual depravity, bears a steady and invariable relation to the production and distribution of staple food supplies, a thing over which society itself at times can have no control (as on the occasion of great natural disturbances), and in general does not yet know how to manage wisely: how much less, then, the individual! This regularity of the recurrence of crime was pointed out long before by the greatest statisticians of Europe, who, indeed, did not go so far as to question why it was so, nor to compare these regularities with other regularities, but upon whom the constant repetition of certain figures in the statistics of murder, suicide, assault, etc., made a profound impression. It was left to the new historians, the great pioneer among whom was H. T. Buckle in England, to make the comparisons in the statistics, and show that individual crimes as well as virtues are always calculable from general material conditions.

This is the basis from which we argue, and it is a basis established by the comparative history of civilizations. In no other way could it have been really established. It might have been guessed at, and indeed was. But only when the figures are before us, figures obtained "by millions of observations extending over different grades of civilization, with different laws, different opinions, different habits, different morals" (I am quoting Buckle), only then are we able to say surely that the human mind proceeds with a regularity of operation overweighing all the creeds and codes ever invented, and that if we would begin to understand the problem of the treatment of crime, we must go to something far larger than the moral reformation of the criminal. No prayers, no legal enactments, will ever rid society of crime. If they would, there have been prayers enough and preachments enough and laws enough and prisons enough to have done it long ago. But pray that the attraction of gravitation shall cease. Will it cease? Enact that water shall freeze at 100° heat. Will it freeze? And no more will men be sane and honest and just when they are compelled to live in an insane, dishonest, and unjust society, when the natural operation of the very elements of their being is warred upon by statutes and institutions which must produce outbursts destructive both to themselves and to others.

Away back in 1835 Quetelet, the French statistician, wrote: "Experience demonstrates, in fact, by every possible evidence, this opinion, which may seem paradoxical at first, that it is society which prepares the crime, and that the guilty one is but the instrument which executes it." Every crime, therefore, is a charge against society which can only be rightly replied to when society consents to look into its own errors and rectify the wrong it has done. This is one of the results which must, in the end, flow from the labors of the real historians; one of the reasons why history was worth writing at all.

Now the next point in the problem is the criminal himself. Admitting what cannot be impeached, that there is cause and sequence in the action of man; admitting the pressure of general causes upon all alike, what is the reason that one man is a criminal and another not?

From the days of the Roman jurisconsults until now the legalists themselves have made a distinction between crimes against the law of nature and crimes merely against the law of society. From the modern scientific standpoint no such distinction can be maintained. Nature knows nothing about crime, and nothing ever was a crime until the social Conscience made it so. Neither is it easy when one reads their law books, even accepting their view-point, to understand why certain crimes were catalogued as against the law of nature, and certain others as of the more artificial character. But I presume what were in general classed as crimes against nature were Acts of Violence committed against persons. Aside from these we have a vast, an almost interminable number of offenses big and little, which are in the main attacks upon the institution of property, concerning which some very different things have to be said than concerning the first. As to these first there is no doubt that these are real crimes, by which I mean simply anti-social acts. Any action which violates the life or liberty of any individual is an anti-social act, whether done by one person, by two, or by a whole nation. And the greatest crime that ever was perpetrated, a crime beside which all individual atrocities diminish to nothing, is War; and the greatest, the least excusable of murderers are those who order it and those who execute it. Nevertheless, this chiefest of murderers, the Government, its own hands red with the blood of hundreds of thousands, assumes to correct the individual offender, enacting miles of laws to define the varying degrees of his offense and punishment, and putting beautiful building stone to very hideous purposes for the sake of caging and tormenting him therein.

We do get a fig from a thistle—sometimes! Out of this noisome thing, the prison, has sprung the study of criminology. It is very new, and there is considerable painstaking nonsense about it. But the main results are interesting and should be known by all who wish to form an intelligent conception of what a criminal is and how he should be treated. These men who are cool and quiet and who move among criminals and study them as Darwin did his plants and animals, tell us that these prisoners are reducible to three types: The

Born Criminal, the Criminaloid, and the Accidental Criminal. I am inclined to doubt a great deal that is said about the born criminal. Prof. Lombroso gives us very exhaustive reports of the measurements of their skulls and their ears and their noses and their thumbs and their toes, etc. But I suspect that if a good many respectable, decent, never-did-a-wrong-thing-in-their-lives people were to go up for measurement, malformed ears and disproportionately long thumbs would be equally found among them if they took the precaution to represent themselves as criminals first. Still, however few in number (and they are really very few), there are some born criminals,—people who through some malformation or deficiency or excess of certain portions of the brain are constantly impelled to violent deeds. Well, there are some born idiots and some born cripples. Do you punish them for their idiocy or for their unfortunate physical condition? On the contrary, you pity them, you realize that life is a long infliction to them, and your best and tenderest sympathies go out to them. Why not to the other, equally a helpless victim of an evil inheritance? Granting for the moment that you have the right to punish the mentally responsible, surely you will not claim the right to punish the mentally irresponsible! Even the law does not hold the insane man guilty. And the born criminal is irresponsible; he is a sick man, sick with the most pitiable chronic disease; his treatment is for the medical world to decide, and the best of them,—not for the prosecutor, the judge, and the warden.

It is true that many criminologists, including Prof. Lombroso himself, are of opinion that the best thing to do with the born criminal is to kill him at once, since he can be only a curse to himself and others. Very heroic treatment. We may inquire, Is he to be exterminated at birth because of certain physical indications of his criminality? Such neo-Spartanism would scarcely commend itself to any modern society. Moreover the diagnosis might be wrong, even though we had a perpetual and incorruptible commission of the learned to sit in inquiry upon every pink-skinned little suspect three days old! What then? Is he to be let go, as he is now, until he does some violent deed and then be judged more hardly because of his natural defect? Either proposition seems not only heartless and wicked but,—what the respectable world is often more afraid of being than either,—ludicrous. If one is really a born criminal he will manifest criminal tendencies in early life, and being so recognized should be cared for according to the most humane methods of treating the mentally afflicted.

The second, or criminaloid, class is the most numerous of the three. These are criminals, first, because being endowed with strong desires and unequal reasoning powers they cannot maintain the uneven battle against a society wherein the majority of individuals must all the time deny their natural appetites, if they are to remain unstained with crime. They are, in short, the ordinary man (who, it must be admitted, has a great deal of paste in him) plus an excess of wants of one sort and another, but generally physical. Society outside of prisons is full of these criminaloids, who sometimes have in place of the power of genuine moral resistance a sneaking cunning by which they manage to steer a shady course between the crime and the punishment.

It is true these people are not pleasant subjects to contemplate; but then, through that very stage of development the whole human race has had to pass in its progress from the beast to the man,—the stage, I mean, of overplus of appetite opposed by weak moral resistance; and if now some, it is not certain that their number is very great, have reversed the proportion, it is only because they are the fortunate inheritors of the results of thousands of years of struggle and failure, struggle and failure, but *struggle* again. It is precisely these criminaloids who are most sinned against by society, for they are the people who need to have the right of doing things made easy, and who, when they act criminally, need the most encouragement to help the feeble and humiliated moral sense to rise again, to try again.

The third class, the Accidental or Occasional Criminals, are perfectly normal, well balanced people, who, through tremendous stress of outward circumstance, and possibly some untoward mental disturbance arising from those very notions of the conduct of life which form part of their moral being, suddenly commit an act of violence which is at utter variance with their whole former existence; such as, for instance, the murder of a seducer by the father of the injured girl, or of a wife's paramour by her husband. If I believed in severity at all I should say that these were the criminals upon whom society should look with most severity, because they are the ones who have most mental responsibility. But that also is nonsense; for such an individual has within him a severer judge, a more pitiless jailer than any court or prison,—his conscience and his memory. Leave him to these; or no, in mercy take him away from these whenever you can; he will suffer enough, and there is no fear of his action being repeated.

Now all these people are with us, and it is desirable that something be done to help the case. What does Society do? Or rather what does Government do with them? Remember we are speaking now only of crimes of violence. It hangs, it electrocutes, it exiles, it imprisons. Why? For punishment. And why punishment? "Not," says Blackstone, "by way of atonement or expiation for the crime committed, for that must be left to the just determination of the Supreme Being, but as a precaution against future offenses of the same kind." This is supposed to be effected in three ways: either by reforming him, or getting rid of him altogether, or by deterring others by making an example of him.

Let us see how these precautions work. Exile, which is still practised by some governments, and imprisonment are, according to the theory of law, for the purpose of reforming the criminal that he may no longer be a menace to society. Logic would say that anyone who wished to obliterate cruelty from the character of another must himself show no cruelty; one who would teach regard for the rights of others must himself be regardful. Yet the story of exile and prison is the story of the lash, the iron, the chain and every torture that the fiendish ingenuity of *the non-criminal class can devise by way of teaching criminals to be good!* To teach men to be good, they are kept in airless cells, made to sleep on narrow planks, to look at the sky through iron grates, to eat food that revolts their palates, and destroys their stomachs,—battered and broken down in body and soul; and this is what they call reforming men!

Not very many years ago the Philadelphia dailies told us (and while we cannot believe all of what they say, and are bound to believe that such cases are exceptional, yet the bare facts were true) that Judge Gordon ordered an investigation into the workings of the Eastern Penitentiary officials; and it was found that an insane man had been put into a cell with two sane ones, and when he cried in his insane way and the two asked that he be put elsewhere, the warden gave them a strap to whip him with; and they tied him in some way to the heater, with the strap, so that his legs were burned when he moved; all scarred with the burns he was brought into the court, and the other men frankly told what they had done and why they had done it. This is the way they reform men.

Do you think people come out of a place like that better? with more respect for society? with more regard for the rights of their fellow men? I don't. I think they come out of there with their hearts full of bitterness, much harder than when they went in. That this is often the case is admitted by those who themselves believe in punishment, and practice it. For the fact is that out of the Criminaloid class there develops the Habitual Criminal, the man who is perpetually getting in prison; no sooner is he out than he does something else and gets in again. The brand that at first scorched him has succeeded in searing. He no longer feels the ignominy. He is a "jail-bird," and he gets to have a cynical pride in his own degradation. Every man's hand is against him, and his hand is against every man's. Such are the reforming effects of punishment. Yet there was a time when he, too, might have been touched, had the right word been spoken. It is for society to find and speak that word.

This for prison and exile. Hanging? electrocution? These of course are not for the purpose of reforming the criminal. These are to deter others from doing as he did; and the supposition is that the severer the punishment the greater the deterrent effect. In commenting upon this principle Blackstone says: "We may observe that punishments of unreasonable severity ... have less effect in preventing crimes and amending the manners of a people than such as are more merciful in general...." He further quotes Montesquieu: "For the excessive severity of laws hinders their execution; when the punishment surpasses all measure, the public will frequently, out of humanity, prefer impunity to it." Again Blackstone: "It is a melancholy truth that among the variety of actions which men are daily liable to commit, no less than one hundred and sixty have been declared by act of Parliament to be felonies ... worthy of instant death. So dreadful a list instead of diminishing *increases* the number of offenders."

Robert Ingersoll, speaking on "Crimes Against Criminals" before the New York Bar Association, a lawyer addressing lawyers, treating of this same period of which Blackstone writes, says: "There is something in injustice, in cruelty, which tends to defeat itself. There never were so many traitors in England as when the traitor was drawn and quartered, when he was tortured in every possible way,—when his limbs, torn and bleeding, were given to the fury of mobs, or exhibited pierced by pikes or hung in chains. The frightful punishments produced intense hatred of the government, and traitors increased until they became powerful enough to decide what treason was and who the traitors were and to inflict the same torments on others."

The fact that Blackstone was right and Ingersoll was right in saying that severity of punishment increases crime, is silently admitted in the abrogation of those severities by acts of Parliament and acts of Congress. It is also shown by the fact that there are no more murders, proportionately, in States where the death penalty does not exist than in those where it does. Severity is therefore admitted by the State itself to have no deterrent influence on the intending criminal. And to take the matter out of the province of the State, we have only to instance the horrible atrocities perpetrated by white mobs upon negroes charged with outrage. Nothing more fiendishly cruel can be imagined; yet these outrages multiply. It would seem, then, that the notion of making a horrible example of the misdoer is a complete failure. As a specific example of this, Ingersoll (in this same lecture) instanced that "a few years before a man was hanged in Alexandria, Va. One who witnessed the execution on that very day murdered a peddler in the Smithsonian grounds at Washington. He was tried and executed; and one who witnessed his hanging went home and on the same day murdered his wife." Evidently the brute is rather aroused than terrified by scenes of execution.

What then? If extreme punishments do not deter, and if what are considered mild punishments do not reform, is any measure of punishment conceivable or attainable which will better our case?

Before answering this question let us consider the class of crimes which so far has not been dwelt upon, but which nevertheless comprises probably nine-tenths of all offenses committed. These are all the various forms of stealing,—robbery, burglary, theft, embezzlement, forgery, counterfeiting, and the thousand and one ramifications and offshoots of the act of taking what the law defines as another's. It is impossible to consider crimes of violence apart from these, because the vast percentage of murders and assaults committed by the criminaloid class are simply incidental to the commission of the so-called lesser crime. A man often murders in order to escape with his booty, though murder was no part of his original intention. Why, now, have we such a continually increasing percentage of stealing?

Will you persistently hide your heads in the sand and say it is because men grow worse as they grow wiser? that individual wickedness is the result of all our marvelous labors to compass sea and land, and make the earth yield up her wealth to us? Dare you say that?

It is not so. THE REASON MEN STEAL IS BECAUSE THEIR RIGHTS ARE STOLEN FROM THEM BEFORE THEY ARE BORN.

A human being comes into the world; he wants to eat, he wants to breathe, he wants to sleep; he wants to use his muscles, his brain; he wants to love, to dream, to create. These wants constitute him, the whole man; he can no more help expressing these activities than water can help running down hill. If the freedom to do any of these things is denied him, then by so much he is a crippled creature, and his energy will force itself into some abnormal channel or be killed altogether. Now I do not mean that he has a "natural right" to do these things inscribed on any lawbook of Nature. Nature knows nothing of rights, she knows power only, and a louse has as much natural right as a man to the extent of its power. What I do mean to say is that man, in common with many other animals, has found that by associative life he conquers the rest of nature, and that this society is slowly being perfected; and that this perfectionment consists in realizing that the solidarity and safety of the whole arises from the freedom of the parts; that such freedom constitutes Man's Social Right; and that any institution which interferes with this right will be destructive of the association, will breed criminals, will work its own ruin. This is the word of the sociologist, of the greatest of them, Herbert Spencer.

Now do we see that all men eat,—eat well? You know we do not. Some have so much that they are sickened with the extravagance of dishes, and know not where next to turn for a new palatal sensation. They cannot even waste their wealth. Some, and they are mostly the hardest workers, eat poorly and fast, for their work allows them no time to enjoy even what they have. Some,—I have seen them myself in the streets of New York this winter, and the look of their wolfish eyes was not pleasant to see—stand in long lines waiting for midnight and the plate of soup dealt out by some great newspaper office, stretching out, whole blocks of them, as other men wait on the first night of some famous star at the theater! Some die because they cannot eat at all. Pray tell me what these last have to lose by becoming thieves. And why shall they not become thieves? And is the action of the man who takes the necessities which have been denied to him really criminal? Is he morally worse than the man who crawls in a cellar and dies of starvation? I think not. He is only a little more assertive. Cardinal Manning said: "A starving man has a natural right to his neighbor's bread." The Anarchist says: "A hungry man has a social right to bread." And there have been whole societies and races among whom that right was never questioned. And whatever were the mistakes of those societies, whereby they perished, this was not a mistake, and we shall do well to take so much wisdom from the dead and gone, the simple ethics of the stomach which with all our achievement we cannot despise, or despising, shall perish as our reward.

"But," you will say, and say truly, "to begin by taking loaves means to end by taking everything and murdering, too, very often." And in that you draw the indictment against your own system. If there is no alternative between starving and stealing (and for thousands there is none), then there is no alternative between society's murdering its members, or the members disintegrating society. Let Society consider its own mistakes, then: let it answer itself for all these people it has robbed and killed: let it cease its own crimes first!

To return to the faculties of Man. All would breathe; and some do breathe. They breathe the air of the mountains, of the seas, of the lakes,—even the atmosphere in the gambling dens of Monte Carlo, for a change! Some, packed thickly together in closed rooms where men must sweat and faint to save tobacco, breathe the noisome reek that rises from the spittle of their consumptive neighbors. Some, mostly babies, lie on the cellar doors along Bainbridge street, on summer nights, and bathe their lungs in that putrid air where a thousand lungs have breathed before, and grow up pale and decayed looking as the rotting vegetables whose exhalations they draw in. Some, far down underground, meet the choke-damp, and—do not breathe at all! Do you expect healthy morals out of all these poisoned bodies?

Some sleep. They have so much time that they take all manner of expensive drugs to try what sleeping it off a different way is like! Some sleep upon none too easy beds a few short hours, too few not to waken more tired than ever, and resume the endless grind of waking life. Some sleep bent over the books they are too tired to study, though the mind clamors for food after the long day's physical toil. Some sleep with hand upon the throttle of the engine, after twenty-six hours of duty, and—crash!—they have sleep enough!

Some use their muscles: they use them to punch bags, and other gentlemen's stomachs when their heads are full of wine. Some use them to club other men and women, at $2.50 a day. Some exhaust them welding them into iron, or weaving them into wool, for ten or eleven hours a day. And some become atrophied sitting at desks till they are mere specters of men and women.

Some love; and there is no end to the sensualities of their love, because all normal expressions have lost their savor through excess. Some love, and see their love tried and worn and threadbare, a skeleton of love, because the practicality of life is always there to repress the purely emotional. Some are stricken in health, so robbed of power to feel, that they never love at all.

And some dream, think, create; and the world is filled with the glory of their dreams. But who knows the glory of the dream that never was born, lost and dead and buried away somewhere there under the roofs where the exquisite brain was ruined by the heavy labor of life? And what of the dream that turned to madness and destroyed the thing it loved the best?

These are the things that make criminals, the perverted forces of man, turned aside by the institution of property, which is the giant social mistake to-day. It is your law which keeps men from using the sources and the means of wealth production unless they pay tribute to other men; it is this, and nothing else, which is responsible for all the second class of crimes and all those crimes of violence incidentally committed while carrying out a robbery. Let me quote here a most sensible and appropriate editorial which recently appeared in the Philadelphia *North American*, in comment upon the proposition of some foolish preacher to limit the right of reproduction to rich families:

"The earth was constructed, made habitable, and populated without the advice of a commission of superior persons, and until they appeared and began meddling with affairs, making laws and setting themselves up as rulers, poverty and its evil consequences were unknown to humanity. When social science finds a way to remove obstructions to the operation of natural law and to the equitable distribution of the products of labor, poverty will cease to be the condition of the masses of people, and misery, CRIME and problems of population will disappear."

And they will never disappear until it does. All hunting down of men, all punishments, are but so many ineffective efforts to sweep back the tide with a broom. The tide will fling you, broom and all, against the idle walls that you have built to fence it in. Tear down those walls or the sea will tear them down for you.

Have you ever watched it coming in,—the sea? When the wind comes roaring out of the mist and a great bellowing thunders up from the water? Have you watched the white lions chasing each other towards the walls, and leaping up with foaming anger as they strike, and turn and chase each other along the black bars of their cage in rage to devour each other? And tear back? And leap in again? Have you ever wondered in the midst of it all *which particular drops of water* would strike the wall? If one could know all the factors one might calculate even that. But who can know them all? Of one thing only we are sure: *some must strike it.*

They are the criminals, those drops of water pitching against that silly wall and broken. Just why it was these particular ones we cannot know; but some had to go. Do not curse them; you have cursed them enough. Let the people free.

There is a class of crimes of violence which arises from another set of causes than economic slavery—acts which are the result of an antiquated moral notion of the true relations of men and women. These are the Nemesis of the institution of property in love. If every one would learn that the limit of his right to demand a certain course of conduct in sex relations is himself; that the relation of his beloved ones to others is not a matter for him to regulate, any more than the relations of those whom he does not love; if the freedom of each is unquestioned, and whatever moral rigors are exacted are exacted of oneself only; if this principle is accepted and followed, crimes of jealousy will cease. But religions and governments uphold this institution and constantly tend to create the spirit of ownership, with all its horrible consequences.

Ah, you will say, perhaps it is true; perhaps when this better social condition is evolved, and this freer social spirit, we shall be rid of crime,—at least nine-tenths of it. But meanwhile must we not punish to protect ourselves?

The protection does not protect. The violent man does not communicate his intention; when he executes it, or attempts its execution, more often than otherwise it is some unofficial person who catches or stops him. If he is a born criminal, or in other words an insane man, he should, I reiterate, be treated as a sick person—not punished, not made to suffer. If he is one of the accidental criminals, his act will not be repeated; his punishment will always be with him. If he is of the middle class, your punishment will not reform him, it will only harden him; and it will not deter others.

As for thieves, the great thief is within the law, or he buys it; and as for the small one, see what you do! To protect yourself against him, you create a class of persons who are sworn to the service of the club and the revolver; a set of spies; a set whose business it is to deal constantly with these unhappy beings, who in rare instances are softened thereby, but in the majority of cases become hardened to their work as butchers to the use of the knife; a set whose business it is to serve cell and lock and key; and lastly, the lowest infamy of all, the hangman. Does any one want to shake his hand, the hand that kills for pay?

Now against all these persons individually there is nothing to be said: they may probably be very humane, well-intentioned persons when they start in; but the end of all this is imbrutement. One of our dailies recently observed that "the men in charge of prisons have but too often been men who ought themselves to have been prisoners." The Anarchist does not agree with that. He would have no prisons at all. But I am quite sure that if that editor himself were put in the prison-keeper's place, he too would turn hard. And the opportunities of the official criminal are much greater than those of the unofficial one. Lawyer and governmentalist as he was, Ingersoll said: "It is safe to say that governments have committed far more crimes than they have prevented." Then why create a second class of parasites worse than the first? Why not put up with the original one?

Moreover, you have another thing to consider than the simple problem of a wrong inflicted upon a guilty man. How many times has it happened that the innocent man has been convicted! I remember an instance of a man so convicted of murder in Michigan. He had served twenty-seven years in Jackson penitentiary (for Michigan is not a hang-State) when the real murderer, dying, confessed. And the State *pardoned* that innocent man! Because it was the quickest legal way to let him out! I hope he has been able to pardon the State.

Not very long ago a man was hanged here in this city. He had killed his superintendent. Some doctors said he was insane; the government experts said he was not. They said he was faking insanity when he proclaimed himself Jesus Christ. And he was hanged. Afterwards the doctors found two cysts in his brain. The State of Pennsylvania had killed a sick man! And as long as punishments exist, these mistakes will occur. If you accept the principle at all, you must accept with it the blood-guilt of innocent men.

Not only this, but you must accept also the responsibility for all the misery which results to others whose lives are bound up with that of the convict, for even he is loved by some one, much loved perhaps. It is a foolish thing to turn adrift a house full of children, to become criminals in turn, perhaps, in order to frighten some indefinite future offender by making an example of their father or mother. Yet how many times has it not happened!

And this is speaking only from the practical, selfish side of the matter. There is another, one from which I would rather appeal to you, and from which I think you would after all prefer to be appealed to. Ask yourselves, each of you, whether you are quite sure that you have feeling enough, understanding enough, and *have you suffered enough*, to be able to weigh and measure out another man's life or liberty, no matter what he has done? And if you have not yourself, are you able to delegate to any judge the power which you have not? The great Russian novelist, Dostoyevsky, in his psychological study of this same subject, traces the sufferings of a man who had committed a shocking murder; his whole body and brain are a continual prey to torture. He gives himself up, seeking relief in confession. He goes to prison, for in barbarous Russia they have not the barbarity of capital punishment for murderers, unless political ones. But he finds no relief. He remains for a year, bitter, resentful, a prey to all miserable feelings. But at last he is touched by love, the silent, unobtrusive, all-conquering love of one who knew it all and forgave it all. And the regeneration of his soul began.

"The criminal slew," says Tolstoy: "are you better, then, when you slay? He took another's liberty; and is it the right way, therefore, for you to take his? Violence is no answer to violence."

"Have good will
To all that lives, letting unkindness die,
And greed and wrath; so that your lives be made
As soft airs passing by."

So said Lord Buddha, the Light of Asia.

And another said: "Ye have heard that it hath been said 'an eye for an eye, and a tooth for a tooth'; but I say unto you, resist not him that is evil."

Yet the vengeance that the great psychologist saw was futile, the violence that the greatest living religious teacher and the greatest dead ones advised no man to wreak, that violence is done daily and hourly by every little-hearted prosecutor who prosecutes at so much a day, by every petty judge who buys his way into office with common politicians' tricks, and deals in men's lives and liberties as a trader deals in pins, by every neat-souled and cheap-souled member of the "unco guid" whose respectable bargain-counter maxims of morality have as much effect to stem the great floods and storms that shake the human will as the waving of a lady's kid glove against the tempest. Those who have not suffered cannot understand how to punish; those who have understanding *will* not.

I said at the beginning and I say again, I believe that in every one of us all things are germinal: in judge and prosecutor and prison-keeper too, and even in those small moral souls who cut out one undeviating pattern for all men to fit, even in them there are the germs of passion and crime and sympathy and forgiveness. And some day things will stir in them and accuse them and awaken them. And that awakening will come when suddenly one day there breaks upon them with realizing force the sense of the unison of life, the irrevocable relationship of the saint to the sinner, the judge to the criminal; that all personalities are intertwined and rushing upon doom together. Once in my life it was given to me to see the outward manifestation of this unison. It was in 1897. We stood upon the base of the Nelson monument in Trafalgar Square. Below were ten thousand people packed together with upturned faces. They had gathered to

219

hear and see men and women whose hands and limbs were scarred all over with the red-hot irons of the tortures in the fortress of Montjuich. For the crime of an unknown person these twenty-eight men and women, together with four hundred others, had been cast into that terrible den and tortured with the infamies of the inquisition to make them reveal that of which they knew nothing. After a year of such suffering as makes the decent human heart sick only to contemplate, with nothing proven against them, some even without trial, they were suddenly released with orders to leave the country within twenty-four hours. They were then in Trafalgar Square, and to the credit of old England be it said, harlot and mother of harlots though she is, for there was not another country among the great nations of the earth to which those twenty-eight innocent people could go. For they were paupers impoverished by that cruel State of Spain in the terrible battle for their freedom; they would not have been admitted to free America. When Francesco Gana, speaking in a language which most of them did not understand, lifted his poor, scarred hands, the faces of those ten thousand people moved together like the leaves of a forest in the wind. They waved to and fro, they rose and fell; the visible moved in the breath of the invisible. It was the revelation of the action of the Unconscious, the fatalistic unity of man.

Sometimes, even now as I look upon you, it is as if the bodies that I see were as transparent bubbles where through the red blood boils and flows, a turbulent stream churning and tossing and leaping, and behind us and our generation, far, far back, endlessly backwards, where all the bubbles are broken and not a ripple remains, the silent pouring of the Great Red River, the unfathomable River,—backwards through the unbroken forest and the untilled plain, backwards through the forgotten world of savagery and animal life, back somewhere to its dark sources in deep Sea and old Night, the rushing River of Blood—no fancy—real, tangible blood, the blood that hurries in your veins while I speak, bearing with it the curses and the blessings of the Past. Through what infinite shadows has that river rolled! Through what desolate wastes has it not spread its ooze! Through what desperate passages has it been forced! What strength, what invincible strength is in that hot stream! You are just the bubble on its crest; where will the current fling you ere you die? At what moment will the fierce impurities borne from its somber and tenebrous past be hurled up in you? Shall you then cry out for punishment if they are hurled up in another? if, flung against the merciless rocks of the channel, while you swim easily in the midstream, they fall back and hurt other bubbles?

Can you not feel that

"Men are the heart-beats of Man, the plumes that feather his wings,

Storm-worn since being began with the wind and the thunder of things.

Things are cruel and blind; their strength detains and deforms.

And the wearying wings of the mind still beat up the stream of their storms.

Still, as one swimming up-stream, they strike out blind in the blast,

In thunder of vision and dream, and lightning of future and past.

We are baffled and caught in the current and bruised upon edges of shoals:

As weeds or as reeds in the torrent of things are the wind-shaken souls.

Spirit by spirit goes under, a foam-bell's bubble of breath,

That blows and opens asunder and blurs not the mirror of Death."

Is it not enough that "things are cruel and blind"? Must we also be cruel and blind? When the whole thing amounts to so little at the most, shall we embitter it more, and crush and stifle what must so soon be crushed and stifled anyhow? Can we not, knowing what remnants of things dead and drowned are floating through us, haunting our brains with specters of old deeds and scenes of violence, can we not learn to pardon our brother to whom the specters are more real, upon whom greater stress was laid? Can we not, recalling all the evil things that we have done, or left undone only because some scarcely perceptible weight struck down the balance, or because some kindly word came to us in the midst of our bitterness and showed that not all was hateful in the world; can we not understand him for whom the balance was not struck down, the kind word unspoken? Believe me, forgiveness is better than wrath,—better for the wrong-doer, who will be touched and regenerated by it, and better for you. And you are wrong if you think it is hard: it is easy, far easier than to hate. It may sound like a paradox, but the greater the injury the easier the pardon.

Let us have done with this savage idea of punishment, which is without wisdom. Let us work for the freedom of man from the oppressions which make criminals, and for the enlightened treatment of all the sick. And though we may never see the fruit of it, we may rest assured that the great tide of thought is setting our way, and that

"While the tired wave, vainly breaking,
Seems here no painful inch to gain,
Far back, through creeks and inlets making,
Comes silent, flooding in, the main."

PART NINE

LUCY PARSONS
(1853–1942)

Lucy Parsons argues that government is power reduced to science, especially so in an industrial age. Government is legalized force. From this flows misery, poverty, and crime itself. The system of government must be removed to remove the systems of imposed force—police, courts, jails, prisons, etc. Only when the prison, stake, and scaffold are gone will progress have been made.

Parsons observes insightfully that the presence of these authorities leads people to believe that they would "go bad" in their absence. She makes the keen point that people become unconscious of their own motives in doing good (and doing so on a regular, everyday, basis). They believe some outside power is keeping them on the right track rather than their own sentiments and relationships with those around them. In cases where new freedoms emerge (abortion, marijuana use, queer rights, relationship openness, etc.) people do not become more engaged in crime or assaults on their and others' freedoms. Yet all the laws, courts, guns, penalties, armies, etc., do not and have not prevented crime—because they cannot. They merely maintain conditions where crime will persist. Social conditions must be developed to allow better sentiments to flourish and build.

Chapter 13 was published as a pamphlet of the same name variously between 1905 and 1910 and appears in the collection of Parsons's writing edited by Gale Ahrens, entitled *Lucy Parsons: Freedom, Equality & Solidarity, Writings & Speeches, 1878–1937* (Chicago: Charles H. Kerr, 2004).

CHAPTER 13

The Principles of Anarchism
Lucy Parsons

Comrades and Friends:

I think I cannot open my address more appropriately than by stating my experience in my long connection with the reform movement.

It was during the great railroad strike of 1877 that I first became interested in what is known as the "Labor Question." I then thought as many thousands of earnest, sincere people think, that the aggregate power, operating in human society, known as government, could be made an instrument in the hands of the oppressed to alleviate their sufferings. But a closer study of the origin, history and tendency of governments, convinced me that this was a mistake.

I came to understand how organized governments used their concentrated power to retard progress by their ever-ready means of silencing the voice of discontent if raised in vigorous protest against the machinations of the scheming few, who always did, always will and always must rule in the councils of nations where majority rule is recognized as the only means of adjusting the affairs of the people.

I came to understand that such concentrated power can be always wielded in the interest of the few and at the expense of the many. Government in its last analysis is this power reduced to a science. Governments never lead; they follow progress. When the prison, stake or scaffold can no longer silence the voice of the protesting minority, progress moves on a step, but not until then.

I will state this contention in another way: I learned by close study that it made no difference what fair promises a political party, out of power, might make to the people in order to secure their confidence, when once securely established in control of the affairs of society; that they were after all but human, with all the human attributes of the politician. Among these are: First, to remain in power at all hazards; if not individually, then those holding essentially the same views as the administration must be kept in control. Second, in order

227

to keep in power, it is necessary to build up a powerful machine; one strong enough to crush all opposition and silence all vigorous murmurs of discontent, or the party machine might be smashed and the party thereby lose control.

When I came to realize the faults, failings, shortcomings, aspirations and ambitions of fallible man, I concluded that it would not be the safest nor best policy for society, as a whole, to entrust the management of all its affairs, with all their manifold deviations and ramifications in the hands of finite man, to be managed by the party which happened to come into power, and therefore was the majority party, nor did it then, nor does it now make one particle of difference to me what a party, out of power may promise; it does not tend to allay my fears of a party, when entrenched and securely seated in power might do to crush opposition, and silence the voice of the minority, and thus retard the onward step of progress.

My mind is appalled at the thought of a political party having control of all the details that go to make up the sum total of our lives. Think of it for an instant, that the party in power shall have all authority to dictate the kind of books that shall be used in our schools and universities, government officials editing, printing, and circulating our literature, histories, magazines and press, to say nothing of the thousand and one activities of life that a people engage in, in a civilized society.

To my mind, the struggle for liberty is too great and the few steps we have gained have been won at too great a sacrifice, for the great mass of the people of this twentieth century to consent to turn over to any political party the management of our social and industrial affairs. For all who are at all familiar with history know that men will abuse power when they possess it. For these and other reasons, I, after careful study, and not through sentiment, turned from a sincere, earnest, political Socialist to the non-political phase of Socialism—Anarchism—because in its philosophy I believe I can find the proper conditions for the fullest development of the individual units in society, which can never be the case under government restrictions.

The philosophy of anarchism is included in the word "Liberty," yet it is comprehensive enough to include all things else that are conducive to progress. No barriers whatever to human progression, to thought, or investigation are placed by anarchism; nothing is considered so true or so certain, that future discoveries may not prove it false; therefore, it has but one infallible, unchangeable motto, "Freedom": Freedom to discover any truth, freedom to develop, to live naturally and fully. Other schools of thought are composed of crystallized ideas—principles that are caught and impaled between the planks of long platforms, and considered too sacred to be disturbed by a close investigation. In all other "issues" there is always a limit; some imaginary boundary line beyond which the searching mind dare not penetrate, lest some pet idea melt into a myth. But anarchism is the usher of science—the master of ceremonies to all forms of truth. It would remove all barriers between the human being and natural development. From the natural resources of the earth, all artificial restrictions, that the body might be nurtures, and from universal truth, all bars of prejudice and superstition, that the mind may develop symmetrically.

Anarchists know that a long period of education must precede any great fundamental change in society, hence they do not believe in vote begging, nor political campaigns, but rather in the development of self-thinking individuals.

We look away from government for relief, because we know that force (legalized) invades the personal liberty of man, seizes upon the natural elements and intervenes between man and natural laws; from this exercise of force through governments flows nearly all the misery, poverty, crime and confusion existing in society.

So, we perceive, there are actual, material barriers blockading the way. These must be removed. If we could hope they would melt away, or be voted or prayed into nothingness, we would be content to wait and vote and pray. But they are like great frowning rocks towering between us and a land of freedom, while the dark chasms of a hard-fought past yawn behind us. Crumbling they may be with their own weight and the decay of time, but to quietly stand under until they fall is to be buried in the crash. There is something to be done in a case like this—the rocks must be removed. Passivity while slavery is stealing over us is a crime. For the moment we must forget that was are anarchists—when the work is accomplished we may forget that we were revolutionists—hence most anarchists believe the coming change can only come through a revolution, because the possessing class will not allow a peaceful change to take place; still we are willing to work for peace at any price, except at the price of liberty.

And what of the glowing beyond that is so bright that those who grind the faces of the poor say it is a dream? It is no dream, it is the real, stripped of brain-distortions materialized into thrones and scaffolds, mitres and guns. It is nature acting on her own interior laws as in all her other associations. It is a return to first principles; for were not the land, the water, the light, all free before governments took shape and form? In this free state we will again forget to think of these things as "property." It is real, for we, as a race, are growing up to it. The idea of less restriction and more liberty, and a confiding trust that nature is equal to her work, is permeating all modern thought.

From the dark year—not so long gone by—when it was generally believed that man's soul was totally depraved and every human impulse bad; when every action, every thought and every emotion was controlled and restricted; when the human frame, diseased, was bled, dosed, suffocated and kept as far from nature's remedies as possible; when the mind was seized upon and distorted before it had time to evolve a natural thought—from those days to these years the progress of this idea has been swift and steady. It is becoming more and more apparent that in every way we are "governed best where we are governed least."

Still unsatisfied perhaps, the inquirer seeks for details, for ways and means, and whys and wherefores. How will we go on like human beings—eating and sleeping, working and loving, exchanging and dealing—without government? So used have we become to "organized authority" in every department of life that ordinarily we cannot conceive of the most common-place avocations being carried on without their interference and "protection." But anarchism is not compelled to outline a complete organization of a free society. To do so with any assumption of authority would be to place another barrier in the way of coming generations. The best thought of today may become the useless vagary of tomorrow, and to crystallize it into a creed is to make it unwieldy.

We judge from experience that man is a gregarious animal, and instinctively affiliates with his kind—co-operates, unites in groups, works to better advantage, combined with his fellow men than when alone. This would point to the formation of co-operative communities, of which our present trades-unions are embryonic patterns. Each branch of industry will no doubt have its own organization, regulations, leaders, etc.; it will institute methods of direct communications with every member of that industrial branch in the world, and establish equitable relations with all other branches. There would probably be conventions of industry which delegates would attend, and where they would transact such business as was necessary, adjourn and from that moment be delegates no longer, but simply members of a group. To remain permanent members of a continuous congress would be to establish a power that is certain soon or later to be abused.

No great, central power, like a congress consisting of men who know nothing of their constituents' trades, interests, rights or duties, would be over the various organizations or groups; nor would they employ sheriffs, policemen, courts or jailers to enforce the conclusions arrived at while in session. The members of groups might profit by the knowledge gained through mutual interchange of thought afforded by conventions if they choose, but they will not be compelled to do so by any outside force.

Vested rights, privileges, charters, title deeds, upheld by all the paraphernalia of government—the visible symbol of power—such as prison, scaffold and armies will have no existence. There can be no privileges bought or sold, and the transaction kept sacred at the point of the bayonet. Every man will stand on an equal footing with his brother in the race of life, and neither chains of economic thralldom nor menial drags of superstition shall handicap the one to the advantage of the other.

Property will lose a certain attribute which sanctifies it now. The absolute ownership of it—"the right to use or abuse"—will be abolished, and possession, use, will be the only title. It will be seen how impossible it would be for one person to "own" a million acres of land, without a title deed, backed by a government ready to protect the title at all hazards, even to the loss of thousands of lives. He could not use the million acres himself, nor could he wrest from its depths the possible resources it contains.

People have become so used to seeing the evidences of authority on every hand that most of them honestly believe that they would go utterly to the bad if it were not for the policeman's club or the soldier's bayonet. But the anarchist says, "Remove these evidences of brute force, and let man feel the revivifying influences of self responsibility and self control, and see how we will respond to these better influences."

The belief in a literal place of torment has nearly melted away; and instead of the direful results predicted, we have a higher and truer standard of manhood and womanhood. People do not care to go to the bad when they find they can as well as not. Individuals are unconscious of their own motives in doing good. While acting out their natures according to their surroundings and conditions, they still believe they are being kept in the right path by some outside power, some restraint thrown around them by church or state. So the objector believes that with the right to rebel and secede, sacred to him, he would forever be rebelling and seceding, thereby creating constant confusion and turmoil.

Is it probable that he *would*, merely for the reason that he *could* do so? Men are to a great extent creatures of habit, and grow to love associations; under reasonably good conditions, he would remain where he commences, if he wished to, and, if he did not, who has any natural right to force him into relations distasteful to him? Under the present order of affairs, persons do unite with societies and remain good, disinterested members for life, where the right to retire is always conceded.

What we anarchists contend for is a larger opportunity to develop the units in society, that mankind may possess the right as a sound being to develop that which is broadest, noblest, highest and best, unhandicapped by any centralized authority, where he shall have to wait for his permits to be signed, sealed, approved and handed down to him before he can engage in the active pursuits of life with his fellow beings. We know that after all, as we grow more enlightened under this larger liberty, we will grow to care less and less for that exact distribution of material wealth, which, on our greed-nurtured senses, seems now so impossible to think upon carelessly. The man and woman of loftier intellects, in the present, think not so much of the riches to be gained by their efforts as of the good they can do for their fellow creatures.

There is an innate spring of healthy action in every human being who has not been crushed and pinched by poverty and drudgery from before his birth, that impels him onward and upward. He cannot be idle, if he would; it is as natural for him to develop, expand, and use the powers within him when not repressed, as it is for the rose to bloom in the sunlight and fling its fragrance on the passing breeze.

The grandest works of the past were never performed for the sake of money. Who can measure the worth of a Shakespeare, a Michelangelo or Beethoven in dollars and cents? Agassiz said, "he had no time to make money"; there were higher and better objects in life than that. And so will it be when humanity is once relieved from the pressing fear of starvation, want, and slavery, it will be concerned, less and less, about the ownership of vast accumulations of wealth. Such possessions would be but an annoyance and trouble. When two or three or four hours a day of easy, of healthful labor will produce all the comforts and luxuries one can use, and the opportunity to labor is never denied, people will become indifferent as to who owns the wealth they do not need.

Wealth will be below par, and it will be found that men and women will not accept it for pay, or be bribed by it to do what they would not willingly and naturally do without it. Some higher incentive must, and will, supersede the greed for gold. The involuntary aspiration born in man to make the most of one's self, to be loved and appreciated by one's fellow-beings, to "make the world better for having lived in it," will urge him on the nobler deeds than ever the sordid and selfish incentive of material gain has done.

If, in the present chaotic and shameful struggle for existence, when organized society offers a premium on greed, cruelty, and deceit, men can be found who stand aloof and almost alone in their determination to work for good rather than gold, who suffer want and persecution rather than desert principle, who can bravely walk to the scaffold for the good they can do humanity, what may we expect from men when freed from the grinding necessity of selling the better part of themselves for bread? The terrible conditions under which labor is performed, the awful alternative if one does not prostitute talent and morals in the service of mammon; and the power acquired with the wealth obtained by ever so unjust means, combined to make the conception of free and voluntary labor almost an impossible one.

And yet, there are examples of this principle even now. In a well-bred family each person has certain duties, which are performed cheerfully, and are not measured out and paid for according to some pre-determined standard; when the united members sit down to the well-filled table, the stronger do not scramble to get the most, while the weakest do without, or gather greedily around them more food than they can possibly consume. Each patiently and politely awaits his turn to be served, and leaves what he does not want; he is certain that when again hungry plenty of good food will be provided. This principle can be extended to include all society, when people are civilized enough to wish it.

Again, the utter impossibility of awarding to each an exact return for the amount of labor performed will render absolute communism a necessity sooner or later. The land and all it contains, without which labor cannot be exerted, belong to no one man, but to all alike. The inventions and discoveries of the past are the common inheritance of the coming generations; and when a man takes the tree that nature furnished free, and fashions it into a useful article, or a machine perfected and bequeathed to him by many past generations, who is to determine what proportion is his and his alone? Primitive man would have been a week fashioning a rude resemblance to the article with his clumsy tools, where the modern worker has occupied an hour. The finished article is of far more real value than the rude one made long ago, and yet the primitive man toiled the longest and hardest.

Who can determine with exact justice what is each one's due? There must come a time when we will cease trying. The earth is so bountiful, so generous; man's brain is so active, his hands so restless, that wealth will spring like magic, ready for the use of the world's inhabitants. We will become as much ashamed to quarrel over its possession as we are now to squabble over the food spread before us on a loaded table.

"But all this," the objector urges, "is very beautiful in the far off future, when we become angels. It would not do now to abolish governments and legal restraints; people are not prepared for it."

This is a question. We have seen, in reading history, that wherever an old-time restriction has been removed the people have not abused their newer liberty. Once it was considered necessary to compel men to save their souls, with the aid of governmental scaffolds, church racks and stakes. Until the foundation of the American republic it was considered absolutely essential that governments should second the efforts of the church in forcing people to attend the means of grace; and yet it is found that the standard of morals among the masses is raised since they are left free to pray as they see fit, or not at all, if they prefer it. It was believed the chattel slaves would not work if the overseer and whip were removed; they are so much more a source of profit now that ex-slave owners would not return to the old system if they could.

So many able writers have shown that the unjust institutions which work so much misery and suffering to the masses have their root in governments, and owe their whole existence to the power derived from government we cannot help but believe that were every law, every title deed, every court, and every police officer or soldier abolished tomorrow with one sweep, we would be better off than now. The actual, material things that man needs would still exist; his strength and skill would remain and his instinctive social inclinations retain their force and the resources of life made free to all the people that they would need no force but that of society and the opinion of fellow beings to keep them moral and upright.

Freed from the systems that made him wretched before, he is not likely to make himself more wretched for lack of them. Much more is contained in the thought that conditions make man what he is, and not the laws and penalties made for his guidance, than is supposed by careless observation. We have laws, jails, courts, armies, guns and armories enough to make saints of us all, if they were the true preventives of crime; but we know they do not prevent crime; that wickedness and depravity exist in spite of them, nay, increase as the struggle between classes grows fiercer, wealth greater and more powerful and poverty more gaunt and desperate.

To the governing class the anarchists say: "Gentlemen, we ask no privilege, we propose no restriction; nor, on the other hand, will we permit it. We have no new shackles to propose, we seek emancipation from shackles. We ask no legislative sanction, for co-operation asks only for a free field and no favors; neither will we permit their interference. It asserts that in freedom of the social unit lies the freedom of the social state. It asserts that in freedom to possess and utilize soil lie social happiness and progress and the death of rent. It asserts that order can only exist where liberty prevails, and that progress leads and never follows order. It asserts, finally, that this emancipation will inaugurate liberty, equality, fraternity." That the existing industrial system has outgrown its usefulness, if it ever had any is I believe admitted by all who have given serious thought to this phase of social conditions.

The manifestations of discontent now looming upon every side show that society is conducted on wrong principles and that something has got to be done soon or the wage class will sink into a slavery worse than was the feudal serf. I say to the wage class: Think clearly and act quickly, or you are lost. Strike not for a few cents more an hour, because the price of living will be raised faster still, but strike for all you earn, be content with nothing less.

* * *

Following are definitions which will appear in all of the new standard dictionaries:

Anarchism: The philosophy of a new social order based on liberty unrestricted by man made law, the theory that all forms of government are based on violence—hence wrong and harmful, as well as unnecessary.

Anarchy: Absence of government; disbelief in and disregard of invasion and authority based on coercion and force; a condition of society regulated by voluntary agreement instead of government.

Anarchist: No. 1. A believer in Anarchism; one opposed to all forms of coercive government and invasive authority. 2. One who advocates Anarchy, or absence of government, as the ideal of political liberty and social harmony.

PART TEN

ALEXANDER BERKMAN
(1870–1936)

Alexander Berkman contends that punishment is founded on two assumptions central in classical criminology. First, that people are rational, calculating actors responsible solely for all their actions. And secondly, that punishment maintains and asserts the spirit of retaliation or revenge even as it claims otherwise. In modern liberal democracies, personal revenge is delegated to the state. The state becomes the "sole legal avenger" of "the collective citizen." The mode has changed but the barbaric spirit (of feudal trial by ordeal, for example) remains for Berkman. Law itself is now being vindicated. That—as classical criminology would have it—the punishment must be adequate to the crime shows further that the spirit of an "eye for an eye, a tooth for a tooth," still predominates, motivating so-called criminal justice.

Berkman prefigures labeling theory by discussing effects of what today is termed *stigma* and outlines how those who have had "hands turned against them" turn their hand against everyone else. Berkman notes that prisons become "veritable schools of crime and immorality," as are so-called reformatories. Reform is still based on fear rather than kindness. Only kindness is truly reformatory.

Berkman also makes an important observation regarding corporate practices as crime. He points to exploitation and the theft of labor and asks how this differs from straight up robbery.

Chapter 14 originally appeared in *Mother Earth* I, no. 6, 1906. Chapter 15 was originally published as Chapter III of *What is Communist Anarchism?* (New York: Vanguard, 1929).

CHAPTER 14

Prisons and Crime

Alexander Berkman

Modern philanthropy has added a new rôle to the repertoire of penal institutions. While, formerly, the alleged necessity of prisons rested, solely, upon their penal and protective character, today a new function, claiming primary importance, has become embodied in these institutions—that of reformation.

Hence, three objects—reformative, penal, and protective— are now sought to be accomplished by means of enforced physical restraint, by incarceration of a more or less solitary character, for a specific, or more or less indefinite period.

Seeking to promote its own safety, society debars certain elements, called criminals, from participation in social life, by means of imprisonment. This temporary isolation of the offender exhausts the protective rôle of prisons. Entirely negative in character, does this protection benefit society? Does it protect?

Let us study some of its results.

First, let us investigate the penal and reformative phases of the prison question.

Punishment, as a social institution, has its origin in two sources; first, in the assumption that man is a free moral agent and, consequently, responsible for his demeanor, so far as he is supposed to be *compos mentis*; and, second, in the spirit of revenge, the retaliation of injury. Waiving, for the present, the debatable question as to man's free agency, let us analyze the second source.

The spirit of revenge is a purely animal proclivity, primarily manifesting itself where comparative physical development is combined with a certain degree of intelligence. Primitive man is compelled, by the conditions of his environment, to take the law into his own hands, so to speak, in furtherance of his instinctive desire of self-assertion, or protection, in coping with the animal or human aggressor, who is wont to injure or jeopardize his person or his interests. This proclivity, born of the instinct of self-preservation and developed in the battle for existence and supremacy, has become, with uncivilized man, a second instinct, almost as potent in its vitality as the source it primarily developed from, and occasionally even transcending the same in its ferocity and conquering, for the moment, the dictates of self-preservation.

Even animals possess the spirit of revenge. The ingenious methods frequently adopted by elephants in captivity, in avenging themselves upon some particularly hectoring spectator, are well known. Dogs and various other animals also often manifest the spirit of revenge. But it is with man, at certain stages of his intellectual development, that the spirit of revenge reaches its most pronounced character. Among barbaric and semicivilized races the practice of personally avenging one's wrongs—actual or imaginary—plays an all-important rôle in the life of the individual. With them, revenge is a most vital matter, often attaining the character of religious fanaticism, the holy duty of avenging a particularly flagrant injury descending from father to son, from generation to generation, until the insult is extirpated with the blood of the offender or of his progeny. Whole tribes have often combined in assisting one of their members to avenge the death of a relative upon a hostile neighbor, and it is always the special privilege of the wronged to give the deathblow to the offender.

Even in certain European countries the old spirit of blood-revenge is still very strong. The semibarbarians of the Caucasus, the ignorant peasants of Southern Italy, of Corsica and Sicily, still practice this form of personal vengeance; some of them, as the Cherkess, for instance, quite openly; others, as the Corsicans, seeking safety in secrecy. Even in our so-called enlightened countries the spirit of personal revenge, of sworn, eternal enmity, still exists. What are the secret organizations of the Mafia type, so common in all South European lands, but the manifestations of this spirit?! And what is the underlying principle of duelling in its various forms—from the armed combat to the fistic encounter—but this spirit of direct vengeance, the desire to personally avenge an insult or an injury, fancied or real: to wipe out the same, even with the blood of the antagonist. It is this spirit that actuates the enraged husband in attempting the life of the "robber of his honor and happiness." It is this spirit that is at the bottom of all lynch law atrocities, the frenzied mob seeking to avenge the bereaved parent, the young widow, or the outraged child.

Social progress, however, tends to check and eliminate the practice of direct, personal revenge. In so-called civilized communities the individual does not, as a rule, personally avenge his wrongs. He has delegated his "rights" in that direction to the State, the government; and it is one of the "duties" of the latter to avenge the wrongs of its citizens by punishing the guilty parties. Thus we see that punishment, as a social institution, is but another form of revenge, with the State in the rôle of the sole legal avenger of the collective citizen—the same well-defined spirit of barbarism in disguise. The penal powers of the State rest, theoretically, on the principle that, in organized society, "an injury to one is the concern of all"; in the wronged citizen society as a whole is attacked. The culprit must be punished in order to avenge outraged society, that "the majesty of the Law be vindicated." The principle that the punishment must be adequate to the crime still further proves the real character of the institution of punishment: it reveals the Old Testamental spirit of "an eye for an eye, a tooth for a tooth"—a spirit still alive in almost all so-called civilized countries, as witness capital punishment: a life for a life. The "criminal" is not punished for his offence, as such, but rather according to the nature, circumstances, and character of the same, as viewed by society; in other words, the penalty is of a nature calculated to balance the intensity of the local spirit of revenge, aroused by the particular offence.

This, then, is the nature of punishment. Yet, strange to say—or naturally, perhaps—the results attained by penal institutions are the very opposite of the ends sought. The modern form of "civilized" revenge kills, figuratively speaking, the enemy of the individual citizen, but breeds in his place the enemy of society. The prisoner of the State no longer regards the person he injured as his particular enemy, as the barbarian does, fearing the wrath and revenge of the wronged one. Instead, he looks upon the State as his direct punisher; in the representatives of the law he sees his personal enemies. He nurtures his wrath, and wild thoughts of revenge fill his mind. His hate toward the persons, directly responsible, in his estimation, for his misfortune—the arresting officer, the jailer, the prosecuting attorney, judge and jury—gradually widens in scope, and the poor unfortunate becomes an enemy of society as a whole. Thus, while the penal institutions on the one hand protect society from the prisoner so long as he remains one, they cultivate, on the other hand, the germs of social hatred and enmity.

Deprived of his liberty, his rights, and the enjoyment of life; all his natural impulses, good and bad alike, suppressed; subjected to indignities and disciplined by harsh and often inhumanely severe methods, and generally maltreated and abused by official brutes whom he despises and hates, the young prisoner, utterly miserable, comes to curse the fact of his birth, the woman that bore him, and all those responsible, in his eyes, for his misery. He is brutalized by the treatment he receives and by the revolting sights he is forced to witness in prison. What manhood he may have possessed is soon eradicated by the "discipline." His impotent rage and bitterness are turned into hatred toward everything and everybody, growing in intensity as the years of misery come and go. He broods over his troubles and the desire to revenge himself grows in intensity, his until then perhaps undefined inclinations are turned into strong antisocial desires, which gradually become a fixed determination. Society had made him an outcast; it is his natural enemy. Nobody had shown him either kindness or mercy; he will be merciless to the world.

Then he is released. His former friends spurn him; he is no more recognized by his acquaintances; society points its finger at the ex-convict; he is looked upon with scorn, derision, and disgust; he is distrusted and abused. He has no money, and there is no charity for the "moral leper." He finds himself a social Ishmael, with everybody's hand turned against him—and he turns his hand against everybody else.

The penal and protective functions of prisons thus defeat their own ends. Their work is not merely unprofitable, it is worse than useless; it is positively and absolutely detrimental to the best interests of society.

It is no better with the reformative phase of penal institutions. The penal character of all prisons—workhouses, penitentiaries, state prisons—excludes all possibility of a reformative nature. The promiscuous mingling of prisoners in the same institution, without regard to the relative criminality of the inmates, converts prisons into veritable schools of crime and immorality.

The same is true of reformatories. These institutions, specifically designed to reform, do as a rule produce the vilest degeneration. The reason is obvious. Reformatories, the same as ordinary prisons, use physical restraint and are purely penal institutions—the very idea of punishment precludes true reformation. Reformation that does not emanate from the voluntary impulse of the inmate, one which is the result of fear—the fear of consequences and of probable punishment—is no real reformation; it lacks the very essentials of the latter, and so soon as the fear has been conquered, or temporarily emancipated from, the influence of the pseudo-reformation will vanish like smoke. *Kindness alone is truly reformative*, but this quality is an unknown quantity in the treatment of prisoners, both young and old.

Some time ago[1] I read the account of a boy, thirteen years old, who had been confined in chains, night and day for three consecutive weeks, his particular offence being the terrible crime of an attempted escape from the Westchester, N. Y., Home for Indigent Children (Weeks case, Superintendent Pierce, Christmas, 1895). That was by no means an exceptional instance in that institution. Nor is the penal character of the latter exceptional. There is not a single prison or reformatory in the United States where either flogging and clubbing, or the straightjacket, solitary confinement, and "reduced" diet (semistarvation) are not practiced upon the unfortunate inmates. And though reformatories do not, as a rule, use the "means of persuasion" of the notorious Brockway, of Elmira, N. Y., yet flogging is practiced in some, and starvation and the dungeon are a permanent institution in all of them.

Aside from the penal character of reformatories and the derogatory influence the deprivation of liberty and enjoyment exercise on the youthful mind, the associations in those institutions preclude, in the majority of cases, all reformation. Even in the reformatories no attempt is made to classify the inmates according to the comparative gravity of their offenses, necessitating different modes of treatment and suitable companionship. In the so-called reform schools and reformatories children of all ages—from five to twenty-five—are kept in the same institution, congregated for the several purposes of labor, learning, and religious service, and allowed to mingle on the playing

---

1   The above article is compiled from notes made by me in prison, in 1895. A.B.

grounds and associate in the dormitories. The inmates are often classified according to age or stature, but no attention is paid to their relative depravity. The absurdity of such methods is simply astounding. Pause and consider. The youthful culprit, who is such probably chiefly in consequence of bad associations, is put among the choicest assortment of viciousness and is expected to reform! And the fathers and mothers of the nation calmly look on, and either directly further this species of insanity or by their silence approve and encourage the State's work of breeding criminals. But such is human nature—we swear it is daytime, though it be pitch-dark; the old spirit of *credo quia absurdum est.*

It is unnecessary, however, to enlarge further upon the debasing influence those steeped in crime exert over their more innocent companions. Nor is it necessary to discuss further the reformative claims of reformatories. The fact that fully 60 percent of the male prison population of the United States are graduates of "reformatories" conclusively proves the reformative pretentions of the latter absolutely groundless. The rare cases of youthful prisoners having really reformed are in no sense due to the "beneficial" influence of imprisonment and of penal restraint, but rather to the innate powers of the individual himself.

Doubtless there exists no other institution among the diversified "achievements" of modern society, which, while assuming a most important rôle in the destinies of mankind, has proven a more reprehensible failure in point of attainment than the penal institutions. Millions of dollars are annually expended throughout the "civilized" world for the maintenance of these institutions, and notwithstanding each successive year witnesses additional appropriations for their improvement, yet the results tend to retrograde rather than advance the purports of their founding.

The money annually expended for the maintenance of prisons could be invested, with as much profit and less injury, in government bonds of the planet Mars, or sunk in the Atlantic. No amount of punishment can obviate crime, so long as prevailing conditions, in and out of prison, drive men to it.

CHAPTER 15

Law and Government

Alexander Berkman

Yes, you are right: the law forbids theft.

If I should steal something from you, you can call a policeman and have me arrested. The law will punish the thief, and the government will return to you the stolen property, if possible, because the law forbids stealing. It says that no one has a right to take anything from you without your consent.

But your employer takes from you what you produce. The whole wealth produced by labor is taken by the capitalists and kept by them as their property.

The law says that your employer does not steal anything from you, because it is done with your consent. You have agreed to work for your boss for certain pay, he to have all that you produce. Because you *consented* to it, the law says that he does not steal anything from you.

But did you really consent?

When the highwayman holds his gun to your head, you turn your valuables over to him. You 'consent' all right, but you do so because you cannot help yourself, because you are *compelled* by his gun.

Are you not *compelled* to work for an employer? Your need compels you, just as the highwayman's gun. You must live, and so must your wife and children. You can't work for yourself, under the capitalist industrial system you must work for an employer. The factories, machinery, and tools belong to the employing class, so you *must* hire yourself out to that class in order to work and live. Whatever you work at, whoever your employer may be, it always comes to the same: you must work for *him*. You can't help yourself. You are *compelled*.

In this way the whole working class is compelled to work for the capitalist class. In this manner the workers are compelled to give up all the wealth they produce. The employers keep that wealth as their profit, while the worker gets only a wage, just enough to live on, so he can go on producing more wealth for his employer. Is that not cheating, robbery?

The law says it is a "free agreement." Just as well might the highwayman say that you "agreed" to give up your valuables. The only difference is that the highwayman's way is called stealing and robbery, and is forbidden by law. While the capitalist way is called business, industry, profit making, and is protected by law.

But whether it is done in the highwayman's way or in the capitalist way, you know that you are *robbed*.

The whole capitalist system rests on such robbery.

The whole system of law and government upholds and justifies this robbery.

That's the order of things called capitalism, and law and government are there to protect this order of things.

Do you wonder that the capitalist and employer, and all those who profit by this order of things, are strong for "law and order"?

But where do you come in? What benefit have you from that kind of "law and order"? Don't you see that this 'law and order' only robs you, fools you, and just enslaves you?

"Enslave me?" you wonder. "Why, I am a free citizen!"

Are you free, really? Free to do what? To live as you please? To do what you please?

Let's see. How do you live? What does your freedom amount to?

You *depend* on your employer for your wages or your salary, don't you? And your wages determine your way of living, don't they? The conditions of your life, even what you eat and drink, where you go and with whom you associate—all of it *depends on your wages*.

No, you are not a free man. You are *dependent* on your employer and on your wages. You are really a wage slave. The whole working class, under the capitalist system, is dependent on the capitalist class. The workers are wage slaves.

So, what becomes of your freedom? What can you do with it? Can you do more with it than your wages permit?

Can't you see that your wage—your salary or income—is all the freedom that you have? Your freedom, your liberty, don't go a step further than the wages you get.

The freedom that is given you on paper, that is written down in law books and constitutions, does not do you a bit of good. Such freedom only means that you have the *right* to do a certain thing. But it doesn't mean that you *can* do it. To be able to do it, you must have the chance, the opportunity. You have a *right* to eat three fine meals a day, but if you haven't the means, the *opportunity* to get those meals, then what good is that right to you?

So freedom really means opportunity to satisfy your needs and wants. If your freedom does not give you that opportunity, than it does you no good. Real freedom means opportunity and well-being. If it does not mean that, it means nothing.

You see, then, that the whole situation comes to this: Capitalism robs you and makes a wage slave of you. The law upholds and protects that robbery.

The government fools you into believing that you are independent and free.

In this way you are fooled and duped every day of your life. But how does it happen that you didn't think of it before? How is it that most other people don't see it, either?

It is because you and every one else are lied to about this all the time, from your earliest childhood.

You are told to be honest, while you are being robbed all your life.

You are commanded to respect the law, while the law protects the capitalist who is robbing you.

You are taught that killing is wrong, while the government hangs and electrocutes people and slaughters them in war.

You are told to obey the law and government, though law and government stand for robbery and murder.

Thus all through life you are lied to, fooled, and deceived, so that it will be easier to make profits out of you, to *exploit* you.

Because it is not only the employer and the capitalist who make profits out of you. The government, the church, tend the school— they all live on your labor. You support them all. That is why all of them teach you to be content with your lot and behave yourself.

"Is it really true that I support them all?" you ask in amazement.

Let us see. They eat and drink and are clothed, not to speak of the luxuries they enjoy. Do *they* make the things they use and consume, do *they* do the planting and sowing and building and so on?

"But they pay for those things," your friend objects.

Yes, they pay. Suppose a fellow stole fifty dollars from you and then went and bought with it a suit of clothes for himself. Is that suit by right his? Didn't he pay for it? Well, just so the people who don't produce anything or do no useful work pay for things. Their money is the profits they or their parents before them squeezed out of you, out of the workers.

"Then it is not my boss who supports me, but I him?"

Of course. He gives you a job; that is, permission to work in the factory or mill which was not built by him but by other workers like yourself. And for that permission you help to support him for the rest of your life or as long as you work for him. You support him so generously that he can afford a mansion in the city and a home in the country, even several of them, and servants to attend to his wants and those of his family, and for the entertainment of his friends, and for horse races and for boat races, and for a hundred other things. But it is not only to him that you are so generous. Out of your labor, by direct and indirect taxation, are supported the entire government, local, state, and national, the schools and the churches, and all the other institutions whose business it is to protect profits and keep you fooled. You and your fellow workers, labor as a whole, support them all. Do you wonder that they all tell you that everything is all right and that you should be good and keep quiet?

It is good for *them* that you should keep quiet, because they could not keep on duping and robbing you once you open your eyes and see what's happening to you.

That's why they are all strong for this capitalist system, for "law and order."

But is that system good for *you*? Do you think it right and just? If not, then why do you put up with it? Why do you support it? "What can I do?" you say; "I'm only one."

Are you really only one? Are you not rather one out of many thousands, out of millions, all of them exploited and enslaved the same as you are? Only they don't know it. If they knew it, they wouldn't stand for it. That's sure. So the thing is to make them know it.

Every workingman in your city, every toiler in your country, in every country, in the whole world, is exploited and enslaved the same as you are.

250

And not only the workingmen. The farmers are duped and robbed in the same manner.

Just like the workingmen, the farmer is dependent on the capitalist class. He toils hard all his life, but most of his labor goes to the trusts and monopolies of the land which by right is no more theirs than the moon is.

The farmer produces the food of the world. He feeds all of us. But before he can get his goods to us, he is made to pay tribute to the class that lives by the work of others, the profit-making, capitalist class. The farmer is mulcted out of the greater part of his product just as the worker is. He is mulcted by the land owner and by the mortgage holder; by the steel trust and the railroad. The banker, the commission merchant, the retailer, and a score of other middlemen squeeze their profits out of the farmer before he is allowed to get his food to you.

Law and government permit and help this robbery by ruling that:
the land, which no man created,
belongs to the landlord; the railroads, which the workers built,
belong to the railroad magnates;
the warehouses, grain elevators, and storehouses,
erected by the workers, belong to the capitalists;
all those monopolists and capitalists have a right to
get profits from the farmer for using the railroads
and other facilities before he can get his food to you.

You can see then, how the farmer is robbed by big capital and business, and how the law helps in that robbery, just as with the workingman.

But it is not only the worker and the farmer who are exploited and forced to give up the greater part of their product to the capitalists, to those who have monopolized the land, the railroads, the factories, the machinery, and all natural resources. The entire country, the whole world is made to pay tribute to the kings of finance and industry.

The small business man depends on the wholesaler; the wholesaler on the manufacturer; the manufacturer on the trust magnates of his industry; and all of them on the money lords and banks for their credit. The big bankers and financiers can put any man out of business by just withdrawing their credit from him. They do so whenever they want to squeeze any one out of business. The business man is entirely at their mercy. If he does not play the game as they want it, to *suit their interests*, then they simply drive him out of the game.

Thus the whole of mankind is dependent upon and enslaved by just a handful of men who have monopolized almost the entire wealth of the world, but who have themselves never created anything.

"But those men work hard," you say.

Well, some of them don't work at all. Some of them are just idlers, whose business is managed by others. Some of them *do* work. But what kind of work do they do? Do they produce anything, as the worker and the farmer do? No, they produce nothing, though they may work. They work to mulct people, to get profits out of them. Does their work benefit *you*? The highwayman also works hard and takes great risks to boot. His "work," like the capitalist's, gives employment to lawyers, jailers, and a host of other retainers, all of whom *your* toil supports.

It seems indeed ridiculous that the whole world should slave for the benefit of a handful of monopolists, and that all should have to depend upon them for their right and opportunity to live. But the fact is just that. And it is the more ridiculous when you consider that the workers and farmers, who alone create all wealth, should be the most dependent and the poorest of all the other classes in society.

It is really monstrous, and it is very sad. Surely your common sense must tell you that such a situation is nothing short of madness. If the great masses of people, the millions throughout the world, could see how they are fooled, exploited and enslaved, as *you* see it now, would they stand for such goings on? Surely they would not!

The capitalists know they wouldn't. That is why they need the government to legalize their methods of robbery, to protect the capitalist system.

And that is why the government needs laws, police and soldiers, courts and prisons to protect capitalism.

But who are the police and the soldiers who protect the capitalists against you, against the people?

If they were capitalists themselves, then it would stand to reason why they want to protect the wealth they have stolen, and why they try to keep up, even by force, the system that gives them the privilege of robbing the people.

But the police and the soldiers, the defenders of "law and order," are not of the capitalist class. They are men from the ranks of the people, poor men who for pay protect the very system that keeps them poor. It is unbelievable, is it not? Yet it is true. It just comes down to this: some of the slaves protect their masters in keeping them and the rest of the people in slavery. In the same way Great Britain, for instance, keeps the Hindoos in India in subjection by a police force of the natives, of the Hindoos themselves. Or as Belgium does with the black men in the Congo. Or as any government does with a subjugated people.

It is the same system. Here is what it amounts to:

Capitalism robs and exploits the whole of the people;

the laws legalize and uphold this capitalist robbery;

the government uses one part of the people to aid and protect the capitalists in robbing the whole of the people.

The entire thing is kept up by educating the people to believe that capitalism is right, that the law is just, and that the government must be obeyed.

Do you see through this game now?

PART ELEVEN

EMMA GOLDMAN
(1869–1940)

Emma Goldman's contributions to social analysis in social sciences stand with those of Kropotkin. Goldman also offered sharp condemnation of state punishment and prison systems, which she also experienced first hand, along with deportations. Goldman was innovative in her analysis of moral regulation and particularly the constraining and shaping of women's lives and labor through moral regulation and the basis of criminal justice and laws in the moral biases of bourgeois advocates (what today criminologists would call moral entrepreneurs) rather than with concerns of social protection, service, or safety. In this her work prefigures much of current social analysis on the productive power of class norms and values, backed by the force of the bourgeois state, since Michel Foucault and Pierre Bourdieu.

Goldman, in particular, focused on the hypocrisy of state practices prohibiting prostitution and birth control as elements, not of public safety, but as the control of working-class women's bodies and labor. Goldman offers an early criticism, from a radical social feminist perspective, of what is today called "carceral feminism," or the mobilization of state repressive force against women in the name of protecting them.

Chapters 16 and 17 were originally published in *Anarchism and Other Essays* (New York: Mother Earth Publishing Group, 1911).

CHAPTER 16

The Traffic in Women
Emma Goldman

OUR REFORMERS have suddenly made a great discovery—the white slave traffic. The papers are full of these "unheard-of conditions," and lawmakers are already planning a new set of laws to check the horror.

It is significant that whenever the public mind is to be diverted from a great social wrong, a crusade is inaugurated against indecency, gambling, saloons, etc. And what is the result of such crusades? Gambling is increasing, saloons are doing a lively business through back entrances, prostitution is at its height, and the system of pimps and cadets is but aggravated.

How is it that an institution, known almost to every child, should have been discovered so suddenly? How is it that this evil, known to all sociologists, should now be made such an important issue?

To assume that the recent investigation of the white slave traffic (and, by the way, a very superficial investigation) has discovered anything new, is, to say the least, very foolish. Prostitution has been, and is, a widespread evil, yet mankind goes on its business, perfectly indifferent to the sufferings and distress of the victims of prostitution. As indifferent, indeed, as mankind has remained to our industrial system, or to economic prostitution.

Only when human sorrows are turned into a toy with glaring colors will baby people become interested—for a while at least. The people are a very fickle baby that must have new toys every day. The "righteous" cry against the white slave traffic is such a toy. It serves to amuse the people for a little while, and it will help to create a few more fat political jobs—parasites who stalk about the world as inspectors, investigators, detectives, and so forth.

What is really the cause of the trade in women? Not merely white women, but yellow and black women as well. Exploitation, of course; the merciless Moloch of capitalism that fattens on underpaid labor, thus driving thousands of women and girls into prostitution. With Mrs. Warren these girls feel, "Why waste your life working for a few shillings a week in a scullery, eighteen hours a day?"

Naturally our reformers say nothing about this cause. They know it well enough, but it doesn't pay to say anything about it. It is much more profitable to play the Pharisee, to pretend an outraged morality, than to go to the bottom of things.

However, there is one commendable exception among the young writers: Reginald Wright Kauffman, whose work *The House of Bondage* is the first earnest attempt to treat the social evil—not from a sentimental Philistine viewpoint. A journalist of wide experience, Mr. Kauffman proves that our industrial system leaves most women no alternative except prostitution. The women portrayed in *The House of Bondage* belong to the working class. Had the author portrayed the life of women in other spheres, he would have been confronted with the same state of affairs.

Nowhere is woman treated according to the merit of her work, but rather as a sex. It is therefore almost inevitable that she should pay for her right to exist, to keep a position in whatever line, with sex favors. Thus it is merely a question of degree whether she sells herself to one man, in or out of marriage, or to many men. Whether our reformers admit it or not, the economic and social inferiority of woman is responsible for prostitution.

Just at present our good people are shocked by the disclosures that in New York City alone one out of every ten women works in a factory, that the average wage received by women is six dollars per week for forty-eight to sixty hours of work, and that the majority of female wage workers face many months of idleness which leaves the average wage about $280 a year. In view of these economic horrors, is it to be wondered at that prostitution and the white slave trade have become such dominant factors?

Lest the preceding figures be considered an exaggeration, it is well to examine what some authorities on prostitution have to say:

"A prolific cause of female depravity can be found in the several tables, showing the description of the employment pursued, and the wages received, by the women previous to their fall, and it will be a question for the political economist to decide how far mere business consideration should be an apology on the part of employers for a reduction in their rates of remuneration, and whether the savings of a small percentage on wages is not more than counterbalanced by the enormous amount of taxation enforced on the public at large to defray the expenses incurred on account of a system of vice, *which is the direct result, in many cases, of insufficient compensation of honest labor.*"[1]

Our present-day reformers would do well to look into Dr. Sanger's book. There they will find that out of 2,000 cases under his observation, but few came from the middle classes, from well-ordered conditions, or pleasant homes. By far the largest majority were working girls and working women; some driven into prostitution through sheer want, others because of a cruel, wretched life at home, others again because of thwarted and crippled physical natures (of which I shall speak later on). Also it will do the maintainers of purity and morality good to learn that out of two thousand cases, 490 were married women, women who lived with their husbands. Evidently there was not much of a guaranty for their "safety and purity" in the sanctity of marriage.[2]

Dr. Alfred Blaschko, in *Prostitution in the Nineteenth Century*, is even more emphatic in characterizing economic conditions as one of the most vital factors of prostitution.

"Although prostitution has existed in all ages, it was left to the nineteenth century to develop it into a gigantic social institution. The development of industry with vast masses of people in the competitive market, the growth and congestion of large cities, the insecurity and uncertainty of employment, has given prostitution an impetus never dreamed of at any period in human history."

And again Havelock Ellis, while not so absolute in dealing with the economic cause, is nevertheless compelled to admit that it is indirectly and directly the main cause. Thus he finds that a large percentage of prostitutes is recruited from the servant class, although the latter have less care and greater security. On the other hand, Mr. Ellis does not deny that the daily routine, the drudgery, the monotony of the servant girl's lot, and especially the fact that she may never partake of the companionship and joy of a home, is no mean factor

1   Dr. Sanger, *The History of Prostitution.*
2   It is a significant fact that Dr. Sanger's book has been excluded from the U.S. mails. Evidently the authorities are not anxious that the public be informed as to the true cause of prostitution.

in forcing her to seek recreation and forgetfulness in the gaiety and glimmer of prostitution. In other words, the servant girl, being treated as a drudge, never having the right to herself, and worn out by the caprices of her mistress, can find an outlet, like the factory or shop-girl, only in prostitution.

The most amusing side of the question now before the public is the indignation of our "good, respectable people," especially the various Christian gentlemen, who are always to be found in the front ranks of every crusade. Is it that they are absolutely ignorant of the history of religion, and especially of the Christian religion? Or is it that they hope to blind the present generation to the part played in the past by the Church in relation to prostitution? Whatever their reason, they should be the last to cry out against the unfortunate victims of today, since it is known to every intelligent student that prostitution is of religious origin, maintained and fostered for many centuries, not as a shame, but as a virtue, hailed as such by the Gods themselves.

"It would seem that the origin of prostitution is to be found primarily in a religious custom, religion, the great conserver of social tradition, preserving in a transformed shape a primitive freedom that was passing out of the general social life. The typical example is that recorded by Herodotus, in the fifth century before Christ, at the Temple of Mylitta, the Babylonian Venus, where every woman, once in her life, had to come and give herself to the first stranger, who threw a coin in her lap, to worship the goddess. Very similar customs existed in other parts of western Asia, in North Africa, in Cyprus, and other islands of the eastern Mediterranean, and also in Greece, where the temple of Aphrodite on the fort at Corinth possessed over a thousand hierodules, dedicated to the service of the goddess.

"The theory that religious prostitution developed, as a general rule, out of the belief that the generative activity of human beings possessed a mysterious and sacred influence in promoting the fertility of Nature, is maintained by all authoritative writers on the subject. Gradually, however, and when prostitution became an organized institution under priestly influence, religious prostitution developed utilitarian sides, thus helping to increase public revenue.

"The rise of Christianity to political power produced little change in policy. The leading fathers of the Church tolerated prostitution. Brothels under municipal protection are found in the thirteenth century. They constituted a sort of public service, the directors of them being considered almost as public servants."[3]

To this must be added the following from Dr. Sanger's work:

"Pope Clement II. issued a bull that prostitutes would be tolerated if they pay a certain amount of their earnings to the Church.

"Pope Sixtus IV. was more practical; from one single brothel, which he himself had built, he received an income of 20,000 ducats."

In modern times the Church is a little more careful in that direction. At least she does not openly demand tribute from prostitutes. She finds it much more profitable to go in for real estate, like Trinity Church, for instance, to rent out death traps at an exorbitant price to those who live off and by prostitution.

Much as I should like to, my space will not admit speaking of prostitution in Egypt, Greece, Rome, and during the Middle Ages. The conditions in the latter period are particularly interesting, inasmuch as prostitution was organized into guilds, presided over by a brothel queen. These guilds employed strikes as a medium of improving their condition and keeping a standard price. Certainly that is more practical a method than the one used by the modern wage-slave in society.

It would be one-sided and extremely superficial to maintain that the economic factor is the only cause of prostitution. There are others no less important and vital. That, too, our reformers know, but dare discuss even less than the institution that saps the very life out of both men and women. I refer to the sex question, the very mention of which causes most people moral spasms.

It is a conceded fact that woman is being reared as a sex commodity, and yet she is kept in absolute ignorance of the meaning and importance of sex. Everything dealing with that subject is suppressed, and persons who attempt to bring light into this terrible darkness are persecuted and thrown into prison. Yet it is nevertheless true that so long as a girl is not to know how to take care of herself, not to know the function of the most important part of her life, we need not be surprised if she becomes an easy prey to prostitution, or to any other form of a relationship which degrades her to the position of an object for mere sex gratification.

3   Havelock Ellis, *Sex and Society*.

It is due to this ignorance that the entire life and nature of the girl is thwarted and crippled. We have long ago taken it as a self-evident fact that the boy may follow the call of the wild; that is to say, that the boy may, as soon as his sex nature asserts itself, satisfy that nature; but our moralists are scandalized at the very thought that the nature of a girl should assert itself. To the moralist prostitution does not consist so much in the fact that the woman sells her body, but rather that she sells it out of wedlock. That this is no mere statement is proved by the fact that marriage for monetary considerations is perfectly legitimate, sanctified by law and public opinion, while any other union is condemned and repudiated. Yet a prostitute, if properly defined, means nothing else than "any person for whom sexual relationships are subordinated to gain."[4]

"Those women are prostitutes who sell their bodies for the exercise of the sexual act and make of this a profession."[5]

In fact, Banger goes further; he maintains that the act of prostitution is "intrinsically equal to that of a man or woman who contracts a marriage for economic reasons."

Of course, marriage is the goal of every girl, but as thousands of girls cannot marry, our stupid social customs condemn them either to a life of celibacy or prostitution. Human nature asserts itself regardless of all laws, nor is there any plausible reason why nature should adapt itself to a perverted conception of morality.

Society considers the sex experiences of a man as attributes of his general development, while similar experiences in the life of a woman are looked upon as a terrible calamity, a loss of honor and of all that is good and noble in a human being. This double standard of morality has played no little part in the creation and perpetuation of prostitution. It involves the keeping of the young in absolute ignorance on sex matters, which alleged "innocence," together with an overwrought and stifled sex nature, helps to bring about a state of affairs that our Puritans are so anxious to avoid or prevent.

Not that the gratification of sex must needs lead to prostitution; it is the cruel, heartless, criminal persecution of those who dare divert from the beaten track, which is responsible for it.

Girls, mere children, work in crowded, over-heated rooms ten

4   Guyot, *La Prostitution*.
5   Banger, *Criminalité et Condition Economique*.

to twelve hours daily at a machine, which tends to keep them in a constant over-excited sex state. Many of these girls have no home or comforts of any kind; therefore the street or some place of cheap amusement is the only means of forgetting their daily routine. This naturally brings them into close proximity with the other sex. It is hard to say which of the two factors brings the girl's over-sexed condition to a climax, but it is certainly the most natural thing that a climax should result. That is the first step toward prostitution. Nor is the girl to be held responsible for it. On the contrary, it is altogether the fault of society, the fault of our lack of understanding, of our lack of appreciation of life in the making; especially is it the criminal fault of our moralists, who condemn a girl for all eternity, because she has gone from the "path of virtue"; that is, because her first sex experience has taken place without the sanction of the Church.

The girl feels herself a complete outcast, with the doors of home and society closed in her face. Her entire training and tradition is such that the girl herself feels depraved and fallen, and therefore has no ground to stand upon, or any hold that will lift her up, instead of dragging her down. Thus society creates the victims that it afterwards vainly attempts to get rid of. The meanest, most depraved and decrepit man still considers himself too good to take as his wife the woman whose grace he was quite willing to buy, even though he might thereby save her from a life of horror. Nor can she turn to her own sister for help. In her stupidity the latter deems herself too pure and chaste, not realizing that her own position is in many respects even more deplorable than her sister's of the street.

"The wife who married for money, compared with the prostitute," says Havelock Ellis, "is the true scab. She is paid less, gives much more in return in labor and care, and is absolutely bound to her master. The prostitute never signs away the right over her own person, she retains her freedom and personal rights, nor is she always compelled to submit to man's embrace."

Nor does the better-than-thou woman realize the apologist claim of Lecky that "though she may be the supreme type of vice, she is also the most efficient guardian of virtue. But for her, happy homes would be polluted, unnatural and harmful practice would abound."

Moralists are ever ready to sacrifice one-half of the human race for the sake of some miserable institution which they can not outgrow. As a matter of fact, prostitution is no more a safeguard for the purity of the home than rigid laws are a safeguard against prostitution. Fully fifty per cent. of married men are patrons of brothels. It is through this virtuous element that the married women—nay, even the children—are infected with venereal diseases. Yet society has not a word of condemnation for the man, while no law is too monstrous to be set in motion against the helpless victim. She is not only preyed upon by those who use her, but she is also absolutely at the mercy of every policeman and miserable detective on the beat, the officials at the station house, the authorities in every prison.

In a recent book by a woman who was for twelve years the mistress of a "house," are to be found the following figures: "The authorities compelled me to pay every month fines between $14.70 to $29.70, the girls would pay from $5.70 to $9.70 to the police." Considering that the writer did her business in a small city, that the amounts she gives do not include extra bribes and fines, one can readily see the tremendous revenue the police department derives from the blood money of its victims, whom it will not even protect. Woe to those who refuse to pay their toll; they would be rounded up like cattle, "if only to make a favorable impression upon the good citizens of the city, or if the powers needed extra money on the side. For the warped mind who believes that a fallen woman is incapable of human emotion it would be impossible to realize the grief, the disgrace, the tears, the wounded pride that was ours every time we were pulled in."

Strange, isn't it, that a woman who has kept a "house" should be able to feel that way? But stranger still that a good Christian world should bleed and fleece such women, and give them nothing in return except obloquy and persecution. Oh, for the charity of a Christian world!

Much stress is laid on white slaves being imported into America. How would America ever retain her virtue if Europe did not help her out? I will not deny that this may be the case in some instances, any more than I will deny that there are emissaries of Germany and other countries luring economic slaves into America; but I absolutely deny that prostitution is recruited to any appreciable extent from Europe. It may be true that the majority of prostitutes of New York City are foreigners, but that is because the majority of the population is foreign. The moment we go to any other American city, to Chicago or the Middle West, we shall find that the number of foreign prostitutes is by far a minority.

Equally exaggerated is the belief that the majority of street girls in this city were engaged in this business before they came to America. Most of the girls speak excellent English, are Americanized in habits and appearance,—a thing absolutely impossible unless they had lived in this country many years. That is, they were driven into prostitution by American conditions, by the thoroughly American custom for excessive display of finery and clothes, which, of course, necessitates money,—money that cannot be earned in shops or factories.

In other words, there is no reason to believe that any set of men would go to the risk and expense of getting foreign products, when American conditions are overflooding the market with thousands of girls. On the other hand, there is sufficient evidence to prove that the export of American girls for the purpose of prostitution is by no means a small factor.

Thus Clifford G. Roe, ex-Assistant State Attorney of Cook County, Ill., makes the open charge that New England girls are shipped to Panama for the express use of men in the employ of Uncle Sam. Mr. Roe adds that "there seems to be an underground railroad between Boston and Washington which many girls travel." Is it not significant that the railroad should lead to the very seat of Federal authority? That Mr. Roe said more than was desired in certain quarters is proved by the fact that he lost his position. It is not practical for men in office to tell tales from school.

The excuse given for the conditions in Panama is that there are no brothels in the Canal Zone. That is the usual avenue of escape for a hypocritical world that dares not face the truth. Not in the Canal Zone, not in the city limits,—therefore prostitution does not exist.

Next to Mr. Roe, there is James Bronson Reynolds, who has made a thorough study of the white slave traffic in Asia. As a staunch American citizen and friend of the future Napoleon of America, Theodore Roosevelt, he is surely the last to discredit the virtue of his country. Yet we are informed by him that in Hong Kong, Shanghai, and Yokohama, the Augean stables of American vice are located. There American prostitutes have made themselves so conspicuous that in the Orient "American girl" is synonymous with prostitute. Mr. Reynolds reminds his countrymen that while Americans in China are under the protection of our consular representatives, the Chinese in America have no protection at all. Every one who knows the brutal and barbarous persecution Chinese and Japanese endure on the Pacific Coast, will agree with Mr. Reynolds.

In view of the above facts it is rather absurd to point to Europe as the swamp whence come all the social diseases of America. Just as absurd is it to proclaim the myth that the Jews furnish the largest contingent of willing prey. I am sure that no one will accuse me of nationalistic tendencies. I am glad to say that I have developed out of them, as out of many other prejudices. If, therefore, I resent the statement that Jewish prostitutes are imported, it is not because of any Judaistic sympathies, but because of the facts inherent in the lives of these people. No one but the most superficial will claim that Jewish girls migrate to strange lands, unless they have some tie or relation that brings them there. The Jewish girl is not adventurous. Until recent years she had never left home, not even so far as the next village or town, except it were to visit some relative. Is it then credible that Jewish girls would leave their parents or families, travel thousands of miles to strange lands, through the influence and promises of strange forces? Go to any of the large incoming steamers and see for yourself if these girls do not come either with their parents, brothers, aunts, or other kinsfolk. There may be exceptions, of course, but to state that large numbers of Jewish girls are imported for prostitution, or any other purpose, is simply not to know Jewish psychology.

Those who sit in a glass house do wrong to throw stones about them; besides, the American glass house is rather thin, it will break easily, and the interior is anything but a gainly sight.

To ascribe the increase of prostitution to alleged importation, to the growth of the cadet system, or similar causes, is highly superficial. I have already referred to the former. As to the cadet system, abhorrent as it is, we must not ignore the fact that it is essentially a phase of modern prostitution,—a phase accentuated by suppression and graft, resulting from sporadic crusades against the social evil.

The procurer is no doubt a poor specimen of the human family, but in what manner is he more despicable than the policeman who takes the last cent from the street walker, and then locks her up in the station house? Why is the cadet more criminal, or a greater menace to society, than the owners of department stores and factories, who grow fat on the sweat of their victims, only to drive them to the streets? I make no plea for the cadet, but I fail to see why he should be mercilessly hounded, while the real perpetrators of all social iniquity enjoy immunity and respect. Then, too, it is well to remember that it is not the cadet who makes the prostitute. It is our sham and hypocrisy that create both the prostitute and the cadet.

Until 1894 very little was known in America of the procurer. Then we were attacked by an epidemic of virtue. Vice was to be abolished, the country purified at all cost. The social cancer was therefore driven out of sight, but deeper into the body. Keepers of brothels, as well as their unfortunate victims, were turned over to the tender mercies of the police. The inevitable consequence of exorbitant bribes, and the penitentiary, followed.

While comparatively protected in the brothels, where they represented a certain monetary value, the girls now found themselves on the street, absolutely at the mercy of the graft-greedy police. Desperate, needing protection and longing for affection, these girls naturally proved an easy prey for cadets, themselves the result of the spirit of our commercial age. Thus the cadet system was the direct outgrowth of police persecution, graft, and attempted suppression of prostitution. It were sheer folly to confound this modern phase of the social evil with the causes of the latter.

Mere suppression and barbaric enactments can serve but to embitter, and further degrade, the unfortunate victims of ignorance and stupidity. The latter has reached its highest expression in the proposed law to make humane treatment of prostitutes a crime, punishing any one sheltering a prostitute with five years' imprisonment and $10,000 fine. Such an attitude merely exposes the terrible lack of understanding of the true causes of prostitution, as a social factor, as well as manifesting the Puritanic spirit of the Scarlet Letter days.

There is not a single modern writer on the subject who does not refer to the utter futility of legislative methods in coping with the issue. Thus Dr. Blaschko finds that governmental suppression and moral crusades accomplish nothing save driving the evil into secret channels, multiplying its dangers to society. Havelock Ellis, the most thorough and humane student of prostitution, proves by a wealth of data that the more stringent the methods of persecution the worse the condition becomes. Among other data we learn that in France, "in 1560, Charles IX. abolished brothels through an edict, but the numbers of prostitutes were only increased, while many new brothels appeared in unsuspected shapes, and were more dangerous. In spite of all such legislation, or because of it, there has been no country in which prostitution has played a more conspicuous part."[6]

An educated public opinion, freed from the legal and moral hounding of the prostitute, can alone help to ameliorate present conditions. Wilful shutting of eyes and ignoring of the evil as a social factor of modern life, can but aggravate matters. We must rise above our foolish notions of "better than thou," and learn to recognize in the prostitute a product of social conditions. Such a realization will sweep away the attitude of hypocrisy, and insure a greater understanding and more humane treatment. As to a thorough eradication of prostitution, nothing can accomplish that save a complete transvaluation of all accepted values especially the moral ones—coupled with the abolition of industrial slavery.

6   *Sex and Society.*

CHAPTER 17

PRISONS: A SOCIAL CRIME AND FAILURE
Emma Goldman

IN 1849 Feodor Dostoyevsky wrote on the wall of his prison cell the following story of *The Priest and the Devil*:

"'Hello, you little fat father!' the devil said to the priest. 'What made you lie so to those poor, misled people? What tortures of hell did you depict? Don't you know they are already suffering the tortures of hell in their earthly lives? Don't you know that you and the authorities of the State are my representatives on earth? It is you that make them suffer the pains of hell with which you threaten them. Don't you know this? Well, then, come with me!'

"The devil grabbed the priest by the collar, lifted him high in the air, and carried him to a factory, to an iron foundry. He saw the workmen there running and hurrying to and fro, and toiling in the scorching heat. Very soon the thick, heavy air and the heat are too much for the priest. With tears in his eyes, he pleads with the devil: 'Let me go! Let me leave this hell!'

"'Oh, my dear friend, I must show you many more places.' The devil gets hold of him again and drags him off to a farm. There he sees workmen threshing the grain. The dust and heat are insufferable. The overseer carries a knout, and unmercifully beats anyone who falls to the ground overcome by hard toil or hunger.

"Next the priest is taken to the huts where these same workers live with their families—dirty, cold, smoky, ill-smelling holes. The devil grins. He points out the poverty and hardships which are at home here.

"'Well, isn't this enough?' he asks. And it seems as if even he, the devil, pities the people. The pious servant of God can hardly bear it. With uplifted hands he begs: 'Let me go away from here. Yes, yes! This is hell on earth!'

"'Well, then, you see. And you still promise them another hell. You torment them, torture them to death mentally when they are already all but dead physically! Come on! I will show you one more hell—one more, the very worst.'

"He took him to a prison and showed him a dungeon, with its foul air and the many human forms, robbed of all health and energy, lying on the floor, covered with vermin that were devouring their poor, naked, emaciated bodies.

"'Take off your silken clothes,' said the devil to the priest, 'put on your ankles heavy chains such as these unfortunates wear; lie down on the cold and filthy floor—and then talk to them about a hell that still awaits them!'

"'No, no!' answered the priest, 'I cannot think of anything more dreadful than this. I entreat you, let me go away from here!'

"'Yes, this is hell. There can be no worse hell than this. Did you not know it? Did you not know that these men and women whom you are frightening with the picture of a hell hereafter—did you not know that they are in hell right here, before they die?'"

This was written fifty years ago in dark Russia, on the wall of one of the most horrible prisons. Yet who can deny that the same applies with equal force to the present time, even to American prisons?

With all our boasted reforms, our great social changes, and our far-reaching discoveries, human beings continue to be sent to the worst of hells, wherein they are outraged, degraded, and tortured, that society may be "protected" from the phantoms of its own making.

Prison, a social protection? What monstrous mind ever conceived such an idea? Just as well say that health can be promoted by a widespread contagion.

After eighteen months of horror in an English prison, Oscar Wilde gave to the world his great masterpiece, *The Ballad of Reading Gaol*:

> The vilest deeds, like poison weeds
> Bloom well in prison air;
> It is only what is good in Man
> That wastes and withers there.
> Pale Anguish keeps the heavy gate,
> And the Warder is Despair.

Society goes on perpetuating this poisonous air, not realizing that out of it can come naught but the most poisonous results.

We are spending at the present $3,500,000 per day, $1,000,095,000 per year, to maintain prison institutions, and that in a democratic country,—a sum almost as large as the combined output of wheat, valued at $750,000,000, and the output of coal, valued at $350,000,000. Professor Bushnell of Washington, D.C., estimates the cost of prisons at $6,000,000,000 annually, and Dr. G. Frank Lydston, an eminent American writer on crime, gives $5,000,000,000 annually as a reasonable figure. Such unheard-of expenditure for the purpose of maintaining vast armies of human beings caged up like wild beasts![1]

Yet crimes are on the increase. Thus we learn that in America there are four and a half times as many crimes to every million population today as there were twenty years ago.

The most horrible aspect is that our national crime is murder, not robbery, embezzlement, or rape, as in the South. London is five times as large as Chicago, yet there are one hundred and eighteen murders annually in the latter city, while only twenty in London. Nor is Chicago the leading city in crime, since it is only seventh on the list, which is headed by four Southern cities, and San Francisco and Los Angeles. In view of such a terrible condition of affairs, it seems ridiculous to prate of the protection society derives from its prisons.

The average mind is slow in grasping a truth, but when the most thoroughly organized, centralized institution, maintained at an excessive national expense, has proven a complete social failure, the dullest must begin to question its right to exist. The time is past when we can be content with our social fabric merely because it is "ordained by divine right," or by the majesty of the law.

The widespread prison investigations, agitation, and education during the last few years are conclusive proof that men are learning to dig deep into the very bottom of society, down to the causes of the terrible discrepancy between social and individual life.

Why, then, are prisons a social crime and a failure? To answer this vital question it behooves us to seek the nature and cause of crimes, the methods employed in coping with them, and the effects these methods produce in ridding society of the curse and horror of crimes.

1   W. C. Owen, *Crime and Criminals.*

First, as to the *nature* of crime:

Havelock Ellis divides crime into four phases, the political, the passional, the insane, and the occasional. He says that the political criminal is the victim of an attempt of a more or less despotic government to preserve its own stability. He is not necessarily guilty of an unsocial offense; he simply tries to overturn a certain political order which may itself be anti-social. This truth is recognized all over the world, except in America where the foolish notion still prevails that in a Democracy there is no place for political criminals. Yet John Brown was a political criminal; so were the Chicago Anarchists; so is every striker. Consequently, says Havelock Ellis, the political criminal of our time or place may be the hero, martyr, saint of another age. Lombroso calls the political criminal the true precursor of the progressive movement of humanity.

"The criminal by passion is usually a man of wholesome birth and honest life, who under the stress of some great, unmerited wrong has wrought justice for himself."[2]

Mr. Hugh C. Weir, in *The Menace of the Police*, cites the case of Jim Flaherty, a criminal by passion, who, instead of being saved by society, is turned into a drunkard and a recidivist, with a ruined and poverty-stricken family as the result.

A more pathetic type is Archie, the victim in Brand Whitlock's novel, *The Turn of the Balance*, the greatest American exposé of crime in the making. Archie, even more than Flaherty, was driven to crime and death by the cruel inhumanity of his surroundings, and by the unscrupulous hounding of the machinery of the law. Archie and Flaherty are but the types of many thousands, demonstrating how the legal aspects of crime, and the methods of dealing with it, help to create the disease which is undermining our entire social life.

"The insane criminal really can no more be considered a criminal than a child, since he is mentally in the same condition as an infant or an animal."[3]

The law already recognizes that, but only in rare cases of a very flagrant nature, or when the culprit's wealth permits the luxury of criminal insanity. It has become quite fashionable to be the victim of paranoia. But on the whole the "sovereignty of justice" still continues

2   *The Criminal*, Havelock Ellis.
3   *The Criminal*.

to punish criminally insane with the whole severity of its power. Thus Mr. Ellis quotes from Dr. Richter's statistics showing that in Germany one hundred and six madmen, out of one hundred and forty-four criminally insane, were condemned to severe punishment.

The occasional criminal "represents by far the largest class of our prison population, hence is the greatest menace to social well-being." What is the cause that compels a vast army of the human family to take to crime, to prefer the hideous life within prison walls to the life outside? Certainly that cause must be an iron master, who leaves its victims no avenue of escape, for the most depraved human being loves liberty.

This terrific force is conditioned in our cruel social and economic arrangement. I do not mean to deny the biologic, physiologic, or psychologic factors in creating crime; but there is hardly an advanced criminologist who will not concede that the social and economic influences are the most relentless, the most poisonous germs of crime. Granted even that there are innate criminal tendencies, it is none the less true that these tendencies find rich nutrition in our social environment.

There is close relation, says Havelock Ellis, between crimes against the person and the price of alcohol, between crimes against property and the price of wheat. He quotes Quetelet and Lacassagne, the former looking upon society as the preparer of crime, and the criminals as instruments that execute them. The latter find that "the social environment is the cultivation medium of criminality; that the criminal is the microbe, an element which only becomes important when it finds the medium which causes it to ferment; *every society has the criminals it deserves*."[4]

The most "prosperous" industrial period makes it impossible for the worker to earn enough to keep up health and vigor. And as prosperity is, at best, an imaginary condition, thousands of people are constantly added to the host of the unemployed. From East to West, from South to North, this vast army tramps in search of work or food, and all they find is the workhouse or the slums. Those who have a spark of self-respect left, prefer open defiance, prefer crime to the emaciated, degraded position of poverty.

4   *The Criminal.*

Edward Carpenter estimates that five-sixths of indictable crimes consist in some violation of property rights; but that is too low a figure. A thorough investigation would prove that nine crimes out of ten could be traced, directly or indirectly, to our economic and social iniquities, to our system of remorseless exploitation and robbery. There is no criminal so stupid but recognizes this terrible fact, though he may not be able to account for it.

A collection of criminal philosophy, which Havelock Ellis, Lombroso, and other eminent men have compiled, shows that the criminal feels only too keenly that it is society that drives him to crime. A Milanese thief said to Lombroso: "I do not rob, I merely take from the rich their superfluities; besides, do not advocates and merchants rob?" A murderer wrote: "Knowing that three-fourths of the social virtues are cowardly vices, I thought an open assault on a rich man would be less ignoble than the cautious combination of fraud." Another wrote: "I am imprisoned for stealing a half dozen eggs. Ministers who rob millions are honored. Poor Italy!" An educated convict said to Mr. Davitt: "The laws of society are framed for the purpose of securing the wealth of the world to power and calculation, thereby depriving the larger portion of mankind of its rights and chances. Why should they punish me for taking by somewhat similar means from those who have taken more than they had a right to?" The same man added: "Religion robs the soul of its independence; patriotism is the stupid worship of the world for which the well-being and the peace of the inhabitants were sacrificed by those who profit by it, while the laws of the land, in restraining natural desires, were waging war on the manifest spirit of the law of our beings. Compared with this," he concluded, "thieving is an honorable pursuit."[5]

Verily, there is greater truth in this philosophy than in all the law-and-moral books of society.

The economic, political, moral, and physical factors being the microbes of crime, how does society meet the situation?

The methods of coping with crime have no doubt undergone several changes, but mainly in a theoretic sense. In practice, society

5   *The Criminal.*

has retained the primitive motive in dealing with the offender; that is, revenge. It has also adopted the theologic idea; namely, punishment; while the legal and "civilized" methods consist of deterrence or terror, and reform. We shall presently see that all four modes have failed utterly, and that we are today no nearer a solution than in the dark ages.

The natural impulse of the primitive man to strike back, to avenge a wrong, is out of date. Instead, the civilized man, stripped of courage and daring, has delegated to an organized machinery the duty of avenging his wrongs, in the foolish belief that the State is justified in doing what he no longer has the manhood or consistency to do. The "majesty of the law" is a reasoning thing; it would not stoop to primitive instincts. Its mission is of a "higher" nature. True, it is still steeped in the theologic muddle, which proclaims punishment as a means of purification, or the vicarious atonement of sin. But legally and socially the statute exercises punishment, not merely as an infliction of pain upon the offender, but also for its terrifying effect upon others.

What is the real basis of punishment, however? The notion of a free will, the idea that man is at all times a free agent for good or evil; if he chooses the latter, he must be made to pay the price. Although this theory has long been exploded, and thrown upon the dustheap, it continues to be applied daily by the entire machinery of government, turning it into the most cruel and brutal tormentor of human life. The only reason for its continuance is the still more cruel notion that the greater the terror punishment spreads, the more certain its preventative effect.

Society is using the most drastic methods in dealing with the social offender. Why do they not deter? Although in America a man is supposed to be considered innocent until proven guilty, the instruments of law, the police, carry on a reign of terror, making indiscriminate arrests, beating, clubbing, bullying people, using the barbarous method of the "third degree," subjecting their unfortunate victims to the foul air of the station house, and the still fouler language of its guardians. Yet crimes are rapidly multiplying, and society is paying the price. On the other hand, it is an open secret that when the unfortunate citizen has been given the full "mercy" of the law, and for the sake of safety is hidden in the worst of hells, his real Calvary begins. Robbed of his rights as a human being, degraded to a mere automaton without will or feeling, dependent entirely upon the mercy of brutal keepers, he daily goes through a process of dehumanization, compared with which savage revenge was mere child's play.

There is not a single penal institution or reformatory in the United States where men are not tortured "to be made good," by means of the black-jack, the club, the strait-jacket, the water-cure, the "humming bird" (an electrical contrivance run along the human body), the solitary, the bull-ring, and starvation diet. In these institutions his will is broken, his soul degraded, his spirit subdued by the deadly monotony and routine of prison life. In Ohio, Illinois, Pennsylvania, Missouri, and in the South, these horrors have become so flagrant as to reach the outside world, while in most other prisons the same Christian methods still prevail. But prison walls rarely allow the agonized shrieks of the victims to escape—prison walls are thick, they dull the sound. Society might with greater immunity abolish all prisons at once, than to hope for protection from these twentieth-century chambers of horrors.

Year after year the gates of prison hells return to the world an emaciated, deformed, will-less, ship-wrecked crew of humanity, with the Cain mark on their foreheads, their hopes crushed, all their natural inclinations thwarted. With nothing but hunger and inhumanity to greet them, these victims soon sink back into crime as the only possibility of existence. It is not at all an unusual thing to find men and women who have spent half their lives—nay, almost their entire existence—in prison. I know a woman on Blackwell's Island, who had been in and out thirty-eight times; and through a friend I learn that a young boy of seventeen, whom he had nursed and cared for in the Pittsburg penitentiary, had never known the meaning of liberty. From the reformatory to the penitentiary had been the path of this boy's life, until, broken in body, he died a victim of social revenge. These personal experiences are substantiated by extensive data giving overwhelming proof of the utter futility of prisons as a means of deterrence or reform.

Well-meaning persons are now working for a new departure in the prison question,—reclamation, to restore once more to the prisoner the possibility of becoming a human being. Commendable as this is, I fear it is impossible to hope for good results from pouring good wine into a musty bottle. Nothing short of a complete reconstruction of society will deliver mankind from the cancer of crime. Still, if the dull edge of our social conscience would be sharpened, the penal institutions might be given a new coat of varnish. But the first step to be taken is the renovation of the social consciousness, which is in a rather dilapidated condition. It is sadly in need to be awakened to the fact that crime is a question of degree, that we all have the rudiments of crime in us, more or less, according to our mental, physical, and social environment; and that the individual criminal is merely a reflex of the tendencies of the aggregate.

With the social consciousness wakened, the average individual may learn to refuse the "honor" of being the bloodhound of the law. He may cease to persecute, despise, and mistrust the social offender, and give him a chance to live and breathe among his fellows. Institutions are, of course, harder to reach. They are cold, impenetrable, and cruel; still, with the social consciousness quickened, it might be possible to free the prison victims from the brutality of prison officials, guards, and keepers. Public opinion is a powerful weapon; keepers of human prey, even, are afraid of it. They may be taught a little humanity, especially if they realize that their jobs depend upon it.

But the most important step is to demand for the prisoner the right to work while in prison, with some monetary recompense that would enable him to lay aside a little for the day of his release, the beginning of a new life.

It is almost ridiculous to hope much from present society when we consider that workingmen, wage-slaves themselves, object to convict labor. I shall not go into the cruelty of this objection, but merely consider the impracticability of it. To begin with, the opposition so far raised by organized labor has been directed against windmills. Prisoners have always worked; only the State has been their exploiter, even as the individual employer has been the robber of organized labor. The States have either set the convicts to work for the government, or they have farmed convict labor to private individuals. Twenty-nine of the States pursue the latter plan. The Federal government and seventeen States have discarded it, as have the leading nations of Europe, since it leads to hideous overworking and abuse of prisoners, and to endless graft.

"Rhode Island, the State dominated by Aldrich, offers perhaps the worst example. Under a five-year contract, dated July 7th, 1906, and renewable for five years more at the option of private contractors, the labor of the inmates of the Rhode Island Penitentiary and the Providence County Jail is sold to the Reliance-Sterling Mfg. Co. at the rate of a trifle less than 25 cents a day per man. This Company is really a gigantic Prison Labor Trust, for it also leases the convict labor of Connecticut, Michigan, Indiana, Nebraska, and South Dakota penitentiaries, and the reformatories of New Jersey, Indiana, Illinois, and Wisconsin, eleven establishments in all.

"The enormity of the graft under the Rhode Island contract may be estimated from the fact that this same Company pays 62 1/2 cents a day in Nebraska for the convict's labor, and that Tennessee, for example, gets $1.10 a day for a convict's work from the Gray-Dudley Hardware Co.; Missouri gets 70 cents a day from the Star Overall Mfg. Co.; West Virginia 65 cents a day from the Kraft Mfg. Co., and Maryland 55 cents a day from Oppenheim, Oberndorf & Co., shirt manufacturers. The very difference in prices points to enormous graft. For example, the Reliance-Sterling Mfg. Co. manufactures shirts, the cost by free labor being not less than $1.20 per dozen, while it pays Rhode Island thirty cents a dozen. Furthermore, the State charges this Trust no rent for the use of its huge factory, charges nothing for power, heat, light, or even drainage, and exacts no taxes. What graft!"[6]

It is estimated that more than twelve million dollars' worth of workingmen's shirts and overalls is produced annually in this country by prison labor. It is a woman's industry, and the first reflection that arises is that an immense amount of free female labor is thus displaced. The second consideration is that male convicts, who should be learning trades that would give them some chance of being self-supporting after their release, are kept at this work at which they can not possibly make a dollar. This is the more serious when we consider that much of this labor is done in reformatories, which so loudly profess to be training their inmates to become useful citizens.

The third, and most important, consideration is that the enormous profits thus wrung from convict labor are a constant incentive

6   Quoted from the publication of the National Committee on Prison Labor.

to the contractors to exact from their unhappy victims tasks altogether beyond their strength, and to punish them cruelly when their work does not come up to the excessive demands made.

Another word on the condemnation of convicts to tasks at which they cannot hope to make a living after release. Indiana, for example, is a State that has made a great splurge over being in the front rank of modern penological improvements. Yet, according to the report rendered in 1908 by the training school of its "reformatory," 135 were engaged in the manufacture of chains, 207 in that of shirts, and 255 in the foundry—a total of 597 in three occupations. But at this so-called reformatory 59 occupations were represented by the inmates, 39 of which were connected with country pursuits. Indiana, like other States, professes to be training the inmates of her reformatory to occupations by which they will be able to make their living when released. She actually sets them to work making chains, shirts, and brooms, the latter for the benefit of the Louisville Fancy Grocery Co. Broom-making is a trade largely monopolized by the blind, shirt-making is done by women, and there is only one free chain-factory in the State, and at that a released convict can not hope to get employment. The whole thing is a cruel farce.

If, then, the States can be instrumental in robbing their helpless victims of such tremendous profits is it not high time for organized labor to stop its idle howl, and to insist on decent remuneration for the convict, even as labor organizations claim for themselves? In that way workingmen would kill the germ which makes of the prisoner an enemy to the interests of labor. I have said elsewhere that thousands of convicts, incompetent and without a trade, without means of subsistence, are yearly turned back into the social fold. These men and women must live, for even an ex-convict has needs. Prison life has made them anti-social beings, and the rigidly closed doors that meet them on their release are not likely to decrease their bitterness. The inevitable result is that they form a favorable nucleus out of which scabs, black-legs, detectives, and policemen are drawn, only too willing to do the master's bidding. Thus organized labor, by its foolish opposition to work in prison, defeats its own ends. It helps to create poisonous fumes that stifle every attempt for economic betterment. If the workingman wants to avoid these effects, he should insist on the right of the convict to work, he should meet him as a brother, take him into his organization, and *with his aid turn against the system which grinds them both.*

Last, but not least, is the growing realization of the barbarity and the inadequacy of the definite sentence. Those who believe in, and earnestly aim at, a change are fast coming to the conclusion that man must be given an opportunity to make good. And how is he to do it with ten, fifteen, or twenty years' imprisonment before him? The hope of liberty and of opportunity is the only incentive to life, especially the prisoner's life. Society has sinned so long against him—it ought at least to leave him that. I am not very sanguine that it will, or that any real change in that direction can take place until the conditions that breed both the prisoner and the jailer will be forever abolished.

Out of his mouth a red, red rose!
Out of his heart a white!
For who can say by what strange way
Christ brings his will to light,
Since the barren staff the pilgrim bore
Bloomed in the great Pope's sight.

AFTERWORD

Luis A. Fernandez

If you are reading my words, then it means you likely waded through the foundational text that outlines the roots of anarchist criminology. In that text, you encountered great thinkers from previous centuries who express sharp critiques on the morality of punishment, the injustice of property, the role of courts in controlling populations, and even early questionings of the function of prisons. As such, you probably saw that many of the issues we face currently, and the critiques that we have of those issues, have deep and complicated roots. This should make us feel simultaneously grateful for our predecessors, but also impatient about how long the struggle is taking to eliminate oppression. This book, then, functions in at least two ways. It helps us look back at our own philosophical history and it also pushes us to confront what we are doing currently to engage liberation struggles. Thus, the past forces us to look to the future.

The last ten years sets the stage for the immediate future. In that time, we experienced a serious economic crisis, a drastic increase in inequity, and the continuation of the carceral state in handing out disproportionate levels of punishment and repression. Much of this has been aimed at communities of color, be it in the form of harsher treatment of undocumented people, the police killings of young black men, or the brutality on native people and the erasure of their cultural past. Given this, we also saw the rise of strong movements, such as Occupy, Black Lives Matter, No DPL, and, more recently, Abolish ICE. Criminology as a field, then, finds itself in the middle of this push from the state agencies and the resistance in the street. As criminologists, we have a great task before us. First, we need to educate ourselves and communities on alternative forms of justice based on collaboration and mutual aid. And we must do this aiming to abolish the criminal justice system entirely. Second, we have to study and engage emerging movements that are already pushing for the abolition of prisons, police, and property, while rethinking the administration of punishment. And both of these tasks have to target the entire criminal justice system and aim to produce better ways to live, love, and work. Not an easy task, but it is the work before us.

In academia, too many professors are using classic criminology textbooks, teaching classical theories, and reinforcing punitive forms of punishment to educate students. This book takes a forceful turn away from these tendencies, pointing us toward other horizons, grounded in different conceptions of social relations, and presenting different ways to collaborate. Given this, this book has to not only be read, but *used*. That is, it has to be studied with an eye to action and implementation. Otherwise, it will not be an important book. We must provide space and place for these ideas, building a common understanding that anarchist criminology is not taboo, but rather based on a set of anarchist principles that date back more than a century.

Looking at the anarchist literature, we know that thinkers developed a thorough analysis of power, the state, property, and cooperation. Yet, they also have a lot to say about the nature of crime and punishment as they relate to domination. Like other anarchist collections, this book points to the oppressive dynamics of the state as it seeks control. However, this collection also shows how these anarchists related these to ending punishment, punitive justice, prisons, and the penal system. At its essence, the writings presented only the sections dealing with criminology-related issues.

As stated previously, anarchists have been fighting to end punitive justice and prisons. And we must continue this tradition. The ideas in this book, then, are just one more step forward in cementing the anarchist criminological tradition in firm ground, a tradition that includes the implementation of restorative, transformative, healing, and community circles as we seek the extinction of subjugation. Anarchist criminologists must seek alternatives in our communities, both inside and outside of academia. In fact, struggles already exist that point the way, including examples from Standing Rock, Youth Justice Coalition, Dignity in Schools, Save the Kids, Philly Stand Up, Critical Resistance, California Coalition Against Sexual Assault, #SayHerName, Bay Area Transformative Justice Coalition, Poetry Behind the Walls, Victim Offender Reconciliation Program, Vision Change Win, Alternatives to Violence Project, American Friends

Service Committee, Racial Justice Now!, Institute for Critical Animal Studies, Black Youth Project 100, and Project NIA to name just a few.

Inside academia, the writings in this book give us the opportunity to introduce key critical views of the criminal justice system. As the reader finishes reading this book, they can also spread the concepts to the broader community. If anarchist criminology is going to take a hold, these theories, methodologies, approaches, and perspectives must grow in collective action and discussion. As a professional criminologist, I take the field seriously and want these ideas to broaden the possibilities, both inside and outside the academic halls. In sum, make sure to take the ideas in this book and share them, leave the book someone where folks can pick it up, or provide it for a course required reading.

As we look beyond this book, I invite the reader to grapple with the ideas. At this moment when we are grappling with the rise of fascist ideologies and movements, when we can see clearly that political turmoil is coming, and when the rise of it is not likely to stop, this book allows us to imagine a different kind of future. If we think hard and act quickly, we could eliminate incarceration, abolish subjugation, build deep-rooted direct democracies, and do it all on the shoulders of our predecessors. We have no time to waste. Read, think, and act!

INDEX

CONTRIBUTORS' BIOGRAPHIES

ANTHONY J. NOCELLA II, PH.D., award-winning author and community organizer, is Assistant Professor of Criminal Justice, Justice Studies, and Criminology in the Institute of Public Safety and the Department of Criminal Justice at Salt Lake Community College. He is the editor of the *Peace Studies Journal*, the *Transformative Justice Journal*, and the book series Poetry Behind the Walls, along with being a co-editor of five book series including Critical Animal Studies and Theory with Lexington Books and Hip Hop Studies and Activism with Peter Lang Publishing. He is the National Coordinator of Save the Kids, Executive Director of the Institute for Critical Animal Studies, and Director of Academy for Peace Education. He has published over fifty peer-reviewed book chapters or articles and over forty books. He has been interviewed by the *Houston Chronicle*, *Durango Herald*, *Fresno Bee*, *Los Angeles Times*, *Washington Post*, CNN, CBS, Fox, and the *New York Times*.

MARK SEIS is Associate Professor of sociology at Fort Lewis College in Durango, Colorado. He has published on a variety of topics ranging from the juvenile death penalty, to environmental topics including the Clean Air Act, global warming, ozone depletion, and acid rain, to various types of environmental crime, to globalization and the environment, to issues concerning radical environmentalism. His primary research interests include sustainable communities, all things environment, anarchist studies, and radical pedagogy.

JEFF SHANTZ is an engaged activist scholar who has taught anarchist theories and practices in a variety of university classes and community-based courses, and who has decades of community organizing experience within social movements. He currently teaches critical theory, elite deviance, community, and human rights in the Department of Criminology at Kwantlen Polytechnic University in Metro Vancouver, Canada. Shantz is the author of numerous books, including *Communist Tendencies: Mutual Aid Beyond Communism* (Punctum, 2013), *Green Syndicalism: An Alternative Red/Green Vision* (Syracuse University Press, 2012), and *Constructive Anarchy* (Ashgate, 2010). Shantz is the

co-founder of the Critical Criminology Working Group (http://www
.radicalcriminology.org/) and the founding editor of the journal *Radical Criminology* (http://journal.radicalcriminology.org/index.php/rc).
Scholarly interests include critical theories, migration, critical surveillance studies, corporate crime, transnational crime, and social movements. Samples of his writing may be found at jeffshantz.ca.

Foreword Author's Biography

Ruth Kinna works at Loughborough University and is the general editor of the journal *Anarchist Studies*. Her recent publications include *Kropotkin: Reviewing the Classical Anarchist Tradition* (Edinburgh University Press) and *Anarchism 1914–18: Internationalism, anti-militarism and war*, co-edited with Matthew S. Adams for Manchester University Press. She is currently working with Uri Gordon to produce an edited collection for Routledge, the *Handbook of Radical Politics* and with Alex Prichard and Thomas Swann on the project Constitutionalising Anarchy. For more information go to www.anarchyrules.info.

Afterword author's biography

Luis A. Fernandez is a Professor in and Chair of the Department of Criminology and Criminal Justice at Northern Arizona University. He is the author and editor of several books, including *Policing Dissent*, *Contemporary Anarchist Studies*, and *Shutting Down the Streets*. His work also appears in various book chapters and journals, including *Social Justice*, *Contemporary Political Theory*, and *Critical Criminology*. His most recent research focuses on the alt-right and the emergence of neo-fascism. Fernandez is served as the President of the Society for the Study of Social Problems in 2017–2018.